Social Security
The First
Half-Century

President Franklin D. Roosevelt signs the Social Security Act of 1935.
Source: Franklin D. Roosevelt Library, Hyde Park, N.Y.

SOCIAL SECURITY
The First Half-Century

EDITED BY

Gerald D. Nash
Noel H. Pugach
Richard F. Tomasson

UNIVERSITY OF NEW MEXICO PRESS
Albuquerque

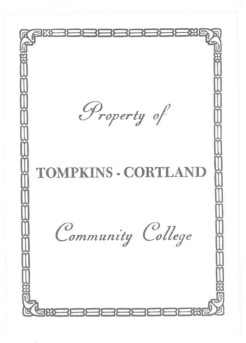

Library of Congress Cataloging-in-Publication Data

Social Security, the first half-century / edited by Gerald D. Nash,
  Noel H. Pugach, Richard F. Tomasson.
    p.   cm.
  Bibliography: p.
  Includes index.
  ISBN 0-8263-1068-0. ISBN 0-8263-1069-9 (pbk.)
  1. Social security—United States—History. I. Nash, Gerald D. II. Pugach, Noel H., 1939– . III. Tomasson, Richard F., 1928–

HD7125.S5994 1988
368.4'3'00973—dc19   87-36853
                                      CIP

Contents

Illustrations following p. 94

Foreword

Fred R. Harris

It is my pleasure to introduce *Social Security: The First Half-Century* as the first volume in the University of New Mexico Public Policy Series. A primary goal of the series is to make available to a wide audience of scholars, students, policy makers, and the public at large recent research and scholarly perspectives on contemporary policy issues of importance to the nation and the Southwest region. A secondary goal of the series is to stimulate participation of scholars from different academic disciplines in the analysis of public policy issues. By their very nature public policies intersect with a variety of academic disciplines and research traditions, beginning with political science but extending to economics, sociology, and history, to name a few. In addition, no analysis or attempt to understand the development and impact of public policies can be complete without some account of the viewpoints and experience of policy makers and program administrators whose acquaintance with the subject is firsthand.

Social Security: The First Half-Century combines all these various elements. There is no question that Social Security is a subject of profound and far-reaching importance: in budgetary terms Old Age, Survivors, Disability, and Health Insurance (OASDHI) is the largest single item in the federal budget. Equally important, the evolution of the Social Security system over the past fifty years encompasses the development of a wide range of other social programs and policies, from Aid to Families with Dependent Children to the unemployment insurance system—both of which trace their current existence to the Social Security Act of 1935. It is no exaggeration to say that one cannot grasp the form and substance of American social policy without first understanding Social Security. The contributors to the present volume represent a rich and varied cross section of perspectives and experiences related to the Social Security system, from renowned scholars to the remarkable men and women who served as pioneers in Franklin D. Roosevelt's New Deal.

The Public Policy Series is sponsored by the University of New Mexico's Institute for Public Policy as part of its mission to promote public policy research and analysis, seminars and symposia, and policy-related publications. The institute gratefully acknowledges financial support of the College of Arts and Sciences to help establish the series. With a grant from the University of New Mexico Foundation, the institute has conducted seminars and symposia on the management of governmental budget cuts, Southwest energy policy, and welfare reform.

Fred R. Harris
Series Editor

Preface

This volume constitutes the proceedings of a conference, "Social Security: The First Half-Century," held at the University of New Mexico, in Albuquerque, on March 29–30, 1985. The conference was designed both to commemorate the fiftieth anniversary of the Social Security Act of 1935 and to evaluate this landmark legislation. The conference planners had three specific goals: To enable veteran social security policymakers to reflect on their handiwork and what has become of it; to provide an opportunity for scholars in the field to summarize their papers; and to allow those individuals and the general public, which was invited to all sessions, to exchange views and engage in frank discussions of the issues relating to the American social security system.

The idea for the conference was initially proposed by Noel Pugach. It was subsequently organized by him, Gerald Nash, and Richard Tomasson, who constituted the Planning Committee. Allan Gerlach, then executive director of the New Mexico Humanities Council, also offered helpful suggestions to the Planning Committee. The successful implementation of the plans and smooth running of the conference, however, would have been impossible without the hard work and contributions of Dr. Michael Welsh and Ms.

Mariana Ibanez. As project director, Dr. Welsh handled, efficiently and imaginatively, the myriad details that a conference of this scope entails. Ms. Ibanez served as the conference secretary, bookkeeper, and general assistant. She also typed several sections of the manuscript for this volume. We are indebted to her fine performance in all these areas. We also wish to thank Professor Howard Rabinowitz, who evaluated the conference for the New Mexico Humanities Council.

The conference could not have taken place without the very generous financial support of the University of New Mexico and its constituent bodies. We wish to single out these former administrators: President John Perovich, Provost McAllister Hull, and Dean of the College of Arts and Sciences, F. Chris Garcia. Each managed to find funds in spite of a very stringent university budget. The European Studies Committee of the University of New Mexico also made a contribution from its limited funds. Two outside sources also provided vital financial support. The New Mexico Humanities Council supplied the conference with a planning grant and the Public Service Company of New Mexico gave the Planning Committee a generous allocation that covered essential expenses. We also thank the New Mexico Chapter of the American Association of Retired Persons, Manzano del Sol Retirement Center, and the Office of Senior Affairs of the City of Albuquerque for sponsoring and publicizing the conference.

Former University of New Mexico President Tom Farer welcomed the conference, hosted a dinner for the participants, and gave the conference his strong moral encouragement. Harry Kinney, the mayor of Albuquerque in 1985, and Congressman Bill Richardson (New Mexico) took time from their busy schedules to address the conference. We appreciate their contributions.

This volume represents the close collaborative efforts of the editors. Gerald Nash and Richard Tomasson wrote the historical overview of American Social Security, 1935–1985. Richard Tomasson edited the panel discussion of the veteran policymakers and moderated the session at the conference; Noel Pugach edited Wilbur Cohen's luncheon address. Although the panel discussion and luncheon address took place on the second day of the conference, the editors thought it appropriate to include them in Part I of the volume. They constituted the highlight of the conference and set its tone. Noel Pugach wrote the introduction for the papers included in

Part II; Gerald Nash provided the introduction for the scholarly papers in Part III. Noel Pugach wrote the Epilogue (Part IV) and Richard Tomasson produced the Appendices.

In closing, we wish to thank all of the participants in the conference. Their thoughtful remarks, candor, and conviviality produced an exciting and stimulating experience. We wish to thank the editors and staff at the University of New Mexico Press. Their cooperation and assistance made our task much easier. Finally, we would like to recognize Lys Ann Shore for her work on the index.

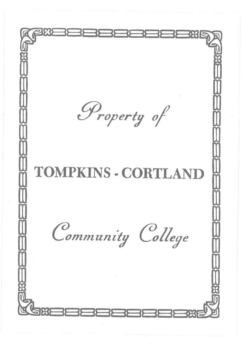

Abbreviations

AALL	American Association for Labor Legislation
AB	Aid to the Blind
ADC	Aid to Dependent Children
AFDC	Aid to Families with Dependent Children
AIME	Average Indexed Monthly Earnings (OASDI)
APTD	Aid to the Permanently and Totally Disabled
COLA	Cost of Living Adjustment
CPI	Consumer Price Index
DI	Disability Insurance
FERA	Federal Emergency Relief Act
FICA	Federal Insurance Contributory Act
FSA	Federal Security Agency
HI	Hospital Insurance (Part A of Medicare)
MFB	Maximum Family Benefit (OASDI)
NRA	Normal Retirement Age
OAA	Old Age Assistance
OAI	Old Age Insurance
OASDHI	Old Age, Survivors, and Disability Insurance and Hospital Insurance
PIA	Primary Insurance Amount (OASDI)
PIB	Primary Insurance Benefit (OASI)
RR	Railroad Retirement
SI	Survivors (and Dependents) Insurance
SSA	Social Security Administration
SSB	Social Security Board
SMI	Supplementary Medical Insurance (Part B of Medicare)
SSI	Supplemental Security Income
UI	Unemployment Insurance
WC	Workers' Compensation

PART I _____

Social Security:
The First Half-Century

1

An Overview of American Social Security, 1935–1985

I

The development of the welfare state has been a major social trend of the twentieth century.[1] By 1900, European governments increasingly assumed responsibilities for social welfare functions that had been largely performed by the family in agrarian societies. The United States was a latecomer to the family of welfare states. Not until the advent of Franklin D. Roosevelt and his New Deal did the federal government enter upon this sphere in any significant way. The passage of the Social Security Act in 1935 launched the American federal welfare state.[2]

But the establishment of the American welfare state was not really a sudden development; it came after three decades of intense discussion and deliberation over the forms social welfare should take in the United States. Many relevant ideas and practices were borrowed from European experience, beginning in the latter nineteenth century. Others emanated from social reformers in the Progressive Era. Some of the proposals envisaged comprehensive social planning. Others were more limited, and affected specific problems that had arisen in an industrial economy, which seemed to call for pragmatic responses. Moreover, reformers differed among themselves as to whether social welfare was to be primarily administered by the state, or whether voluntary associations were to play an important role in its implementation. Deliberations concerned issues such as workmen's compensation, health insurance, mothers' pensions, public health, aid to the disabled, public assistance, unemployment insurance, and old-age pensions. Each had its advocates and critics who in the years before 1935 were engaged in lively debate.

European social welfare legislation aroused interest in the United States as it became caught up in the industrialization process. In 1893 the U.S. Commissioner of Labor published a detailed analysis of the German social insurance system which Chancellor Otto von Bismarck had established in the 1880s.[3] In 1899 the New York State Bureau of Labor Statistics conducted its own independent examination of the German social welfare program.[4] In 1911 the U.S. Commissioner of Labor published a comprehensive survey of European social insurance with detailed descriptions for individual countries.[5]

Meanwhile, Progressive reformers were seeking greater public awareness of the need for governmental social welfare. Among them John B. Andrews was preeminent. A nonprofessional economist, Andrews in 1906 founded the American Association for Labor Legislation (AALL) with the help of some of the leading economists and social workers of his day. The Progressive version of a latter-day think tank, the AALL for more than two decades spearheaded the organized social insurance movement in America. Including prominent social scientists like John R. Commons, Jeremiah Jenks, Richard T. Ely, and Henry Seager, the organization provided consultants for voluntary groups as well as government agencies, drafted legislation for scores of city governments and state legislatures, and publicized the growth of social welfare legislation through lectures and reports. Like many Progressive reformers, the men and women in the AALL tended to be pragmatists rather than ideologues, hoping to improve the efficiency of American society by providing expert advice in the realm of social welfare and social engineering.[6]

In addition to Andrews, Isaac Rubinow became one of the significant pioneers of the American social welfare movement. Born in Russia, Rubinow came to the United States as a youth and earned a medical degree from New York University in 1898. But he soon abandoned medicine to become one of the nation's leading actuaries. Before and after earning his Ph. D. in economics at Columbia University he published a series of monumental studies of social insurance policies in Europe and America. Meanwhile, he held major positions with various federal agencies as well as with private insurance companies. Unlike Andrews, who tended to favor voluntary social services, Rubinow was a strong advocate of government sponsored social programs.[7]

Rubinow and Andrews often collaborated with John R. Commons, a leading economist and specialist in labor relations at the University of Wisconsin. Commons developed what came to be known as the Wisconsin Idea, whereby academic experts provided advice for politicians and public servants in the formulation of political, economic, and social policies. In particular, he believed that administrative commissions staffed by experts could provide solutions to many of the human problems wrought by industrialization. With his special interest in labor relations, Commons became an early supporter of workmen's compensation programs and wrote extensively on the subject while acting as an expert consultant in the field.[8]

The Wisconsin Idea had national reverberations. President Theodore Roosevelt was particularly concerned with the impact of industrialism on America's next generation and used his office to focus attention on the plight of dependent children. In 1909 he called the first White House Conference on Children to which many leading family and child specialists were invited. The conference dramatized the plight of poor, homeless, and abandoned youth and made concrete recommendations for some forms of government assistance. Although Congress itself took no action, the Conference gave impetus to a mothers' pension movement in the ensuing decade as cities and states developed scores of programs to provide some aid to single-head families and abandoned children.[9]

If the First World War slowed the momentum of the movement for social welfare, it received a decided forward thrust from new leaders who emerged in the 1920s. One of these was Abraham Epstein, an emigre from Russia in 1910, who became one of the nation's most prolific writers on social welfare programs, particularly old-age insurance. His many books and articles were widely read, while he also served as a consultant to labor unions and governmental agencies at the state and federal level.[10] In an academic setting, Paul H. Douglas of the University of Chicago, an economist, was a pioneer in the establishment of the field of welfare economics, with books and articles that enjoyed widespread respect during these years. His works clarified the options open to policymakers in the United States and helped to crystallize an emerging consensus on the need for some forms of social welfare.[11] Such a consensus was also furthered by Professor Eveline Burns of Columbia University. An emigre from England in 1926, she became one of the most prolific writers on old-age and social insurance in succeeding years.[12]

By the time of the Great Depression, therefore, the goals as well as the implementation of social welfare proposals had been discussed for more than three decades. The debate had resulted in an extensive literature on the subject and had seen the emergence of acknowledged experts in the field. Before the advent of the New Deal, most social workers were aware of this movement—prominent individuals like Harry Hopkins or New York State Labor Commissioner Frances Perkins—while the general public had remained less concerned.[13]

But the Great Depression changed all that as economic crisis catapulted the issue of social welfare into the mainstream of American politics. A succession of popular political leaders now embraced the cause of social welfare as their principal program. Most important was the U.S. senator from Louisiana, Huey P. Long, an aspirant to the presidency, who founded his Share-the-Wealth movement in 1934. Within a year he enrolled five million members. Before his assassination in 1935 he advocated a wide range of government sponsored welfare programs including old-age pensions, health care, education, unemployment insurance, and public relief. After his death many of his supporters joined the Old Age Revolving Pension Fund movement founded by Francis Townsend, a retired Long Beach, California doctor. Townsend advocated two hundred dollar a month federal pensions for all individuals over sixty and effectively focused the nation's attention on the plight of the elderly. In fact, more than any single individual, he brought the issue into the forthcoming presidential election of 1936.[14]

It was within this context that President Roosevelt decided to preempt and forestall his critics by supporting a comprehensive social welfare program of his own. To achieve this goal he appointed a Committee on Economic Security, chaired by his Secretary of Labor, Frances Perkins, and influenced by Harry Hopkins, an expert assistant to the president on social welfare policies. The committee considered not only the experience of other countries, but also that accumulated in the United States. Moreover, the committee members considered the political and constitutional context of the day, for they were wary of a Supreme Court that had already invalidated important New Deal measures. The fruit of their deliberations was the Social Security Act of 1935.[15]

II

Prior to the election of Roosevelt and the coming of the New Deal in 1933 there had been only two social programs in the twentieth century with federal involvement. Beginning in 1920, the federal government provided grants to the states to cover half the cost of initiating and maintaining vocational rehabilitation programs.[16] The Sheppard-Towner Act, in effect from 1921 to 1929, provided grants to the states for maternal and child welfare through the agency of the U.S. Children's Bureau.[17] The first third of this century, however, did see the passage of some social programs at the state level. Most of the states had passed workmen's compensation laws by 1918. Prior to 1935, thirty-five of the forty-eight states provided noncontributory means-tested pensions for the indigent old at 65 or 70, all but South Carolina had legislated mothers' pensions,[18] and twenty-four states had pension programs for the needy blind. A few states had adopted unemployment insurance before the Social Security Act became law on August 14, 1935.

The term *social security* is problematic. To most contemporary Americans it is immediately synonymous with government old-age pensions. Upon a little reflection most individuals will realize that it is also something more. It comprises all the programs we are taxed for by the FICA (Federal Insurance Contributory Act) deduction: old-age, survivors and dependents, and disability insurance plus Medicare. But this is really not a complete roll call of what social security originally encompassed, what was included in the eleven titles of the original act passed in 1935 and amended in 1939.

The 1935 Act consisted of eleven titles introducing federal involvement into nine programs in which there had been some previous state involvement and one program which was totally new under the American sun: old-age insurance (OAI). The Social Security Act was based on the Report of the Committee on Economic Security created by President Roosevelt on June 29, 1934. Its report was transmitted to Congress six and a half months later, on January 17, 1935. The entire legislative process took another seven months and was signed into law by the president on August 14, 1935. That such a complex and innovative piece of legislation could have been put through in thirteen and a half months is a remarkable phenomenon.

But it is explicable. The United States was in the midst of an extreme economic depression and in a state of social upheaval such as it had not been in since the Civil War. The states were bankrupt and unable to support their modest social programs. Radical prescriptions for impossible programs with large constituencies abounded. In stark contrast, the Committee on Economic Security was passionately pragmatic, ideologically committed to the superiority of social insurance over public assistance, and had the highest degree of support from an enormously popular president. Rarely, if ever, has a president been so intimately involved with such a complex piece of legislation. Rarely has a president shaped a complex piece of legislation the way Roosevelt did the Social Security Act.

The thirty-two-page Social Security Act,[19] as stated in its Prologue, had as its intent

> to provide for the General welfare by establishing a system of Federal old-age benefits, and by enabling the several States to make more adequate provision for aged persons, blind persons, dependent and crippled children, maternal and child welfare, public health, and the administration of their unemployment compensation laws; to establish a Social Security Board; to raise revenue; and for other purposes.

Title I of the act provided grants to the states to pay half the cost of old-age assistance (OAA) "not counting so much of such expenditure with respect to any individual for any month as exceeds $30" (increased to $40 in 1939). It established the general conditions a state must adopt to be eligible for federal monies, how payment to the states was to be made, and how the program was to be administered. Minimal federal regulation was necessary to keep the support of southern representatives. Even the provision that the states must provide sufficient assistance "compatible with decency and health" was removed from the House bill so as not to disturb the racial status quo in the South. Still, it was the least controversial and most popular of the major programs in the act. And that is why it was put first.

Much more controversial than Old-Age Assistance was Old-Age Benefits, now called Old-Age Insurance (OAI), the subject of Title II. This title established how the system of contributory old age pensions was to operate. It specified a formula by which persons with lower earnings would receive a larger replacement of lost earnings than those with higher earnings. OAI provided for coverage of virtually all employees in industry and commerce, a bare majority of the labor force. No benefit could be higher than $85 a month.

Nothing is said in Title II about the taxation of employers and employees to finance OAI. This is the subject of Title VIII. The reason for this separation was the enormous fear of the drafters of the bill that the Supreme Court would rule the program unconstitutional as it had so ruled a number of New Deal programs. The benefits part of the program was thought to be justified under the general welfare clause of the Constitution. And the federal government certainly had the right to tax. But it was thought safest to keep the two sides of the program separate. The same pattern characterizes the unemployment compensation program (Titles III and IX).

OAI was not considered the most important of the several programs in the original act—unemployment insurance was; nor was it the larger of the two programs for the elderly—OAA was. But social insurance pensions for the aged aroused the strongest and most bitter opposition from some business groups, Republican congressmen, and conservatives generally. It was a direct challenge to the pervasive American belief that the federal government had no business being involved in such a scheme and that most individuals could and should provide for their own old age. In an unsuccessful attempt to strike out old-age insurance from the social security bill, Senator Daniel O. Hastings of Delaware predicted that it might "end the progress of a great country and bring its people to the level of the average European."[20] Congressman Daniel Reed of New York predicted "The lash of the dictator will be felt and 25 million American citizens will for the first time submit themselves to a fingerprint test."[21]

That OAI, for which there was little understanding in the country and even less popular demand,[22] was not stricken from the original act was a result of Roosevelt's determination to have the Social

Security Act passed in its entirety. Roosevelt and the framers of the act had an intense commitment to the philosophy of social insurance and believed that contributory old-age pensions would eventually lessen the need for old-age assistance.

The retirement age was set at 65 (60 was thought too expensive and 70 too old), payment of pensions was to begin in 1942 (changed to 1940 by the 1939 Act), with total withdrawal from paid, covered employment a necessary condition for receipt of a pension (much liberalized over this half century). OAI was conceived of as insurance against a loss of earnings, not as an annuity.

OAI was the only one of the various programs in the original act which was to be a wholly federal program.[23] The actuaries who advised the Committee on Economic Security were unanimous in opposition to a state-by-state system. They successfully argued that the great mobility of the population would make it impossible to estimate the future age composition of the working population in each state, and such estimates would be necessary if there were to be a state-by-state system.[24]

Title III provided for grants to the states for unemployment compensation administration. It also specified the provisions that must be present in the state law before a state could receive payment. These provisions were of a very general nature and the states had a great deal of freedom to develop their own laws. As with the previous OAI title, nothing was said about taxation. This was dealt with in Title IX.

There had been much controversy over the form that unemployment insurance was to take. Of the various proposals, the Wisconsin plan which gave the states the maximum role in administration was adopted. Roosevelt and the members of the Committee on Economic Security were strongly committed to this approach in opposition to those who favored a national system administered along lines similar to OAI.

Title IV provided federal grants to the states for Aid to Dependent Children (ADC). It was to provide a federal contribution to what had previously been called mothers' pensions or widows' pensions or mothers' aid. If a state developed an approved plan, the secretary of the treasury would pay one third of the cost of the benefits up to a maximum monthly benefit of $18 for the first dependent child and $12 for subsequent dependent children. As in the law today, there are no federal guidelines as to the size of the benefits. A "dependent child" is defined to mean a child under the age of sixteen who has been deprived of parental support or care by reason of the death, continued absence from the home, or physical or mental incapacity of a parent, and who is living with his father, mother, grandfather, grandmother, brother, sister, stepfather, stepmother, stepbrother, stepsister, uncle, or aunt, in a place of residence maintained by one or more of such relatives as his or their own home.

Many amendments have been made to ADC over the years. The age limit of dependent children has been increased. Various monetary disregards have been introduced to encourage working. In 1950 benefits were allowed to be paid to the caretaker of the dependent child, thus becoming Aid to Families with Dependent Children (AFDC). In 1961 the states were given the option to provide benefits under certain conditions to intact families. Provisions for temporary emergency benefits were introduced in 1967. Many deliberalizations have been made in AFDC since 1981.

Title V contained four different programs. The first program was a revival of the Sheppard-Towner Act, in effect from 1921 to 1929. It provided grants to the states for "promoting the health of mothers and children." The second provides grants to the states for "locating crippled children, and for providing medical, surgical, corrective, and other services and care, . . . for children who are crippled or . . . [with] conditions which lead to crippling." The third provides grants for "the protection and care of homeless, dependent, and neglected children, and children in danger of becoming delinquent." These three programs were to be administered by the U.S. Children's Bureau and were to be operative "especially in rural areas and in areas suffering from severe economic distress."

The fourth program was of a different sort. It provided modest grants to the states for extending and promoting the 1920 act to promote "vocational rehabilitation of persons disabled in industry or otherwise and their return to civil employment." This program, aid to crippled children, and aid to the needy blind (Title X) were the only programs in the original act which dealt with aid to the disabled.

Title VI provided for grants to be made by the surgeon general of the Public Health Service to assist the states in "establishing and maintaining adequate public-health services, including the training of personnel for . . . health work." The title also provided a modest appropriation of funds for the Public Health Service for the "investigation of disease and problems of sanitation."

Title VII established a three-member Social Security Board to administer all of the programs provided for in the Social Security Act and to study and make recommendations as to the "most effective methods of providing economic security through social insurance, . . . [including] old-age pensions, unemployment compensation, accident compensation, and related subjects." This last phrase gave the Social Security Board (from 1946, Social Security Administration) authority to study and create health insurance proposals, which it began to do after passage of the act. While health insurance was recommended by the Committee on Economic Security, there is not even an indirect reference to it in the original act because of the belief that such would doom the entire act.

Title VIII specified the taxes to be paid for OAI (Title II), how they were to be paid, and who was to pay them. Employees and employers were both to pay 1 percent of earnings up to a limit of $3,000 for the years 1937, 1938, and 1939. The tax on both employers and employees was then to increase in ½ percent intervals reaching 3 percent in 1949. Congress, however, continually refused to increase the tax and it remained at 1 percent until 1950 when it rose to 1½ percent. But the pattern of equal contributions from both employer and employee with no contributions from general revenues has continued to the present. Yet in 1944 the act was amended to allow appropriations from general revenues, but this was rescinded in 1950.

The Committee on Economic Security had favored contributions from general revenues to OAI beginning about 1965, but President Roosevelt wanted a completely self-supporting system, and Congress concurred. In defense of his position, Roosevelt proclaimed: "We put those payroll contributions there so as to give the contributors a legal, moral, and political right to collect their pensions. With those taxes in there, no damn politician can ever scrap my Social Security Program."[25]

Two easily overlooked items in this title have had important consequences. First is the stipulation that the tax is not to be allowed as an income tax deduction to the taxpayer, a condition that has continued down to the present. Second is the provision that the commissioner of Internal Revenue "shall make and publish rules and regulations for the enforcement of this title." Rulings in 1939 and 1941 declared benefits as gifts or gratuities from the government and, hence, not subject to the federal income tax. This was modified for upper income beneficiaries in 1983.

Title IX was the taxation title for the administration of unemployment compensation. It provided for an excise tax on all employers of eight or more persons in the industrial and commercial sectors. The method used demonstrates how the federal government can use its power to tax to control the actions of the states. The federal government here taxed employer payrolls but permitted employers to use the tax as an offset against their payments to an approved state unemployment system. This method overcame three problems in the creation of an unemployment system. First, it solved the problem of states without an unemployment system having an advantage over states with such systems; all employers in covered establishments had to pay the tax. Second, it compelled the states to establish an unemployment system because if they did not their taxes would go into the national treasury and be used for other purposes. And, third, the constitutionality of the device seemed secure; its use had been upheld by a unanimous decision of the Supreme Court in 1927 in *Florida v. Mellon,* a case involving a national inheritance tax for which individuals could use a state inheritance tax as an offset.[26] By 1937 all of the states had passed approved unemployment insurance laws.

The tax was established at 1 percent of covered payroll for 1936, 2 percent for 1937, and 3 percent for 1938. (In 1939 earnings in excess of $3,000 in the calendar year were exempted from the tax.) No benefits could be paid before 1938. The details of merit rating were established whereby employers who caused little unemployment would pay lower rates. Conditions were specified whereby a state could not deny unemployment compensation to a person for refusing to take a position vacant because of a labor dispute, where the conditions of work were "substantially less favorable" than those for similar work in the community, and where the individual would be required to join a company union or resign from or refrain from joining a "bona fide labor organization." All money deposited in the Unemployment Trust Fund plus interest must be used to pay benefits.

The subject of Title X was aid to the needy blind, the only categorical kind of disability, other than crippled children, dealt with in the act. As with OAA, the federal government pays half of the cost of benefits to the needy blind "not counting so much of such expenditure with respect to any individual for any month as exceeds $30" (increased to $40 in the 1939 Amendments). Similarly, it pays half of the costs of administration. Both the definition of "needy" and of "blind" were left to the states. An individual could not receive AB for any period for which OAA was received.

The concluding Title XI defined terms used in the act and dealt with administrative details.

Social security became a major issue in the presidential campaign of 1936 when the Republican candidate, Alfred M. Landon, charged it was "a fraud on the working man. The savings it forces on our workers is a cruel hoax."[27] But Roosevelt won mightily and favorable attitudes toward old-age pensions among Americans grew quickly. Support for OAI, which few people really understood, was 68 percent of a national sample in a November 1936 Gallup poll, increasing to an incredible 97 percent in an NORC (National Opinion Research Center) poll taken in 1943.[28] But the fate of social security still depended on its constitutionality.

Clear sailing for social security came after May 24, 1937, the day the Supreme Court in two decisions affirmed the constitutionality of unemployment insurance (Titles III and IX) and OAI (Titles II and VIII).

The 1935 act, it should be emphasized, provided only for old-age pensions for workers at age 65 who retired completely from covered employment. There were no provisions for pensions for widows or other survivors, or for dependents. This great oversight was recognized as such by the important 1937–38 Advisory Council on Social Security whose recommendations formed the basis for the 1939 amendments to the original act. The amendments filled forty-eight pages compared to the thirty-two pages of the original act. Social security now became a family protection plan and had essentially the same structure as what we now call social security, except for the addition of disability insurance (DI) in 1956 and Medicare in 1965.

The 1939 amendments added benefits for survivors and dependents, including the wife aged 65 or over, the child under age 18 of a retired or deceased worker, the widow aged 65 or over, the widowed mother under age 65 with a child under 18, and the surviving dependent parent aged 65 or over. The effective date for the payment of monthly benefits was advanced to 1940 from 1942. A program of lump-sum death benefits was added. And all this was done without much long-term cost to the system by reducing the amount payable to single persons and eliminating the money back guarantee of contributors who died or otherwise did not qualify for a benefit. The OAI trust fund became the OASI trust fund.

A new formula for calculating pensions was also adopted in the 1939 amendments. Interestingly, the relative size of benefits provided by the 1939 formula for the worker with average earnings retiring at age 65 is almost precisely the same as those provided by the current formula. According to the 1939 law the single worker would retire with a benefit of 40.0 percent of previous earnings—assuming constant wages and prices—and with an eligible spouse, 60.0 percent. Under current law the comparable percentages are 40.6 and 60.3 percent.[29] It is therefore not true, as is commonly believed, that social security benefits have somehow become more generous than they were in the past.[30]

From the passage of the 1939 amendments to 1950 not much happened in social security; it "just was not very important" observed Robert Ball about this period.[31] Contributions and benefits in no way kept up with increases in prices and wages. By 1950 the average benefit was only about $26 a month. In 1950 only a quarter of those over age 65 received OAI pensions. In 1985, by contrast, 94 percent of those over 65 received OAI pensions and over 95 percent of children and their mothers were protected by survivors and dependents insurance.

In the years around 1950 there were various proposals from various quarters for adopting a system of flat rate pensions and blanketing in everyone over 65, but they were successfully opposed by the social security leadership and never came to a vote in Congress. Never in the first half century of its history has the fundamental structure of social security been so seriously threatened.

The 1950 amendments revived the ailing social security system. Benefits were increased by a whopping 77 percent. The combined employer-employee tax rate was increased to 3 percent with provisions for the combined rate to increase to 6½ percent by 1970. Compulsory coverage was extended to new categories of the working population. Gratuitous wage credits of $160 a month were granted for service in the Second World War (and later extended for postwar service). Certain changes in beneficiary categories were adopted in this year beginning the trend toward the completely sex blind system we have today.

The 1947–48 Advisory Council, which recommended most of the changes that were adopted in 1950, had proposed a limited program of disability insurance. But because of strong opposition inside and outside of Congress, it was not included in the 1950 bill. In 1954, however, a "disability freeze" became part of the social security law, providing that a period of disability would not be counted in determining the worker's insured status or benefit amounts. DI was finally adopted in 1956 and then only for workers over age 50, but OASI had become OASDI. In 1960 the age qualification was removed and benefits were also provided for dependents of disabled workers. American DI has continued to use a severe definition of disability: an inability to engage in "substantial gainful employment" with a condition expected to last at least 12 months or result in death; and no partial disability is recognized.

III

There has been much continuity over the first half century of OASDI. Equal contributions by employers and employees have continued, with the self-employed contributing at a higher rate than employees (established by legislation at 1½ the employee percentage in 1950 when the self-employed were first covered, lowered in 1965, reestablished in 1977, but changed to double the employee percentage in 1983). Contributions from general revenues, as envisioned for the future by the architects of the original system, have been vigorously opposed by Congress in favor of the original self-supporting mode of financing adopted in 1935. (Though a one-time exception of .3 percent of the employees' contribution from general revenues was legislated in 1983 for 1984). This opposition continued even when the trust funds were close to bankruptcy in the early 1980s. The strong emphasis on social adequacy at the expense of individual equity has continued in the primary insurance amount (PIA) formula adopted in 1977, though with a slightly greater emphasis on individual equity at higher earning levels compared with the operative 1939 formula. (The formula for those having first eligibility in 1985 is 90 percent of the first $280 of averaged indexed monthly earnings [AIME], plus 32 percent of AIME in excess of $280 but not in excess of $1,691, plus 15 percent of AIME in excess of $1,691). The normal retirement age (NRA) remains age 65, but the 1983 legislation will increase this gradually to 67 in the next century; early retirement at ages 62 to 64 with actuarially reduced benefits has been available to women since 1956 and to men since 1961. The earnings or retirement test continues, though it has been weakened by successive legislation beginning in 1939. (The retirement test touches a profound difference in the popular as distinct from the official understanding of OAI. The benefits are popularly interpreted as an annuity, not as insurance against lost earnings.) Even the earnings base of $3,000 in the late 1930s covers about the same percentage of earnings (about 90 percent) in covered employment as did the 1985 earnings base of $39,600.

Most of the changes in OASDI that have occurred up to the legislation of 1977 were expansionary: expansion of coverage; expansion of benefit categories; expansion of flexibility in age at retirement; expansion of exempt amounts under the earnings test; expansion of social adequacy; and, above all, expansion of taxes. There also had been a few contractions in the program before 1977 such as elimination of return of contributions provisions (1939), freezing of the lump-sum death benefit at $255 in the early 1950s, and making earnings in noncovered employment applicable to the earnings test (1954). Legislation in 1977 and particularly 1981 and 1983, however, introduced a number of deliberalizations into OASDI.

The 1935 legislation covered only a bare majority of the labor force, essentially all employees in the nonfarm private sector other than railroad employees who were covered under their own plan. In 1950 compulsory coverage was extended to cover virtually all workers in the private sector, state and local employees not already covered by some type of government retirement system, and the nonfarm self-employed other than those in certain professions. In 1954 self-employed farmers and state and local government employees with a retirement system could be covered on an elective basis. In 1956 the remainder of professional self-employed persons, except self-employed physicians, were compulsorily covered. Physicians were mandatorily covered in 1965. Coverage was extended on a compulsory basis in 1983 to employees of nonprofit organizations and to all federal civilian employees hired after 1983. The president, the vice president, members of Congress, federal judges, and some 8,000 other upper level political appointees and senior government executives were also covered in 1983. Over 90 percent of the workforce is now covered by social security (OASDI); the only sizable categories outside the system are about 29 percent of state and local government employees, most federal civilian employees hired prior to 1984, and low-earnings casual workers.

Benefit categories began to expand even before the first benefits were paid. The 1935 Act provided benefits only for the retired worker at age 65. The 1939 Act added benefits for survivors and dependents as previously noted. In 1950 dependent husbands and widowers were added in addition to wives of any age of retired workers if a child under age 18 was present. In 1965 benefits were added for full-time students aged 18 to 21 and wives' and widows' benefits for divorced wives when the marriage had lasted at least twenty years (reduced to ten years in 1977). In 1972 widows' and dependent widowers' benefits were increased to 100 percent of the PIA when claimed at age 65 or after (increased from the 82½ percent legislated in 1961, which had been increased from the original 75 percent of 1939). Benefits were adjusted to changes in the Consumer Price Index in 1972 to take effect in 1975.

Supreme Court decisions in 1975 and 1977 expanded monthly benefit categories by eliminating the two most important sex differences existing under OASDI. The 1975 decision in *Weinberger v. Wiesenfeld* gave fathers with a deceased, disabled, or retired wife the same benefits as a mother in a comparable situation. The 1977 decision in *Califano v. Goldfarb* did away with the dependency requirement for aged husbands and widowers on the grounds that none existed for aged wives and widows. Later decisions of lower courts required that divorced men receive benefits under the same conditions applicable to divorced women. No other social security system in the world is now as fully devoid of sexual differentiation as the American.

In 1956 women became eligible for actuarially reduced benefits at ages 62 to 64. This first introduction of flexibility in age at retirement was made available to wives, widows, female dependent parents, and working women. The original rationale, though most inadequate, was that wives are commonly younger than their husbands and that it was desirable for both to be able to claim a pension at the same time. The eligibility age for men was reduced in 1961, also with actuarially reduced benefits. An increment of 1 percent of the PIA for each year retirement was delayed between 65 and 72 was legislated in 1972, increased to 3 percent for each year in 1977, and to 8 percent for each year in 1983 (to be phased in over the period 1990–2009 and to be applicable only above the increasing NRA).

Since 1950 legislation has made real increases in the amount of earnings exempt from the retirement test, lessened the amount of reduction in benefits over the annual exempt amount, and lowered the age at which the retirement test no longer applies. In 1985 the annual exempt amount was $7,320 for those over 65 and $5,400 for those under 65 with a $1 reduction in benefits for each $2 earned over the exempt amount (to become $3 in 1990). A lesser amount is exempt for those receiving DI. The age at which the earnings test is no longer applicable became age 75 in 1950, 72, in 1955, and 70 in 1983.

OASDHI taxes (or contributions) as a percentage of covered payroll have increased considerably since 1937 when they were first collected. The rate was 2 percent of the first $3,000 of earnings (1 percent from both employer and employee) through 1949. The combined employer-employee tax for OASDHI for 1985 was 14.1 percent on an earnings base of $39,600. The maximum OAI tax in 1937–1949 for employer and employee combined was $60, or $30 each; the maximum tax for OASDHI in 1985 was $5,583.60 for employer and employee, or $2,791.80 each. The tax rate is scheduled in present law to increase in steps reaching an ultimate rate of 15.3 percent in 1990 and after. The earnings base, however, will be increased only in step with increases in average earnings. The allocation to the three trust funds is:

	OASI	DI	HI	TOTAL
1985	11.4	1.0	2.7	14.1
1990 and after	10.2	2.2	2.9	15.3

Beginning in 1974 the United States, like other industrial nations, began experiencing high rates of inflation and unemployment combined with a slowdown in economic growth, all of which had disastrous and unanticipated effects on the OASDI trust funds. Income showed a relative decline at the same time that outgo in the indexed programs increased. There was an upswing in retirement for reasons of disability and unemployment. The Congress, beginning in 1977, reacted by reversing the expansionist patterns of the previous decades.

As a consequence of the rapid inflation of the 1970s it became clear that the PIA formula adopted in 1972 was resulting in escalating replacement ratios for successive cohorts. A new formula was adopted in 1977 that reduced replacement ratios by around 7 percent for persons born in 1917 and after. The adoption of the 1977 formula, however, had universal support among social security experts, informed opinion, and in Congress because the earlier formula came to be regarded as in "error." But the new formula certainly is regarded as a deliberalization by the "notch babies" born in 1917–1922, who, with similar earnings records, receive substantially smaller pensions than those born in the years before them.

Several other deliberalizations occurred in the 1977 amendments. The minimum benefit was frozen at its December 1977 level of $122. The continuing monthly earnings test was replaced by an annual test, a deliberalization for persons with relatively large earnings in a few months. A government pension offset for spouses with federal, state, or municipal pensions was enacted to take effect in December 1982.

Legislation enacted in 1980 capped disability benefits by a special maximum family benefit (MFB) lower than exists in cases of the retirement or death of a worker. This was done, according to Robert J. Myers, because it was believed the relatively high benefits that could arise "could discourage rehabilitation of disabled workers and thus result in higher costs for the program."[32]

The 1981 and 1983 amendments were more deliberalizing than any earlier social security legislation, but they are minor in light of what was variously proposed by the Reagan Administration during its first year in office. The major provisions relating to OASDI signed into law by President Reagan on August 13, 1981 were these:

1. Benefits for youth aged 18 to 21 who were full-time students (adopted in 1965) were phased out.
2. Minimum benefits were phased out for new beneficiaries and for those already on the rolls. This was later changed to be applicable only to those claiming benefits from 1982.
3. Mothers' and fathers' benefits were terminated when the youngest child reached 16 (had been age 18 since 1950).
4. Benefit amounts were to be rounded to the next lower dime at each step in the application of the PIA formula and to the next lower dollar at the final step. (Previously amounts had been raised to the next higher dime in all steps of the PIA formula.)
5. A disability megagap was introduced whereby total disability benefits under certain federal, state, and local public programs could not exceed 80 percent of previous earnings.[33]

The deliberalizations of the 1983 legislation which successfully and quickly resolved the shortfall of the OASDI trust funds were these:

1. The OASI tax for 1984 was increased by .3 percent for both employer and employee and part of the rate increase for 1990 was moved to 1988. (For 1984, a one-time direct reduction of .3 percent of the employee tax was made up from general revenues.)
2. Cost-of-living adjustments were moved ahead six months to a calendar year basis, from July to January, effective for 1983.
3. Upper income recipients were to pay federal income tax on up to half their benefits. (The unindexed thresholds for tax liability are $25,000 for individuals and $32,000 for couples.)
4. Tax rates for OASDHI for the self-employed were increased to be equal to that of the combined employer-employee rate, effective in 1984.
5. A prohibition on termination of state and local governmental units from coverage after having elected coverage became effective on enactment of the legislation.
6. The benefit formula was modified to provide lower benefits for persons with large pensions from noncovered employment.[34]

All of the foregoing are clear deliberalizations, but most are minor when considering the magnitude of the proposals which emanated from the Reagan Administration in the spring of 1981.[35] The most important of the stillborn proposals were those increasing new pensions by less than the increase in average wages for the years 1982–1986; reducing the benefit rate for early retirement at age 62 from 80 to 55 percent of the PIA, with proportionate changes between ages 62 and 64; decreasing the maximum family benefits for the retired and for survivors as was done for the disabled; elimination of dependent children benefits of retired workers aged 62 to 64; and delaying the automatic cost-of-living adjustments from July to October in 1982 and subsequent years. (This is, by the way, just half the lag actually adopted in 1983.)

Considering that 1981 was a year preceded by half a decade of "crisis" talk about the OASDI trust funds and the year when the prestige of the conservative Reagan administration was at a high point, the changes made in OASDI can only be regarded as minor and peripheral to the core of the programs. The two most important deliberalizations, those which resulted in the greatest savings, were the elimination of student benefits at ages 18 to 21 and the elimination of the minimum benefit. Both the Ford and Carter Administrations attempted unsuccessfully to eliminate student benefits because of their tremendous cost to the program and the introduction of various federal programs to aid students after the passage of OASDI student benefits in 1965.

Elimination of the minimum benefit, originally introduced for administrative reasons and later regarded as a social adequacy benefit for low-earnings workers, was aimed at the much maligned double-dippers who made up the majority of those who received the minimum benefit. (The minority who were poor would be eligible for enhanced Supplemental Security Income benefits.) Individuals could be eligible for the minimum benefit with only a small number of quarters of coverage and very small earnings. For example, a person reaching age 65 in 1978 needed only six years of coverage (twenty-four quarters) under OASDI to be eligible for a pension. Prior to 1978 a quarter of coverage was given for any quarter in which a mere $50 was earned in covered employment. (In 1978 this amount was increased to $250 and is increased annually in relation to increases in average earnings reaching $410 in 1985.)

In late 1981 after President Reagan had shelved his social security proposals, he announced the appointment of a bipartisan fifteen person National Commission on Social Security Reform[36] to seek solutions to both the short-range financial problems of the 1980s and the more distant, but more serious problem of the shortage of funds beginning in the second decade of the next century after the large birth cohorts of 1940–1965 begin to enter upon retirement. The commission was composed of some who were suspicious of the system and some who were supportive of it, of expansionists, moderates, and contractionists. That the commission was able to agree twelve to three on a package of eight core proposals was a remarkable exception to the low degree of consensus achieved by previous committees devoted to making recommendations about the social security system. The previous National Commission on Social Security charged by the 1977 Social Security Amendments to investigate "all aspects of social security and related programs" failed in its 1981 report to achieve consensus on some of the big issues such as age of retirement with full benefits, cost-of-living adjustments, and general revenue financing. So, too, did the recent Advisory Councils on Social Security fail.

How little agreement there really is on the nature of OASDI and its future directions among expert opinion—policymakers and politicians, economists, and actuaries—was observed by Alicia H. Munnell a decade ago in summarizing a Brookings Institution Conference on "The Future of Social Security:"

> One speaker characterized the conference participants as the proverbial blind men feeling the elephant, all holding their own views of what the social security program is. However, the participants had a more difficult problem than the blind men, because they were asked not only to define the social security program as it is today but to propose what it should be in the future. The introductory analogy was indeed prophetic, for participants displayed substantial disagreement on the role of social security, the appropriate benefit structure, and how the program should be financed. The differing recommendations were derived directly from the participants' differing perceptions about the beast. [37]

The lack of consensus on the goals and purposes of our social security system among the experts has always existed and makes the accomplishments of the National Commission on Social Security Reform which prepared the way for the 1983 Amendments a most remarkable success. But, in spite of the experts, the great majority of the American population continues to support social security. [38]

The OASDI trust funds are in stunningly good shape now and are projected to be so for many years in the future, even under poor economic conditions. But the American public has been so bombarded with dire predictions about "the bankruptcy of social security" for so many years that they can't believe it. Consider the observation made in late 1985 by Claire Longden, a financial planner with the Philadelphia firm of Butcher & Singer: "We have no way of knowing where we will be 10 years from now. . . . For instance, there's a great disbelief in social security. I'm not sure it's going to be around in eight or 10 years. If I'm wrong, it's wonderful. If I'm right, it could be horrible." [39]

Future OASDI income and outgo will depend on a number of economic and demographic factors such as economic conditions, inflation, employment, mortality, and fertility. Four alternative sets of assumptions are prepared by the Social Security Administration in projecting the future financial status of OASDI. Two sets, Alternatives II-A and II-B, are called "intermediate." Both use the same demographic assumptions, but Alternative II-B assumes slower economic growth than Alternative II-A. Alternative I is designated "optimistic," Alternative III "pessimistic."

Under Alternative II-B assumptions OASDI cost rates are projected to be *lower* than income rates for a third of a century. According to Harry C. Ballantyne, Chief Actuary of the Social Security Administration, writing about the actuarial status of the OASI and DI trust funds over the 75-year period 1985–2060: "During the first half of this period, the estimates indicate that income will generally exceed outgo, resulting in substantial surpluses each year. After about 2020, the reverse is true, with outgo exceeding income, thus resulting in substantial deficits."[40]

Because of the healthy prospects for future decades of the OASDI trust funds, it is unlikely that there will be any basic changes in the system. Social security has the largest public of any domestic political issue and the large majority of that public supports the essentials of the existing program. In presenting the 1977 Social Security Amendments to the House of Representatives, Al Ullman, Chairman of the Ways and Means Committee, warned there would be "no more easy votes on social security."[41] I would now say there will be no votes on social security in the foreseeable future unless and until an issue can be defined as a crisis. And that is unlikely.

Acknowledgements

Some of the material in this introduction has been taken from Richard F. Tomasson "Old Age Pensions under Social Security: Past and Future," *American Behavioral Scientist*, vol. 26, no. 4 (July/August 1983), pp. 699–723 and "Government Old-Age Pensions under Affluence and Austerity: West Germany, Sweden, the Netherlands, and the United States," in Michael Lewis (ed.), *Research in Social Problems and Public Policy*, vol. 3 (Greenwich, CT: JAI Press, 1984), pp. 217–272. The U.S. part of this latter article was commented on in great detail by Robert J. Myers; many of his suggestions and corrections have been incorporated into this essay.

Notes

1. For general surveys see Gaston V. Rimlinger, *Welfare Policy and Industrialization in Europe, America, and Russia* (New York: John Wiley, 1971); Richard F. Tomasson, ed., *The Welfare State, 1883–1983*, volume 6

of *Comparative Social Research* (Greenwich, CT: JAI Press, 1983); and Roy Lubove, *The Struggle for Social Security, 1900–1935* (Cambridge, MA: Harvard University Press, 1968).

2. Christopher Leman, *The Collapse of Welfare Reform: Political Institutions, Policy, and the Poor in Canada and the United States* (Cambridge, MA: MIT Press, 1980), p. 23.

3. John G. Brooks, *Compulsory Insurance in Germany, Including an Appendix Relating to Compulsory Insurance in Other Countries in Europe*, Fourth Special Report of the [U.S.] Commissioner of Labor (Washington, DC: Government Printing Office, 1893).

4. Adna F. Weber, "Industrial Accidents and Employers' Responsibility for their Compensation," State of New York, *Seventeenth Annual Report of the Bureau of Labor Statistics for the Year 1899* (Albany, 1900).

5. US Commissioner of Labor, "Workmen's Insurance and Compensation Systems in Europe," *Twenty-fourth Annual Report*, two volumes (Washington, DC: Government Printing Office, 1911).

6. A good brief discussion of the AALL is Lubove, *The Struggle for Social Security, 1900–1935*, pp. 29–34; for a fuller account, see John A. Fitch, "The American Association for Labor Legislation," in *John B. Andrews Memorial Symposium on Labor Legislation and Social Security* (Madison: University of Wisconsin Press, 1949), pp. 81ff.

7. Writings by and about Rubinow are extensive. An excellent summary of his views is I. M. Rubinow, *The Quest for Security* (New York: Henry Holt, 1934).

8. See his autobiography, *Myself* (Madison: University of Wisconsin Press, 1934) and the biography by L. G. Harter, *John R. Commons: His Assault on Laissez-faire* (Corvallis: Oregon State University Press, 1962).

9. *Proceedings of the Conference on the Care of Dependent Children held at Washington, DC, January 25, 26, 1909* (Washington, DC: Government Printing Office, 1909) and Harold A. Jambor, "Theodore Dreiser, the *Delineator* Magazine, and Dependent Children: A Background Note on the Calling of the 1909 White House Conference," *Social Service Review* 32 (1): 33–40.

10. On Epstein see Lubove, *The Struggle for Social Security, 1900–1935*, pp. 128–143. One of his best known works was *Insecurity: A Challenge to America: A Study of Social Insurance in the United States and Abroad* (New York: Random House, 1938).

11. See, for example, Paul H. Douglas and Aaron Director, *The Problem of Unemployment* (New York: Macmillan, 1931), Paul H. Douglas, *Social Security in the United States*, 2nd edition, New York: McGraw-Hill, 1939), and his memoirs, *In the Fullness of Time* (New York: Harcourt Brace Jovanovich, 1972).

12. Lubove, *The Struggle for Social Security, 1900–1935*, p. 113. Her

extensive writings include *Toward Social Security* (New York: McGraw-Hill, 1936), *The American Social Security System* (Boston: Houghton Mifflin, 1949), and *Social Security and Public Policy* (New York: McGraw-Hill, 1956).

13. Searle F. Charles, *Harry Hopkins: Minister of Relief* (Syracuse: Syracuse University Press, 1963) and Frances Perkins, *The Roosevelt I Knew* (New York: Viking, 1946) touch on their roles in the formulation of the social security legislation.

14. A colorful discussion of these movements can be found in Arthur M. Schlesinger, Jr., *The Politics of Upheaval* (Boston: Houghton Mifflin, 1963), pp. 29–41.

15. Edwin E. Witte, *The Development of the Social Security Act* (Madison, University of Wisconsin Press, 1962) and Arthur J. Altmeyer, *The Formative Years of Social Security* (Madison: University of Wisconsin Press, 1966) discuss the formative period of the Social Security Act of 1935.

16. Edward D. Berkowitz, "The American Disability System in Historical Perspective," in Edward D. Berkowitz (ed.), *Disability Policies and Government Programs* (New York: Praeger, 1979), p. 18.

17. Walter I. Trattner, *From Poor Law to Welfare State*, 3rd ed. (New York: Free Press, 1984), pp. 207–8.

18. Mark H. Leff, "Consensus for Reform: The Mothers'-Pension Movement in the Progressive Era," *Social Service Review* 47 (September 1973), pp. 397–417.

19. [Public—No. 271—74th Congress], [H.R. 7260]. The Social Security Act and other basic documents relating to the development of the act are to be found in National Conference of Social Work, *The Report of the Committee on Economic Security of 1935 and Other Basic Documents* (Washington, DC: NCSW, 1985).

20. Quoted in Arthur M. Schlesinger, Jr., *The Coming of the New Deal* (Boston: Houghton Mifflin, 1959), p. 312.

21. Quoted in Arthur J. Altmeyer, *The Formative Years of Social Security* (Madison: University of Wisconsin Press, 1966), p. 38.

22. Carolyn Weaver, *The Crisis in Social Security: Economic and Political Origins* (Durham, N.C.: Duke Press Policy Studies, 1982), pp. 94–96.

23. The granting of two million dollars to the U.S. Public Health Service in Title VI is an exception to this statement.

24. Altmeyer, *The Formative Years*, p. 25.

25. Quoted in Robert J. Myers, *Social Security*, 3rd ed. (Homewood, IL: Richard D. Irwin, 1985), pp. 456–57.

26. Lewis Meriam, *Relief and Social Security* (Washington, DC: Brookings Institution, 1946), pp. 184–88.

27. Quoted in Altmeyer, *The Formative Years*, p. 68.

28. Richard M. Coughlin, *Ideology, Public Opinion and Welfare Policy*

(Berkeley: Institute of International Studies, University of California, 1982), pp. 58–59.

29. Calculations made by Myers, *Social Security*, Appendix 3–5, pp. 333–37.

30. OASDI pensions for those born for several years prior to 1917 are more generous than those born in previous and subsequent years because of the operation of the 1972 formula.

31. Robert M. Ball, "The 1939 Amendments to the Social Security Act and What Followed," in National Conference on Social Welfare, p. 167.

32. Myers, *Social Security*, p. 89.

33. John A. Svahn, "Omnibus Reconciliation Act of 1981: Legislative History and Summary of OASDI and Medicare Provisions," *Social Security Bulletin*, vol. 44, no. 10 (October 1981), pp. 3–24.

34. John A. Svahn and Mary Ross, "Social Security Amendments of 1983: Legislative History and Summary of Provisions," *Social Security Bulletin*, vol. 46, no. 7 (July 1983), pp. 3–48.

35. Myers, *Social Security*, Appendix 3–8, pp. 339–43.

36. The president named five members of the National Commission on Social Security Reform, Speaker Thomas P. O'Neill, Jr. named five, and Senate Majority Leader Howard H. Baker, Jr. named five.

37. Alicia H. Munnell, *The Future of Social Security* (Washington, DC: Brookings Institution, 1977), p. 716.

38. Myers, *Social Security*, pp. 417–20.

39. Quoted by Thomas Watterson, "Baby Boomers Face Retirement Pinch," *Albuquerque Journal*, November 24, 1985, p. D12.

40. Harry C. Ballantyne, "Actuarial Status of the OASI and DI Trust Funds," *Social Security Bulletin*, vol. 48, no. 6 (June 1985), p. 31.

41. Quoted in Martha Derthick, *Policymaking for Social Security* (Washington, DC: Brookings Institution, 1979), p. 411.

Update 1988

Rather than "updating" the social security dollar amounts in this introduction and throughout the volume, the editors decided a listing of 1988 dollar amounts was preferable.

The bend points in the universal social security benefit formula (p. 16) for 1988 are $319 and $1,922. Other dollar figures for 1988 are as follows:

Amount needed to earn one quarter of coverage	$470.00
Maximum earnings subject to tax	45,000.00
Maximum individual tax (7.51% of earnings)	3,379.50
Exempt earnings for beneficiaries 65–69	8,400.00

Social Security

Exempt earnings for beneficiaries under 65	6,120.00
Maximum benefit, worker who retired at 65 in 1987	822.00
Maximum family benefit, first combined in 1988	1,879.80
Average benefit, all retired workers	513.00
Average benefit, couple, both beneficiaries	876.00
Average benefit, widowed mother, with two children	1,077.00
Average benefit, aged widow alone	468.00
Average benefit, disabled worker, spouse, children	919.00
Average benefit, all disabled workers	508.00
Maximum federal SSI payments, individual	354.00
Maximum federal SSI payments, couple	532.00

All benefit amounts above are monthly amounts.

2

Social Security
The First Half-Century, A Discussion

Panelists: *Eveline M. Burns,*
Wilbur J. Cohen, Thomas H. Eliot,
Robert J. Myers, and
Charles I. Schottland

Moderator: *Richard F. Tomasson*

Moderator: Today I am going to introduce the shapers of our social security system in reverse alphabetical order, from left to right. On my far left is Charles I. Schottland, Commissioner of Social Security under President Eisenhower from 1954 to 1959. During 1933–1934 he was head of Federal Emergency Relief in California, later he was Director of Welfare for the State of California, and President of Brandeis University. Next to him is Robert J. Myers, long time Chief Actuary of Social Security and most recently Executive Director of the 1983 National Commission on Social Security Reform. He has just published the definitive book on social security, which I hold up in my hand. It is 1076 pages long. (*Social Security*, 3rd ed., Homewood, IL: Richard D. Irwin, 1985).

On my right is Thomas H. Eliot, chief draftsman of the 1935 Social Security Act. Later he was Congressman from Massachusetts and Chancellor of Washington University. Next is Wilbur J. Cohen, about whom we have said so many times that he was the first employee of the Social Security Administration. He has been continuously involved with social security since he was twenty-one years old. In the 1960s he was Lyndon Johnson's Secretary of Health Education and Welfare. He is currently Professor of Public Affairs at the Lyndon B. Johnson School of Public Affairs at the University of Texas. And on the far right is Eveline M. Burns, Professor Emeritus of Social Welfare at Columbia University, who, beginning in the late 1920s, has written a small library on social security and social welfare.

I have asked each of these founders and shapers of social security to talk for about five minutes on a subject of their choice regarding the first half century of social security. I told them that the question is very general, but their answers may be quite specific and they may deal with any issue they choose. Continuing in reverse alphabetical order, we begin with Mr. Schottland.

Schottland: Thank you. It is a pleasure to be here and to discuss social security over the last fifty years. A five minute presentation means one minute for each decade of social security.

I want to emphasize that social security in the United States was a new phenomenon; however, we were the Johnny-come-lately in the social security field among the industrialized nations. Many countries are now celebrating their one-hundredth anniversaries of such legislation. It was born in controversy in the United States and controversy has continued through the entire fifty years. Some of you may have tuned in on "Wall Street Week" last night. Social security was very prominent in the discussions with Louis Rukeyser,* who took the president to task for his lack of knowledge about the relationship of social security to the deficit. Alan Greenspan,† the guest on the program, came out in favor of freezing the COLA which is now a major political issue in the congressional arena. And although I agree that Alan Greenspan has the right to freedom of speech and to his own opinion, he also has a right to be wrong; and as far as I'm concerned, he is.

I want to congratulate the organizers of this program for bringing together the people who make up this panel today. I was going to say old timers, but last night Wilbur Cohen objected to our using the word old timers, so I shall not describe the old timers as old timers because of his objection.

*Louis Rukeyser is an economic commentator, nationally syndicated economic columnist, and host of "Wall Street Week."

†Alan Greenspan is an economist and was Chairman of the National Commission on Social Security Reform, 1981–1983. In August 1987, he assumed the position of Chairman of the Federal Reserve Board.

I'd like to emphasize just two or three things in this brief five minutes. First, the great battles of social security, like the other great battles of public policy, are being fought in the political arena. And those of us who are interested in promoting programs and changing public policy, or establishing public policy, had better recognize that our role has to be played out in the political arena. Second, I want to emphasize the importance of individuals both inside and outside of government in those political arenas. Yesterday this subject was touched upon lightly by Gary Freeman and Charles McClelland* and I would like to emphasize it by using one of our panel members, Wilbur Cohen, as the subject of my comment on the role of the individual. Gary Freeman developed for us in the summary of his paper some models that influence public policy. For many years I taught a course in public policy, and I, too, developed models along parallel lines: one on mass movements, and the influence mass movements had on policy; second, the role of bureaucracies—Congress as a bureaucracy, the executive branches as a bureaucracy, the courts as a bureaucracy and increasingly the role of the courts in developing policy, particularly in social security; and, finally, individuals as influencers of public policy. And I used a number of individuals. Those of you in the mental health field will know the name Dorothea Dix. I had a model of what she did in the field of mental health a hundred years ago. I had a model for Mary Lasker and her role of promoting mental health and public health, and then of Wilbur Cohen and social security. One of my students in asking a question said, "referring to the Wilbur Cohen model;" and after that we called it the "Wilbur Cohen Model."

I think its very important for us to recognize the contributions of individuals, including some of the people at this table, to social security in the last fifty years. There has not been any major controversy in social security that persons at this table have not participated in and been influential in. But I think that seventy-five or one hundred years from now when all of the people here are no longer with us—and I believe that the actuary on my right, as competent as he is, will agree with my assumption of their not being with us seventy-five or one hundred years from now is correct—people may not be aware of the contributions made by individuals. I would like

*Both Freeman's paper and McClelland's comments are in this volume.

to mention the contributions of Wilbur Cohen as illustrative of the contributions of many dedicated people who helped formulate the social security program, who had much to do with the writing of the various amendments over fifty years, and who initiated lobbying and public support for these amendments. It has been said that Wilbur Cohen was the father of Medicare, but a lot of people contributed to it. Yet there is no question that he made a major contribution in formulating the specifics of the Medicare program and in helping get it through Congress. But if he was the father of Medicare, he was really the father and mother of Medicaid, if that is biologically possible.

I think that it is the dedication of individuals and the leadership of social security over the years that has distinguished the administration of this program from the administration of other programs, where persons involved were managers and not dedicated proponents of the particular program.

I would also like to point out the role that social security has played in the lives of the American people. It has lifted more people out of poverty than all of the antipoverty programs of the federal government put together. Thirty-seven million people now receive social security checks, and for many it is their floor of security and keeps them out of poverty. And Medicare and Medicaid have kept the high cost of medical care from reducing many families to poverty. It has made an invaluable contribution to eliminating poverty and is thoroughly accepted by the American people. And the attacks upon it have not been very successful, except in a few cases. And in every administration, until the present one, from the beginning and through all of the Democratic and Republican administrations, social security has been advanced.

Just one further comment, and that is to repeat that individuals can make a great deal of difference. And I have noted Wilbur as one person who, both inside and outside of government, did make a great deal of difference.

Moderator: Mr. Myers.

Myers: As an actuary I see the developments in social security in the last fifty years in terms of numbers. And I hope I won't bore you if I give you a few numbers, at least I won't give you any intricate actuarial formulas. There are three particular statistics that I think indicate very well the growth of the Old Age, Survivors, and Disability Insurance Program [OASDI] over these fifty years. The number of covered persons, that is the people who had taxable and creditable wages in a year, rose from 32 million in the first year of operation [1937] to 119 million currently. The number of people receiving monthly benefits started at zero, was only 1 million in 1945, and currently is 36½ million. Another figure, from an economic standpoint, that is good to keep in mind to indicate how things have changed over the years is the level of average wages. In the late 1930s the average annual wage in the country was around $900, in 1985 it is about $16,500, almost a twenty-fold increase.

Now let's look at something else—what was the actual situation in 1980 compared with the original estimates made in 1935 for that distant future year? Perhaps the most important element in my view is what is the cost of the program as it relates to taxable payroll? That indicates what tax rate is necessary to finance the program. Here I'm considering only Old-Age and Survivors Insurance [OASI] and not Disability Insurance [DI], because the estimates made for 1980 included only Old-Age Insurance. The addition of survivors benefits in 1939 was not an expansion of the program, but rather a readjustment. The level of retirement benefits was reduced to provide supplementary benefits for spouses and children, and the lump-sum death payments that were a sort of "return of contributions," and that would have been a sizable amount in later years, were eliminated and instead monthly survivor benefits were put in that gave good protection, very good protection to those who needed it, but did not provide this return of contributions for people who really didn't need it. For the OASI program the actual cost in 1980 was 9.4 percent of payroll. The estimated cost—the estimate that was made in 1935—was 9.6 percent. This is an indication that over the years the program has not "over expanded," but rather has remained close to the 1935 estimate.

Let's look at another figure. In the early days there was great controversy over the size of the fund that would be built up, because although the program wasn't fully funded, it was going to be on a partial reserve basis. There was an estimate of forty-seven billion dollars, which was of course a huge amount of money, to be in the fund in 1980. The actual balance of the fund in 1980 was twenty-three billion dollars because the financing had moved more toward a pay-as-you-go approach. Well, that's not too bad; twenty-three billion dollars, forty-seven billion dollars, they're in the same ball park. But don't ask me about other figures such as benefit-outgo and contribution-income because, with the inflation of wages and prices that we've had over the years, these comparisons don't look very good.

As an actuary I don't want to just look backwards, I also want to look ahead and project what's going to happen in the next fifty years. Using the intermediate estimates, in fifty years, in 2035, as compared with the present 36½ million OASI beneficiaries each month, there will be something like 80 million. The number of covered workers will increase from the present 119 million to somewhere around 157 million. Of course, it's an increase that's not nearly as huge as the number of beneficiaries. We've heard many times about the growing load over future years, at least in relative terms. The bottom line of all this is that the cost rate, that is the cost of the benefits as a percentage of taxable payroll will be around 16 percent fifty years from now. The projected tax rates for OASI are somewhat less than this, but the difference will be made up by the present form of financing—which I don't think is a very good one—by drawing on the OASI trust fund. Eventually, when the fund is drawn down another fifteen or twenty years later, higher tax rates on the order of 16 percent, that's 8 percent on both the employer and employee, will have to be levied.

Finally, what about the general structure of the plan fifty years from now? Well, I'm willing to be a "status quoer" and say that I think fifty years from now, when many of the people here will be present, the system will look very much as it does today in its general form. The dollar figures of course won't be at all the same—benefits will be much higher in terms of absolute dollars and similarly the taxes. Maximum taxable earnings will be higher, but I think we will have a social insurance system of the same general type that we have now. The major change that should be made in the program of the future, I think, is in the financing. We should not carry out the procedure that present law contemplates. Some people say—another myth about social security—that its being financed on a pay-as-you-go basis. Under present law it is not pay-as-you-go. I think it should be. Under present law a huge fund will be built up beginning in about the year 1990 and it will reach a peak in perhaps 2025 and then it will begin to be used up. When it's used up we will face the problem of a higher tax rate. I would prefer to see the system financed *really* on a pay-as-you-go basis, by building up a fund to a certain level, say half a year's benefit payments, then having the tax rate automatically adjusted thereafter to keep the funds at about this level. Thank you.

Moderator: Mr. Eliot

Eliot: Bob Myers mentioned that Survivors Insurance was added to the Social Security Act in 1939. When the President's Committee on Economic Security, of which I was counsel, was formulating the program no one was sure exactly how the Old-Age Insurance part of the program would be administered. We had not yet reached the high speed computer era, and we knew that there was going to be a big problem. And so the committee recommended a considerable number of exclusions from the original act—the chief ones, I suppose, being nonprofit organization workers, agricultural workers, and domestic servants—and there was no provision for survivors getting benefits in the original bill. However, when the bill was being considered before the House Ways and Means Committee in executive session, several of the congressmen said, "but what about the poor widow after the man who has been receiving benefits dies?" And so they assigned Mr. Middleton Beman of the House legislative counsel and me to draft an amendment to include survivors in the insurance program. It was quite a job. We had to get a lawyer down from the treasury, because it would probably change the tax rates. We had to get an actuary, though I don't think it was Bob. He was a very young fellow then, even younger than I was, and we worked all weekend and formulated a proper survivors insurance amendment. We brought it back to the committee and presented copies to the members, and Chairman Doughton looked at it and said, "What's this?" And Mr. [Carl] Vincent and Mr. [Jere] Cooper looked at it and said, "What's this?" And somebody said, "I move we table it." And we didn't have survivors insurance until 1939. A bit of congressional history!

Yesterday, in one of the discussions, mention was made of the Townsend Plan and the pressure that plan perhaps caused, resulting in administration support for a major old-age insurance program. I was amused to find after the discussion that when we were listening to this Wilbur Cohen and I had exactly the same reaction, the same name came to our lips, simultaneously we said it—Huey

Long. While some of the congressmen were certainly affected by the increasing political power of the Townsend Club movement—in the minds of the people in the administration and particularly the man at the top, there was always the visible possibility or threat that the Kingfish of Louisiana would organize a presidential opposition ticket against Roosevelt in 1936 and, conceivably with his slogan "Every Man a King," sweep the country.

Mention of Huey Long takes me back to a conference that Arthur Altmeyer*, I think, and I attended in the summer of 1934, nearly fifty-one years ago, at the White House with the two people to whom most of the credit historically should go for the existence of a social security program in the United States: Frances Perkins, secretary of labor, and President Roosevelt. At that meeting, as in most of the discussions in the Committee on Economic Security, which Miss Perkins headed, most of the attention was paid not to what we now call social security, and what we then spoke of loosely as Old-Age Insurance, but rather to unemployment compensation or unemployment insurance. One of the suggestions that was made was that there should be a national scheme of unemployment insurance. To this Mr. Roosevelt said an emphatic, "No!" He added, "We've got to keep a lot of responsibility and a lot of functions in the states." He said, "just think what it would be like to have all the power in the federal government, if Huey Long should become president." He was pretty well committed anyway to unemployment insurance by state law. He had spoken for it when he was governor of New York, he had campaigned for the presidency in 1932 on a platform that called for that specifically, and when he tried to recruit Miss Perkins to his cabinet she had insisted—and I don't believe he resisted too much—that he approve and promise to support a number of programs dear to her heart. One of those was unemployment insurance by state laws.

Actually an attempt to achieve this had begun fifty-one years ago this winter and I was involved in that. That was the drafting of the introduction of a bill imposing a federal tax, a payroll tax, on employers, but allowing employers to offset against that tax whatever they were required to pay under a state unemployment compensation law. No state unemployment compensation law was then in

*Arthur J. Altmeyer was an original member of the Social Security Board 1935–37, Chairman 1937–46, Commissioner of Social Security 1946–53.

effect, although one had been passed in Wisconsin. Its effective date had been postponed because imposing a payroll tax on Wisconsin employers when nobody else had to pay such a tax would leave those employers at a competitive disadvantage with employers in other states.

We needed a scheme that would eliminate that competitive disadvantage for the progressive state, and that would in fact persuade every state to keep the money at home rather than have the payroll tax go into the general funds in the federal treasury; keep the money at home for the benefit and protection of their own unemployed. That bill, which was drafted by the son-in-law of Mr. Justice Brandeis, Paul Rauschenbush,* and me, age 26, was known as the Wagner-Lewis Bill and was introduced in the winter of 1934. It was debated considerably. There were alternative approaches. The president's committee spent a great deal of time battling back and forth with the various approaches that were made. The Wagner-Lewis approach was adhered to partly because of Mr. Roosevelt's belief in one of the objectives of the Wisconsin law, which was the stabilization—the voluntary stabilization—of employment by rewarding the employer who had a good record of not letting many of his employees go and forcing them to apply for unemployment insurance. This came to be known as merit rating and then as experience rating in the unemployment insurance field. Also the president and Miss Perkins, and I at least,—although Roosevelt didn't publicize the fact—had good reason to believe that this particular type of law would be upheld by the Supreme Court in a period when the Supreme Court was busy knocking down one New Deal law after another. The Wagner-Lewis bill didn't get anywhere that year, but it reemerged a year later as Title IX of the Social Security Act. As a result of that title every state passed an unemployment insurance law.

This is the fiftieth year not just of what we now speak of, think of, as social security, but also of all the other parts of the Social Security Act itself: the welfare parts, and especially, in my view, the unemployment insurance part. We've now had half a century of unemployment insurance in this country. There have been abuses. The laws are intended to compensate people with partial replacement of

*Paul A. Rauschenbush was Director, Wisconsin Unemployment Compensation Division of Wisconsin Industrial Commission.

lost wages while they are unemployed and looking for work. Doubtless in numerous cases that provision has not been rigorously enforced and gifts, in effect, have been made to people who prefer to be idle, but they are a small minority. I think of the millions of people over the past fifty years who wanted work and couldn't find it and who have been virtually saved by the existence of these programs in the states. And I wonder too whether without the maintenance of that admittedly fairly low level of purchasing power in times of recession, recession would not more than once have slid down and deepened into depression. For that reason I would like to emphasize—I take this occasion here to emphasize—that over and above the Old-Age Insurance and Disability and all the rest, this is the anniversary of the beginning of unemployment insurance in the United States.

Moderator: Mr. Cohen

Cohen: I am somewhat embarrassed today to be a living example of a bureaucratic model, mainly because I've tried it on my children and grandchildren and they can't believe it. But, more seriously, as I read the political scientists and the books that have been written in connection with the bureaucratic model, I think there is a small footnote that always seems to me to be overlooked when I realize two aspects today of my own and my distinguished colleagues participation. One is that the people who were drawn in in 1934–35 had a social consciousness about the problems of our country. They were not bureaucratic as they came into the program in terms of making a job for themselves or a role for their lifetime occupation. They were concerned, as were the people of the United States between 1929 and 1933, that the social fabric of our nation was in virtual collapse, in a deterioration, in which a man like Huey Long or Gerald Smith,* Father Coughlin† or Doctor Townsend could come in with panaceas that would virtually change the whole nature of our government. I believe, following on what Tom Eliot has said, that with the virtual collapse of the banking system in 1933, the

---

*Gerald L. K. Smith was an anti-Semitic, extreme right wing clergyman with a national following.

†Father Charles Coughlin was an anti-Semitic, pro-German, anti-Roosevelt priest with a huge radio audience.

states were bankrupt, the counties were bankrupt. The farmers, when I was a young student at the University of Wisconsin, carried pitchforks up to the state capitol—which I saw myself—in rebellion. They make the farmers today look like pale copies of their counterparts in 1932. And I believed then and I believe now that our country was on the verge of a social change of radical proportions. Franklin D. Roosevelt said that he had some ideas about security and it gave people a sense of hope, a sense of the future of our country, a sense of community solidarity. And this was embodied in the program.

Now these young people, some of whom you see before you today, at that time were motivated by a social consciousness of preserving the community. If you want to call it a bureaucratic model I have no objection to it, but I don't think it gives the sense of responsibility and the essence of the kind of spirit that Frances Perkins and Arthur Altmeyer and Edwin Witte* had, some of them products of the LaFollette-Progressive period, populists and so on, who were trying to preserve what was good in our social relationships. In fact I would go one step further, perhaps with a little exaggeration, I think Franklin Roosevelt in 1934–35 could have wiped out the states in the United States if he hadn't taken the position he did. The governors that live today don't realize that in 1932–33 the states and the counties were bankrupt sovereignties, they were incomplete sovereignties. Franklin D. Roosevelt could have nationalized the banks in 1933, he could have eliminated the states, he could have nationalized unemployment insurance, and welfare and everything else. I think it would have been accepted because people were homeless, the equivalent of thirty million unemployed today were without work then. And so I believe that Frances Perkins, Franklin Roosevelt, Edwin Witte, Arthur Altmeyer, John Winant†, Republicans and Democrats both, were infused with a sense of trying to keep the body politic, the social fabric, the community solidarity together. This was a social mission that is frequently overlooked in the bureaucratic model. It certainly is consistent with it, but it is frequently overlooked.

---

*Edwin D. Witte was Professor, Department of Economics, University of Wisconsin; Executive Director, Committee on Economic Security.

†John G. Winant, a Republican Governor of New Hampshire, was first Chairman of the Social Security Board, 1935–37.

Second, something in this model that is distinctive, which I think you will see here, is that quite a number of them have stayed involved with the program for fifty years. There are not very many other programs that I'm aware of as a teacher in which a number of the significant people made it a lifetime preoccupation because they believed in it. Not because it was a job. Not because it gave them an income. Not because it gave them power, although you may say that's consistent with the bureaucratic model, but because it was a program that had a mission in society to bridge not merely the problems of our time but to solve some of those problems. Now following on what Mr. Eliot said, I think it is completely overlooked that we are commemorating the Social Security Act today and in this year. Old-age insurance was a rather minor aspect of the Social Security Act fifty years ago. Mr. Eliot's genius, among many of the things that he did, was to put Old-Age Assistance as Title I of the Social Security Act, which was a much more immediate aspect. The states were no longer able to even take care of needy people on welfare who were old. They didn't have the money. The property tax was not a possible basis for financing the care of the aged or the blind or the disabled or the mothers and the children. And because he put that first, the conservatives in Congress, who then dominated the Congress—Southern conservatives were chairmen of the committees, Mr. Doughton* of North Carolina, Pat Harrison† of Mississippi—felt that was a great contribution to preserving the integrity of the states and they went along with Old-Age Insurance simply because they felt that maybe the program might help in the future to take some of the financial burden off the states. So here again we find a rather interesting facet of Franklin D. Roosevelt; he was able to enlist liberals, radicals, and conservatives in this effort. And I think that's one aspect of his political genius, his ability to balance the different groups.

Now one point more. In 1934 or in 1935, in my opinion, President Roosevelt could have gotten the enactment of unemployment insurance as soon as Tom Eliot had finished redrafting it. He could

---

*Robert L. Doughton was a Democratic congressman from North Carolina; Chairman, House Ways and Means Committee, which had jurisdiction over social security.

†Bryon Harrison was a Democratic senator from Mississippi, and Chairman, Senate Finance Committee, when social security was drafted.

have—and Old-Age Assistance, too. But in my opinion, upon the recommendation particularly of Miss Perkins and Harry Hopkins,* he opted for a Committee on Economic Security to study what he already knew was his decision. And by studying it, what happened? We added—not we, but Congress, I mean collectively—Old-Age Insurance, now the biggest social welfare safety net in our nation, and we added Aid to Dependent Children, maternal and child health, crippled children, child welfare services, and grants for public health and vocational rehabilitation, all of which are aspects relatively neglected by the political scientists and the sociologists as part of the Social Security Act. The important point to me, though, is that the people who framed the act were thinking of an inter-generational, cross-generational set of programs. They weren't simply preoccupied with the aged; they wanted to do things for children, and they wanted to do things for rehabilitation, and they wanted to do things for child welfare. And embedded in all these eleven Titles when Tom finished drafting it—eleven titles of the Social Security Act—was a protection over the whole life cycle and upon which further Congresses could build. I think that aspect of the broadness of the act is indeed neglected because of the tendency to think always of the Social Security Act, which now has twenty titles in it, only as a matter of old-age security.

I want to make two more points. One of the most important ways the 1935 act differed from foreign programs is that Congress elected to make the benefits vary with peoples' wages in Old-Age Insurance and Unemployment Insurance rather than have the flat, uniform benefits that the British system had. And that is something that we did without recognizing that there would be inflation, which would cause flat benefits to have to be constantly adjusted. Our system is more related to a capitalistic market system than an egalitarian system which exists in some foreign countries. When we met with Sir William Beveridge,† in 1942, we then exported that approach to the social insurance and social security institutions of the world. It was more or less the United States accepting a variable benefit in relation to earnings that made our character different from others.

---

*Harry Hopkins was Special Assistant to President Roosevelt and Member of the Committee on Economic Security.

†William Beveridge was the author of *Social Insurance and Allied Services* (1942) which outlined the bases of the postwar British Welfare State.

This is, in my opinion, why Bob Myers can say, and with which I wholeheartedly agree, that the social security system will remain for the next fifty years, because the system is adaptable and can be retained indefinitely. There are other characteristics that I will be glad to discuss when we come to them later. But I believe this adaptability together with the variation with wages, an omnibus bill covering all sorts of things, and a program so constructed that future Congresses could build on it incrementally—these were the important contributions in 1934 and 1935.

Moderator: Mrs. Burns.

Burns: I don't know what there is left for me to say after the four people have so adequately covered past, present, and future of the Social Security Act. But it does seem to me that one of the reasons they dug up the five of us—I was going to say disinterred—and a few others, who were alive at that time, to come and talk to you is that it was hoped that we might give you some sense of the significance of what we now take for granted and of what things were like before the Social Security Act came into existence.

I came to this country from England in 1926 as a young economist, and of course I was eager to find out all about the social institutions of this country. I kept wanting to find out what the social insurance system was like. And everybody I asked looked at me rather pityingly and said, "Oh, but that is something for Europe, for effete countries. We don't need that kind of thing in the United States." Well, of course, they were punished because two years later we had the Great Depression. But all the same it does amaze me how much was achieved in 1934–35 by the development and passage of the Social Security Act, which as Wilbur Cohen has told you, covered not only old-age insurance, but also covered many other social problems. And one naturally asks oneself, "who really was responsible for all this?" I would firmly agree and assert that it was President Roosevelt—if there was one single person who could be given the credit, not so much perhaps for conceiving of the problem, but of seeing that a solution to the problem became enacted, and enacted in a way that made it very popular. I suppose there is no piece of federal legislation that is more popular today than the Social Security Act. The first thing every political aspirant and appointee thinks he has to do is to make sure everybody understands that he's all for the Social Security Act and doesn't want it changed; and this is a measure of his responsibility.

While I think President Roosevelt was remarkable in his ability to get things achieved, I think Miss Perkins has a great deal of credit due her, for, after all, helping to educate Mr. Roosevelt when he was governor of New York. Remember, she didn't start the education process when he got into the White House. It was already done, that part of it, and people of that ilk were able to get legislation through. But we also have to give credit to the people who formulated the legislation. Two people whose names should be added to the list of those people we honor for what they did for social security are Professor Barbara Armstrong* of the University of California and Professor J. Douglas Brown† of Princeton. Had he been able to travel, I'm sure Professor Brown would have been with us today. He and Dr. Armstrong were in charge of that part of the staff of the Committee on Economic Security concerned with old age. And they are as responsible as anyone for making sure that we got in protection for the aged in 1935, not just Old-Age Assistance but also Old-Age Insurance. Indeed, the two of them were quite convinced from the beginning that if you were going to do anything serious about old age it would have to be through social insurance.

They went quietly about their work on the Committee on Economic Security when everybody else was quarrelling, as Mr. Eliot I'm sure will agree, about what kind of social insurance system we should have for unemployment. Everybody's attention was paid to that. It's funny, you look back on it now to think that it was on that that everybody was spending their time, research, memoranda, proving to you—the lawyers proving to you—that there couldn't be a federal system of unemployment insurance because it would be declared unconstitutional. This is something, by the way, which we never seem to worry about nowadays. The people now planning various kinds of federal programs never seem to have to worry as we worried in those days about whether they would be declared unconstitutional. As late as November 1934 before the Congressional session opened there was a series of public meetings because the

---

*Barbara Armstrong was a University of California economist and author of *Insuring the Essentials: Minimum Wage, Plus Social Insurance* (1932).

†J. Douglas Brown was a prominent economist at Princeton who wrote many books on Social Security. He was a consultant to the Committee on Economic Security.

Committee was, in addition to everything else, going to report on its programs—really on its nonexistent programs at that time. All they were talking about was unemployment insurance and there was a great riot of attention about it.

But people began to ask, "What about old age?" Well, nobody knew much about old age. What were you going to do about old age? Meanwhile, here were Doug Brown and Barbara Armstrong quietly working away and they said, "Oh, here's a program for old age." They already had a well-worked-out system that ultimately, with certain modifications of the financing, became the famous Old-Age Insurance program. I always use this episode as an example when talking to my students about how you never know when you're going to have a chance to put your ideas into effect. Therefore, be ready with your ideas and don't postpone thinking about the problem or what to do about it because you don't think its possible. Those two, I'm sure, were responsible as much as anyone for the fact that we now have this system.

Now one other thing that occurs to me as I look at what it was like fifty years ago and what it is like to today and has been for some years, is that now we do have a system that covers almost everybody in one way or another. It's a system that isn't only assisting people who get their benefits on the basis of need, but a system that helps people who are affected by things largely beyond their control, what's happening to the economy, what's happening to their ages, and so on. And I think one of the great achievements of the American social security system is the fact that it applies to the middle classes as well as to the workers, as well as to the proven poor, what our president likes to refer to as our ["truly needy"] people. That gives it a basis of strength that I think most other systems don't have and has enabled it to resist so many changes in government and in policy. People sometimes say, "Why do you cover people who are well off?" One reason we cover them is because we have adhered to the objective of universal coverage, including not only the very poor whose influence may not be so great, but the comfortably off as well. We perhaps failed to take advantage, although we are now beginning to do so, of using the tax to reduce the inequality of incomes. We can tax higher incomes rather than merely develop a system for the poor. And it has been said a system for the poor is indeed a poor system. I look forward to growth and continuance of the program.

I am only sorry for you people who are younger than I am, you who are in your twenties and thirties or will be, that you don't have the opportunity that my generation had knowing that there were great problems, national interests involved, and that technical people were needed. We had some training in technique and we knew we could be involved in contributing our bit to the planning. And we knew that if we could come up with something good, we had a chap in the White House who knew how to pull strings and get it done. And I am sorry for you people that you didn't have that enormously exciting experience that I was lucky enough to have in my thirties. Thank you.

Moderator: Now let us introduce some controversy into this discussion. I'll begin with a controversial question. In the first couple of decades of social security, there were a number of proposals for a two tier, a double-decker plan of old-age pensions. The first tier would be a noncontributory universal pension paid for out of general revenues and this would go to everybody, presumably at age sixty-five. And then on top of this universal noncontributory pension would be a strictly earnings related pension. This plan is one that is found in a number of countries and it has a certain clarity. First there's the egalitarian program where everyone gets a pension by virtue of being a citizen or resident national of the country, and then there's the inegalitarian part with the strictly earnings related pension on top. This would resolve the conflict between social adequacy and individual equity that so many people criticize in our system of old-age insurance. I would like to ask the participants how they view such a plan? Forget about the politics. Wouldn't this have been a better system than the one we have now in which there is some relationship—but by no means a clear one—between what one has contributed and the size of one's pension and in which the social adequacy and the individual equity element are not clear.

I know that you have some rather strong views on this topic and I would like to turn to you first, Mr. Myers.

Myers: Thank you. Well, first of all, I'm not worried a bit about the conflict between social adequacy and individual equity. Even in a double-decker plan such as you described there would still be that conflict in the wage related part because although the benefits would be proportional to wages, they wouldn't be what was individually purchasable. I did not particularly like the double-decker plan because I think there would have been a better way than that, which I will describe in a moment. I would oppose the double-decker plan because I believe that financing through general revenues is a fiscally irresponsible thing to do. There are too many people who would put all the emphasis on the flat benefit and say, "Let's increase it. It doesn't cost anything. The money comes from general revenues, that's just money that comes down from heaven." And I believe in a system where the cost is visible and direct. In other words, through payroll taxes.

What would have been the ideal system to have started with, if it had been possible to have completely universal coverage? It would have been to guarantee that everybody in the country, even though they were no longer covered or no longer working, would get the minimum benefit. It's a little something like what was done in 1965 and 1966. The difficulty with this approach, however, would have been that if you didn't have universal coverage then you never would have gotten it because many people would say, "I don't want to be covered and pay taxes, I'll take the minimum benefit." With universal coverage, it would have been perfectly equitable and proper to have financed the minimum benefit to people who already were retired out of the contributions of the employers and the employees because this is just like giving prior service credits that are all paid for by the employer. So ideally that would have been the way, but I think it would have been impossible to administer such a system, so I think we had to go the way that we did.

Cohen: Can I?

Moderator: Yes, please, Mr. Cohen.

Cohen: Like Mr. Myers, I've spent nearly forty years studying every double-decker plan that has ever been, as far as I know, proposed in detail. But the Moderator says, "Why don't you discuss it but leave out politics." Well, that's what you can't leave out. Politics is the very nature of public policy decision making. Now what are the politics of that, when you try to examine it? A large number of people including Mr. Altmeyer, and Mr. Witte, Ida

Merriam*, Dr. Falk†, and all the other people, including Bob Myers, and me, who worked on it all those years, were concerned that the minimum, whatever it was—one hundred dollars a month, two hundred dollars a month—would have had to be financed out of general revenues. We also realized it would have become a political issue in every presidential campaign because every opponent to the incumbent would have said, and I think this is almost predictable, 'whatever the X was I will propose in my administration to increase the X.' Therefore, that bottom part of the deck would have injected social security into every congressional and presidential election, in which candidates would try to outbid each other. Just as Bob Myers says, they'll say, "Well, we'll pay that out of general revenues."

That's one consideration, and you might think that's not the important one. I'll say for myself that the important consideration in President Roosevelt's and other people's minds was that benefits could be cut. This could have become an issue in 1980, it's just the other side of that same thing. If it's easy to raise it, it is equally easy in a period of budget deficit, to cut it. The reason that's unsatisfactory is not whether a minimum benefit is the right amount, but that is not what is security in terms of social security. If the amount can be raised and lowered every presidential or congressional election, how do old people—or disabled people—plan their lives in the future when they don't know what their benefit is going to be? The essence, at least in my opinion, of why the double-decker plan with that large amount in the bottom deck is unacceptable is that it would give people anxiety and insecurity in being able to retire from employment and being sure that they could organize their life and move if they want—to Albuquerque from some other place and buy a house and so on—when they don't know what their pension amount is going to be. So I believe that the reason it became unsatisfactory is because the very nature of the double-decker, particularly the bottom deck, lent itself to such possible political manipulation that it would not have been satisfactory. Finally, I think that what you have to realize in connection with the double-

---

*Ida C. Merriam was head of the Office of Research and Statistics on Social Security during the 1960s and 1970s.

†Isadore S. Falk was head of the Office of Research and Statistics of Social Security (1936–1953).

decker that worried a lot of people, and Bob I think touched on it, is if it did occur that the bottom deck grew by political manipulation to a bigger and bigger one, then the contributory part would become relatively smaller and obviously be something you would eliminate. The net effect would be that people would say social security was a welfare program. If it became a welfare program in their minds, then ultimately there would be a means test or an income test attached to it. There was one thing that the people who were trying to build the social security system were clear about and that was that the American people did not want the primary, basic, fundamental old-age security system to be a welfare system. They wanted it to be some kind of a contributory, wage-related, nonmeans-tested system. So for all these reasons I think that the double-decker found support only among a very few people, largely politicians who wanted to make the bottom deck very low, and largely people and economists who thought it was a way to keep the contributory system down to a very minimum.

Burns: May I?

Moderator: Yes.

Burns: I remember—it must have been about forty years ago, when the double-decker system was very much under discussion—having written a memorandum for the Social Security Board, as it was then called, opposing it and saying why. I'm not sure that I would write that memorandum again today. There are indeed a number of problems in connection with the double-decker program, but also there are a number of problems in connection with our present system. Wilbur [Cohen] says that if there were a double-decker program there would be discussion about what the lower level should be, and I think basically there should be discussion. One of the things that we have failed to get people to think seriously about is the question of what level of living our society should guarantee all its members. At the moment we've evaded that. I think we are going to come to the realization, as wages and therefore benefits increase, people are more and more going to say, "Why are we going to force all these people to guarantee themselves benefits that run into the tens of thousands a year," as under the present system we will. In other words, we've somehow or other buried a part of the understanding of the cost of our social security benefits by saying there's nothing really to decide because it's a certain percentage of earnings as laid down in the law. Now that percentage has changed and I suspect its going to change again in the future. More and more people are going to complain, on the one hand, that in spite of the social security benefit system we have these many thousands of people getting Supplemental Security Income because their social security benefits are too low. Therefore we've got to do something to raise the benefits. On the other hand, more and more are going to say, "is it really fair to ask, to force, the Mr. Rockefellers of this country to put aside this amount of their money to guarantee themselves an adequate benefit out of the public system?" I must say I'm uneasy about this.

I have to confess, I was once very strongly opposed to the idea, perhaps partly because I felt unsure whether the existing system would have enough popular support. Today I think it does have enough popular support for us to think rather seriously about whether we don't need to have some kind of a change in the benefit formula. Wilbur, it doesn't necessarily mean an income test.

I was in Australia two years ago and was impressed by the fact that Australians, who are not anything if not spunky and independent and who will fight anything they don't like, have accepted a system where the benefit is based on a means test. All I would like to suggest is that they have accepted it. My relatives there think nothing of a means test. Which suggests that perhaps when we're thinking about changing the system or improving it—I don't mean abolishing it, but improving it—we should think two or three times more about what it is we don't like about a means test. I hate the means test and I'm glad that Wilbur emphasized the fact. The system we have is one way of avoiding putting everybody through a means test, but if it's more of a formality such as the income tax is— which is a kind of means test when you come to think about it—if we could change . . .

Cohen: I disagree with you violently on this point.
(Laughter)

Burns: As you see you're going to see some fun here. But if we could consider what it is that is offensive and undesirable about the means test, maybe we could free ourselves to think a little bit about whether we couldn't improve the system insofar as the benefits structure is concerned.

Cohen: My only point is please don't do it during the next three and a half years.

Burns: Yes.

Cohen: If you're going to improve the system, do it when you have a much more favorable environment. The present environment, which is antigovernment, which is antisafety net, which is anti–social security in terms of the political framework, in my opinion, is not a good time to do that, Eve [Burns].

Burns: Well I didn't say I was going to do it now, but we've got to do a lot of thinking and it'll take three and a half years, I'm sure.

Moderator: Related to this idea of a system of universal pensions is a criticism that some younger academics have made about social security. They claim that the people who constructed the system have constructed an inegalitarian system, a system that provides social insurance for the deserving majority and public assistance for the less deserving minority. We have in our system this distinction between Old-Age Insurance and Supplemental Security Income, between Medicare and Medicaid, between income tax deductions for children and AFDC. It permeates our whole system of social security and the criticism is that we went the wrong way and we should have constructed a system built on more egalitarian grounds. I ask you to respond to this.

Cohen: You want me to start?

Moderator: You may start.

Cohen: Well, I was brought up in an atmosphere of egalitarianism under the LaFollette-Progressive movement, but this is not exactly a politically viable philosophy today. It is one thing to say it, but something else when it comes to constructing social institutions that people accept. We're a democracy and the people who develop these ideas have to go out and get 218 or more people in the House of Representatives and 51 people in the Senate to vote for them. As much as I would be for the ideas that you mention, I don't think you can do that in the present political climate. So that's one situation that has to be realistically taken into account. The second is why do you expect that when we have an inegalitarian society that people would want to make social security egalitarian? When President Reagan is talking about lowering marginal tax rates so that wealthy people have a lot more money and will go out and invest more, why would you assume that there would be public or political support for injecting egalitarianism as a principle in social security? In the last few years our whole society has become less egalitarian in its objectives. So I think there are separate issues here.

Now when you take just old age and realize that there are only 5 percent of the aged who are receiving ssi—while I would like to see that go down to 4, 3, 2, or zero if that were possible—the fact that 95 percent of the aged are not on welfare is pretty good. That's a pretty good achievement. But this doesn't mean we ought to be satisfied and that we can't do better. I strongly favor raising the ssi payment to above the poverty level so that none of these people would be in poverty and I would even favor a somewhat higher minimum social security benefit. But one doesn't have to go all the way to egalitarianism by saying that everybody ought to get the same, everybody ought to be treated equally. We don't apply that principle in education. We don't apply it in taxation. We don't apply it in wages in the market place. Why do you ask that social security or social policy be the only place in our whole social fabric where egalitarianism should be applied? So it seems to me that this doesn't take into account the reality, even though it may be a desirable objective in some form.

Finally, to the extent that you do this you go in the direction of general revenue financing—and as Bob Myers said when you go into general revenue financing you lead yourself into a position that a new administration can cut back on it as an effort to balance the budget—and this has a lot of political difficulties and I think that is partially the reason that it hasn't been accepted. But if what you're saying when you apply it to Medicare and Medicaid, that you are for a national health insurance system, I'm with you 100 percent. I think the biggest gap we have at the present time is that 100 percent of the population is not covered under a uniform comprehensive national plan in which all people are treated equally in the sense that no matter what their illness is, no matter what their disability is, they have access to the highest quality medical care under a national system. But I'd have to admit I think that's pretty far from reality right now.

Eliot: I think the young critics of today had their counterparts fifty years ago, and certainly some articles were written that were very critical of the Social Security Act because it did not seem to provide an egalitarian society. The fact is that it wasn't supposed to. The earliest draft in its preamble, as I recall it rather fuzzily, said that this was a bill to ameliorate the vicissitudes of economic insecurity. And that's all it was. And it wasn't supposed to create a totally different egalitarian society.

Schottland: I'd like to approach this from the standpoint of the present political situation because I believe it is important for us to discuss in academic circles and in intellectual circles and in forums such as this a variety of proposals, past and present, that can be made to improve our system. But I think we have to recognize that we are where we are and that no country in the world has succeeded in having a completely egalitarian income maintenance program. And I'm not worried about the fact that we have a combination of social insurance and ssi, or that we have Medicare and Medicaid. Our problem, it seems to me, is to improve our system so that we begin to have a secure system. I emphasize the words *secure* and *security*.

I am very much afraid of any program that completely depends for income maintenance on general revenues and the whims and wishes of elected officials, whether presidents or Congress, that gives them the power to raise or lower benefits in a program that ought to be based on income security. So I'm willing to go along with the present system, constantly improving it to eventually do away with some of the insecurity and the gaps in our income maintenance program.

Myers: I also disagree with those critics who say that the present system of social security is inherently inegalitarian. For one thing, I think some of those critics would take the mathematically impossible position that everybody in the country should have above average income.

I think the really key thing, and Wilbur mentioned this too, but since its in the line of figures I want to repeat it. The way the question is stated you might think the deserving majority is 51 percent and the deserving minority is 49 percent. Well if it were that way, that 49 percent of the people had to get SSI in addition to OASDI benefits, there would be something wrong with the OASDI system. And I think that this is one of the things that is wrong with the British system. The British level of benefits as far as old-age pensions is concerned is too low, and a sizeable proportion of the people have to get supplementary assistance. Here in the U.S., where maybe 6 or 7 percent have to get SSI I think that's about the best we can do. It would be desirable if that were lower, but its certainly not putting the OASDI program in a bad light when some 93 percent of the people are making out very well on their own on an insurance benefit and not on an assistance benefit that's subject to a means test and review.

Although I'm in agreement with my good friend Wilbur on this general principle, he brought up a couple of other things where I want to express my dissent without going on at any great length. First, I don't believe that proposals to reform the tax structure, such as moving more toward the flat tax, are necessarily something that is going to benefit the rich at the expense of the poor, although it seems to be on the surface. If a more flat rate tax system is adopted and loopholes are closed it could have just the reverse effect. Second, I do not believe that a national health insurance system or national health service of the type Wilbur is talking about would be desirable. While it might be more egalitarian to divide up a smaller pie into more equal pieces, this may not be nearly as good as having a much larger pie that isn't divided quite as equally. Now I'm not saying that health care should only be given on the basis of ability to pay, but I think there's a good compromise somewhere between that and a completely egalitarian health delivery system.

Cohen: Could I make one more point? I don't want to monopolize, but . . .

Moderator: Yes.

Cohen: I think we ought to say this sometime during this discussion. I think that what we have done in these fifty years with regard to the matter of cash benefits for the aged and disabled has been very constructive. I think the nation has done a responsible job and Congress has. I think the cash benefits situation is in good financial condition. I think Bob would agree with me. Despite people thinking it's bankrupt, it isn't. That's a myth that's been circulated. It's not any longer a problem. The big problem is medical care expenses in the future.

Medicare and Medicaid are going to be big problems for the next fifty years, and you younger people in the room will have to figure out how you're going to pay and how you're going to have access to the highest quality medical care, with all this new technology and the aging population and so on. The problem isn't any more the financing or the administration of old-age security or a double-decker system for social security, it is how to finance, how to provide, how to access, to all of the American people the cost of a high quality medical care system. We haven't touched on that. That I think is the problem for the next fifty years.

Burns: I think you're right.

Moderator: Don't you think that we need a social security simplification act, such as the proposed income tax simplification act? We have the most complex social security system in the world, at least I think we do. The calculation of pensions is complex. There are three different earnings tests. There are three different actuarial reduction rates. There is a different age for pension eligibility for widows than for workers and spouses. Look at the *Social Security Handbook*. How many pages does it have? Five hundred pages of just basic interpretations. The Social Security Law is how long? How many pages of small print?

Burns: Look at the book [Myers, *Social Security*, 1,076 pages]. Like the Bible.

Moderator: Like the Bible. That's right. Doesn't it need to be made simpler? One failure of social security is that very few people have even a primitive understanding of how it works. I'm sure that not one in 100 Americans understands how old-age pensions are calculated. I know you'd want to be first, Bob.

Myers: I'm probably one of the perpetrators of the complexness, although I don't have a license to draft legislation the way Tom does.

I've drafted a lot of legislation in my day and I'm still doing it. I would say this complexity is just fine. It's sort of like the file clerk who can't be disposed of because he or she has the files in such a system that nobody else can understand them. But I give the— perhaps you will say simplistic—answer that it is complex so as to produce desirable results. And there are a great many other things in our society that are the same way. I doubt if there are many people here who know how a television set works. What really makes it work? They know how to get the picture and everybody is satisfied with that; if you turn a few knobs you get reception. You don't know why, but it's the result that counts. Well, I think the results of the OASDI system on the whole are very good. There were a few mistakes that were made like the notch problem* that was brought up yesterday, but by and large I think the results that come out of the machine justify the complexity within it. Thank you.

Cohen: Could I?

Moderator: Yes.

Cohen: I think that different retirement ages are not only justifiable but desirable. I don't think we should have one retirement age as we started out with in 1935 at age sixty-five. There are different retirement ages for different things. People who are disabled can get benefits before sixty-five. People can get an actuarial reduction at sixty-two, and people can continue to work between sixty-five and seventy and later get a bigger benefit. I would say that this is all to the good of the system. It is more complicated, but people have more choices.

Moderator: Why, though, is there a different minimum age for widows' benefits and for spouses' benefits?

Cohen: Well, I'm not justifying every particular age, but as far as I'm concerned my first aim would be to amend the age discrimination law and repeal age seventy for mandatory retirement. I believe

---

*This is a problem of persons born in 1917 receiving substantially smaller pensions than persons born in 1916 with comparable earnings records. This is a consequence of the mandatory use of the 1977 formula for cohorts born in 1917 and subsequent years.

people ought to be able to work as long as they want and as long as they can perform and to choose to retire when they want to retire. And yet I do think there are a lot of special problems that society recognizes, which may be different than mine about the treatment of widows or widowers, or disabled widows. What?

Burns: And women as compared with men?

Cohen: Well, no. Now because of the gender changes we've made the same rule is applicable to widowers and to widows.

Moderator: In every case?

Cohen: In every case, yes. Completely. And I think that, incidentally, where we made a big, big, big improvement over all the foreign systems is that we never had a different retirement age for men and women as do most foreign countries, including the British system. We were not sexist in that one instance anyway. But my answer to you is that I think it would be great if we could simplify the Bible down to two pages. I would understand it a little bit better if it were boiled down, but I don't think you can do it any more with the Bible than you can do it with social security.

Moderator: The official understanding of oasdi is that it's insurance against lost earnings resulting from death, disability, and retirement. Regarding retirement, however, the popular understanding is that the old-age pension is an annuity that you get at age sixty-five. This is the overwhelming popular interpretation of social security old-age pensions, but it is probably not the understanding of the people sitting at this table. And my question is: Isn't it time for the official ideology to be replaced by the popular ideology insofar as retirement pensions are concerned?

Burns: Well, you might formulate your question perhaps even more broadly and say: "Isn't it time that more attention was devoted by the Social Security Administration itself, and by anybody who claims to have some knowledge of the program, to do a little more to educate people about the fundamentals of the program?" The program is misunderstood, the financing of it is misunderstood, the reasons for many of the provisions are misunderstood. For example, a lot of people talk about the earnings test as a means test. It is not.

It is a method of defining who is retired because this is a retirement system. And I think by and large it's shocking that after fifty years, even allowing for the complications that fifty years could introduce, that only a tiny proportion of the population, old or young, understands the rationale and the logic, such as it is, of the program, and how the provisions work today and what they are intended to do. Don't you people find that there's a lot of misunderstanding about it?

Eliot: I don't know whether I've found that exactly, Eve. But responding to Dick's [the Moderator's] question in the beginning, it seems to me that I have heard the program quite frequently described as a required insurance program leading to the payment of annuities upon retirement.

Burns: Yes.

Eliot: That's exactly what the simplest definition to the ordinary layman would seem to be. We didn't quite dare say that at the time the bill was being considered because there was a real possibility that the Supreme Court, as then constituted, would say that the Constitution gives Congress no power whatever to establish a retirement insurance system. But as soon as the Court had been induced to change its mind, after it had upheld the law in 1937, I think that was the most common, brief definition of the old-age insurance program.

Burns: But I don't think that everybody understands that. And talking about lack of understanding, will my colleagues explain if they know the answer, I confess I don't: Why is it that the unemployment insurance system has escaped the scrutiny and criticism that has been directed to OASDI, because if ever there was a lousy system that's our unemployment insurance system?

Myers: I'd like to talk about the original topic about the retirement earnings test. But first I'd like to answer Eve's question. I think the reason people don't pay much attention to the unemployment insurance as against OASDI is that everybody expects to get OASDI at some time and a lot of people say I'm never going to be unemployed, I don't care about that system.

But to get back to the retirement earnings test. There have been frequent proposals to do away with it. And you can look at this in two lights. One way of looking at it is that when people reach sixty-five or whatever the normal retirement age is, benefits would automatically be paid regardless of earnings. Those who oppose this particular argument say, "Look, it doesn't make sense to pay retirement pensions to people who aren't retired."

But another way to look at the retirement earnings test, is as already having been abolished, but this is on a deferred basis. From a cost standpoint, you can say to people, "We will not pay the benefit to you when you reach sixty-five, but if you keep on working we'll pay you an actuarially equivalent larger amount when you do retire." That is in present law. At the moment, people who delay retirement, as you know, get 3 percent more for each year of delay. But present law says that eventually, in the year 2009, people will get 8 percent more per year. That 8 percent more is close to the actuarial equivalent, so that over the long run, from a cost standpoint, the retirement earnings test has been eliminated. Now, personally, I would like to see, even though it will cost some money, that change moved up, at least to 1988 or 1990, but preferably the increment for delaying retirement should go up to 8 percent immediately. In theory I'm opposed. I would say that people who work longer shouldn't get more, that you should have a retirement test, but in practice its a very great disincentive to work for many people. Now those who favor the retirement test will take the example of a $100,000 a year lawyer, or doctor, or university professor . . .

Cohen: . . . at lower salary . . .

Myers: . . . who is going to receive a much larger benefit by delaying retirement and who doesn't really need it. From a needs standpoint people should get the same benefits no matter at what age they retire, but for the average guy who is earning ten to twenty-five thousand dollars a year the way the retirement test works out, the mathematics of it, is horrendous. In some cases people can even work after age sixty-five in this ten to twenty-five thousand dollar range and lose money by working, when you consider the income tax, the social security tax, and so forth. Many people get only maybe 10–15 percent net gain from any income earned at that time, and I think that this disincentive to employment is a bad thing. It's bad for the country as a whole by decreasing productivity. And I think it's even bad for people psychologically and from a health standpoint to say, "Well, I want to work, but I can't afford it. It just doesn't pay me to work. I'll go retire and sit on the porch." So that I think, therefore, what should be done to have better retirement income planning is to give larger deferred retirement credits as the present law will do eventually, but put that into effect as soon as possible and therefore give more incentives to people to work.

Cohen: I'd like to bring up another aspect of this question about educating the public about social security. I don't think we've done enough, and I criticize my own tenure in this, to persuade young people that there are also life insurance and disability benefits in social security. Everybody always starts and stops with old age and doesn't realize that there's a package deal in social security that covers four types of benefits, not only old age with all these different options that we have talked about. There's also life insurance if the breadwinner dies, which is very valuable, especially for young people who don't have the income to provide that. There's disability insurance from twenty-two to sixty-five. And there's Medicare. Now younger people will say "Well, its not going to be there when I get to be sixty-five." I don't happen to agree with them, but they overlook that when they get married and when they have a family there is tremendous family protection in social security. It is a family protection policy in which younger people, when their incomes are lowest and their family obligations are highest, get the greatest amount of protection. Therefore, they get their money's worth out of the system, which they do not believe is true. So I believe in answer to your question that there has been a failure of education, there has been a failure of understanding. Part of it is due to the government. Part of it is due to the media only stressing the old age element, more or less, as of interest. And part of it because young people automatically assume they're never going to get sick, disabled, or die, and they don't even think about ever getting to be sixty-five. So I think we've got a tremendous educational problem for the next fifty years.

Schottland: I agree with both Wilbur Cohen and Eveline Burns on the importance of education, particularly for grammar school and high school students. The problem is not only that they have inadequate information, but they're given wrong information in the textbooks they use in civics classes written by college professors. Bob Myers will remember that many years ago the Social Security Administration examined the seventeen, I think, leading textbooks that mentioned social security. Many other texts never even mentioned social security although they had chapters or many pages on relatively insignificant problems of our national life. And practically every textbook had a major error. I've examined several texts when I've spoken to grammar school and high school students and these texts not only have major errors, but they also have major biases and prejudices. I think it behooves the federal government, the Social Security Administration, and the Department of Education to look into this matter and see if we can't have a broad scale educational program that can simplify, not the law, but simplify the explanation and the basic premises of the law for young people. I have found an eagerness to understand social security on the part of young persons, and an acceptance of it once they do understand it. So I think that we have failed to do what so many other programs have done, get the information to the children going through the educational process.

Moderator: I don't think anybody answered the question, but that's alright. We'll go on to this next question.

Burns: What were we discussing?

Moderator: About accepting the popular view of old-age pensions as the official view.

Myers: Well, Dick, I thought I answered it because what is being done under present law, will eventually get you there. It will give people whenever they retire after the normal retirement age the actuarial equivalent of what would happen if the benefit had been paid at the normal retirement age. And my view was that the phasing in ought to be speeded up some, but eventually we will achieve just this result which happens to be the popular conception. Not, I think, necessarily because the public conceives of it that way, but because it ought to be that way.

Cohen: Mr. Myers and I will tell you that a couple of years ago when we were on one of the national commissions, we did a memorandum that listed a dozen myths. We discovered about a dozen things in which the general population, the media, or somebody completely misunderstood what was in the program. You asked about the popular attitude toward just one thing. There are a whole host of them. I could mention a dozen other things that the average person believes Congress has done in a completely different way from what Congress would ever recognize. I think that's why you need to have a good educational program.

Moderator: You're still not answering the question. I said should the official ideology about retirement be changed?

Cohen: My answer to that is no. If the popular interpretation of something is wrong, I don't think we ought change the explanation to accord with what is wrong, if you are making it a generic question.

Moderator: You've answered the question. (Laughter)

Moderator: I think it's correct to say America is the only industrial society in the world that hasn't come to terms with social security. It's attacked from the right by arguments that it inhibits savings, is a bad deal, is extortionist. It's attacked from the left by arguments that it's financed by a regressive tax, has an inegalitarian benefit structure, and is not conditioned on need. This last charge also comes from the right. Why is this? I think I can say that in all the other industrial societies the right and the left accept social security and it's not a political issue as it is in the United States.

Burns: Well, I think, if there's one single thing that might explain it, it is the fact that other countries believe in their own government much more than America does. And they credit the government with good, on the whole moderately good intentions, but at least a sufficiently close ear to the ground so that the government realizes ultimately what it is people want and tries to provide it. I think it's really surprising how much this shows up in many of our actions, but particularly in social security. I don't think other countries have had this kind of panic reaction to the discovery that for a period of years there's going to be some shortage of funds which is already planned for and which is provided for in the legislation. There is so little real confidence in the government as such—I don't mean Democratic presidents or Republican presidents, I mean in government as such—that I think the people are prepared to believe the worst. They don't think there's any kind of real control of the people over their own government. And this to me is what needs to be explained and what needs to be dealt with.

I think one of the worst things that's happening at the present time—and now I have to introduce a political comment—is the effort to destroy people's faith in the intentions and functioning of government. And so long as we do that we're going to do a lot of other stupid things. (Applause)

Eliot: I agree with this last comment of Eve Burns. I'm not sure, though, that I agree with the underlying assumptions of the question itself. Sure, there are vehement critics on the right and on the left, but as has been said here earlier, the political support for social security is widespread and is something that no political candidate for president or for national office can easily overlook. I'd like to ask a question of Eve or anybody else who would like to answer it. Is there a possibility that the comparatively greater acceptance of social security in other western nations may have some connection with the fact that in most systems, largely contributory though they may be, there is a continuing governmental contribution from general taxation rather than a complete dependence on what is, unarguably, a regressive tax? This is what we have here.

Burns: Well, are you saying that the popular attitude in America prevents us from having some contributions from general revenues in the system?

Eliot: Oh, I'm not saying that. What appears to be preventing us from having some general revenue financing, although there was a tiny bit in the recent amendments, is what appears to be an assumption on the part of many people, including the gentleman, I think, on my right [Cohen] and certainly the gentleman two from me on the left [Myers]. This is the principle that the system should be self-supporting from the taxes on payrolls and wages is graven in stone and can never be changed. Now both of them—both Mr. Myers and Mr. Cohen—have made very cogent and persuasive arguments that to have any general revenue financing would lead to great insecurity in the mind of the potential recipient because Congress might at any time either take away the benefits or ruin the country by raising the benefits irresponsibly in response to political pressure. I ask, then, if they have so little faith in the sense of Congress? Can't Congress now change the rates, change the benefits, wipe out the whole program? Of course it can. Mr. Achenbaum's paper yesterday pointed out very strongly that the courts have already held, more than once, that no enforceable contractual right was established by the Social Security Act. So Congress, which would be so dangerously prone to making mistakes if there were general revenue financing, is still perfectly able to make similar mistakes under the present system.

Burns: That's right.

Cohen: You wrote that in Tom. You wrote it in Title XI of the Act of 1935. You wrote in that Congress can amend or alter this program at anytime.

Eliot: I think that was done in committee. (Laughter)

Burns: I think it shows up again and again. People you expect would have a different point of view, nonetheless, oppose or propose things on the grounds that the Congress and the president can't be trusted. I think Tom's question is good. If it is the case that they are so irresponsible, why haven't they done it before. Why haven't they done more irresponsible things about the program? They haven't. By and large I think the Congress has been very responsible. And I've heard Wilbur say so many times when he's trying to sell people on something or other. (Laughter)

Cohen: Bob and I are going to differ so you'll have to hear two stories. Go ahead, Bob, you start.

Myers: Well, several points. First, I'm afraid I take exception to Tom Eliot's point that the social security taxes are "unarguably" regressive. I say that they are not regressive. You can't just look at the taxes by themselves, you have to look at the entire package of the benefits and the taxes. It's an insurance system.

I also think it's a good thing in this country that people are skeptical or critical about their government instead of just being mildly subservient. And I would disagree that the present administration is wrong for doing this. I don't say that I agree with the present administration in everything, but I think it's a good idea to raise these points. Are we having too much government or are we not? We shouldn't just blindly assume that the more government we have the better it is.

Now about the payroll tax being regressive, I just happen to have a quote from a book I picked up here. [His book, laughter.] FDR said, "I guess you're right on the economics, but those taxes were never a problem of economics. We put those payroll contributions there so as to give the contributors a legal, moral, and political right to collect their pensions. With those taxes in there no damn politician can ever scrap my Social Security program." I think those are words of great wisdom and I think they argue strongly for having as little general revenue financing in the program as possible.

Cohen: If the question about general revenue contributions to social security were just a hypothetical question, I would be strongly for it as was the original Committee on Economic Security in 1935. However, this view of the Committee on Economic Security views was reversed by Morgenthau,* by Roosevelt, and by Congress in 1935 and we've continued on a different basis ever since. And I do not think it is realistic to consider a government contribution into this system at this time with the big budget deficit, nor in the forseeable future.

My view is, if we were in a different situation, that the place we're going to have to use general revenue is in some kind of a health system. In other words, what I would like to do would be to use whatever we were able to get, especially if it were from a progressive revenue, to have a medical system that isn't a two tier system. The worst two tier system is one for poor people and one for other people, and I think it is unconscionable in this country that we do not provide access for every single person by right of citizenship to adequate medical care. I think that, as I said earlier, is the big problem. I think it is going to require massive amounts of money

*Henry Morgenthau, Jr. was Secretary of the Treasury (1933–1945) and a member of the Committee on Economic Security.

that will have to be provided by the younger people and the working people. We've got the contributory, wage related system right this minute on a fairly good financial basis, but we don't have a medical care system in the United States which is equitable, fair, adequate, or comprehensive. It meets no basic condition of equity whatsoever. I hope it'll be answered before fifty years.

Burns: I agree with you that medical care is going to be the big headache of the next fifty years. But the more that is true, the more it behooves those of us who are familiar with the existing program and who see all the misconceptions to do everything we can, because it is clear that the attitude toward government is going to affect greatly what we, in fact, are able to do in the matter of medical care. I'm sure you would agree that we can't conceive of any real solution of the medical care problem if we say right away, the way we said it in regard to social security, "but there's no government contribution." We must not let that idea get around without challenging it. I think that's the job for the present generation of people and the people who are the past generation—I say that in deference to Wilbur's feelings about not wanting to be called an oldster. But I do think this is one of the basic things we've got to change: people's attitudes to the trustworthiness and the responsiveness of government. We must not tie our hands, neither with the cash benefits system nor with the medical care system in the years to come. I'm not only thinking of three and a half years, I'm thinking of time when people grow up and become a little more sensible about what government can do.

Cohen: The point that I feel strongly about is that when you come to health care as against cash benefits, life is not fair in regard to health. You do not know from the point of conception to the point of death what kind of health condition you're going to have. Therefore I think the financing of health care is sui generis, in the sense that people can't predict what their health care costs are going to be and hence the cost of that has to be distributed over the whole community on a completely different basis.

Burns: But, Wilbur, people can't predict when they're going to die.

Cohen: Ah, but we know that everybody is going to die.

Burns: No, but that's another thing.

Cohen: Ah, that's different.

Burns: The thing that worries people is, I think, not the fact that they are going to die, but when they are going to die and lose out on all the fun of being young and growing up and having a family and all that sort of thing. This is very different from the question that I would face when I am going to die. If I'm eighty-five, my Lord, how long have I got.

Cohen: You've got another twenty-five years. I know it. (Laughter)

Burns: Anyway my point is I don't quarrel with you that there is a difference in attitude and the way it hits people in the matter of health care. But if we continue to inculcate in people the feeling that you can't trust government because it is not responsive, if you say you don't like something or other, that you've got no remedies of any kind for persuading other people to vote with you, if we keep that attitude alive on the basis of what we think is evidently happening in regard to the cash benefit system, I don't see how we're ever going to persuade people to face up to the problem of the financing of medical care. That's my point. I think it's a wrong attitude and not enough people are saying so and that's what makes me so cross.

Moderator: Now let's turn the questioning over to you, the audience. Would you come down and speak in the microphone and tell us who you are?

Brake: My name is Susan Brake and I'm a claims representative with social security. Granted that all the commissioners are presidential appointees, do any of you feel strongly that its better to have a professional social security administrator such as we have now, a person who has come up through the ranks, or to have someone appointed from the outside on a purely political basis?

Myers: I think it should be a political appointee because it's a political program, but there's no reason why a political appointee could not also have come up through the ranks as, for example, some of the commissioners have. But basically its a political position, I think, and properly so. Of course I would favor, as Wilbur would, going back to where we started and having a Social Security Board with three political appointees: two representing in essence the majority party as far as the executive branch is concerned, the other being a true appointee of the opposition party.

Cohen: And then the commissioner in effect would be appointed by the board, with the approval of the Senate possibly.

Brake: So you would approve a more professional person, not just a dumb political crony?

Cohen: If you're asking me if I would like Martha McSteen appointed commissioner, the answer is yes. President Reagan has not done so and I think that's a very unfortunate situation to have continued her for over a year now. President Reagan has continued a career woman, Martha McSteen, as acting Social Security Commissioner without giving her a senatorial appointment. I think that's been bad for the program.

Moderator: Yes.

Pino: I'm Mandy Pino from the Albuquerque Office of Senior Affairs. Will you speak to two [questions]: the President's position on the COLA and the deficit and also the unified budget?

Moderator: Wow.

Cohen: First, I think that social security should be taken out of the unified budget completely, and it ought to be effective in 1986. It is now effective under the 1983 amendments for Fiscal 1993. I think that ought to be advanced because it is difficult not only for the people of the United States but for the president of the United States to explain it when it is in the unified budget. And it is confusing. [It's a return to] the way it was from 1935 to 1969. I think that President Lyndon Johnson made a great mistake in changing it and he made that change on the recommendation of the economists. I feel that was a big mistake because it confused people.

With regard now to the COLA and its relation to the budget, the president of the United States, in my opinion, is both correct and in error in the way he has explained it. He has explained it correctly in the sense that since social security is now taking in more money than it is paying out, it is not a cause of a single penny in the deficit. As a matter of fact in the unified budget, roughly in 1987, I think its close to about nine billion dollars. Isn't it, Bob?

Myers: For the whole system.

Cohen: Eight or nine billion dollars for the whole system. Social security is taking in about nine billion dollars more than it is paying out, and when that nine billion dollars is subtracted from the gross deficit, the net unified federal budget deficit is therefore nine billion dollars less. Once you've said that, it is hard for people to understand how subtracting that nine billion dollars from the gross deficit helps anything because the nine billion dollars always stays in the social security trust fund. Obviously both things are true. Namely, it reduces the federal deficit, but at the same time it doesn't help pay one cent toward national defense, because the money doesn't go to the defense department to have nine billion dollars less cost of defense. It goes into the social security trust funds to enhance the reserve. So I favor taking it out of the federal [budget], not to help the economists particularly or anyone else, but in order to help public understanding, which has suffered a great deal of confusion.

On the COLA itself, I am strongly opposed to the senator from New Mexico's [Pete Domenici] position to cut the COLA, because in cutting the COLA he is, in my opinion, going against the commitment that President Reagan and Mr. Mondale made in the political campaign not to cut it. I believe if politicians make a promise in a presidential campaign, they ought to stick to it. That is what undermines people's confidence, I believe, when high political officials in our government make a commitment and then try to back down on it. The COLA is financed by the social security contributions, the system is financially sound at the present time and I think we ought to keep the president, the senator from New Mexico, and the United States Senate committed to what the president of the United States promised in the election campaign. (Applause)

Myers: I'd like to add one thing about the COLA. It is a fact that if the COLA were cut this would reduce the deficit. I'm not saying it should be, in fact I'm opposed to freezing the COLA, but I would go on to say that if the COLA were cut this would mean that social security would have that much more money, money they hadn't counted on. Therefore if you're going to say, "We're going to freeze the COLA," you should at the same time say "We're going to lower the tax rate." If you did that, as far as the budgeteers are concerned you'd be right back at the same place you started from. So there's no point in doing it. Therefore, leave the COLA in.

Moderator: Gil.

Joel: My name is Gil Joel and I'd like to make one quick comment and then ask two quick questions. My comment is about why controversy about social security exists in America, when it doesn't exist in other countries. It is because we're so damned afraid that somebody will get away with something for nothing, that's why we're arguing about it all the time. A quick question, the first one: The tax system can now touch half of social security benefits over $25,000 a year. Isn't that a sort of an introduction to a means test? And my second question is: yesterday the comment was made, and it was on television, that nobody needs to worry about the social security system as it will always be here and so forth. Well, I can visualize a Congress elected by short-sighted people who will allow social security to become a voluntary, rather than a contract of every worker with the Social Security Administration. These are the two things that I'm concerned about.

Moderator: Anyone want to answer the first question?

Myers: Let me answer. As far as the first question is concerned, which is: Does the recent income taxation of social security benefits mean that a means test has been introduced into the system? I suppose this is like the story of the blind man and the elephant, it depends on how you look at the creature. But I don't think it's a means test any more than the fact that private pension plans are subject to income tax means that private pensions are subject to a means test. I think that income taxation of social security benefits is a desirable thing. But I don't think those thresholds should be there. Half of all social security benefits should be subject to the income tax. Of course many people wouldn't pay any income tax on that half anyhow. The only problem I have with the income taxation of benefits is that I didn't think the tax money should go into the trust fund. It should go into the general treasury just as does the tax on a private pension; that doesn't go back to the pension fund, it goes to the general fund of the treasury.

Cohen: Charles, do you want to . . .

Schottland: No, you go ahead. I know what you're going to say.

Cohen: I agree with my good friend, Bob Myers, except on one point. I think the tax should go back into the social security fund simply because the taxation of benefits came so fast that many people could not take that into account in their preparation for retirement. And one rationalization for it was that it helped make the social security financing solvent. Your second question, if I understood correctly, had to do with whether the system should be voluntary?

Moderator: . . . whether the Congress would elect representatives who would vote in a voluntary system.

Cohen: Well, you can elect people to do anything you want that's not unconstitutional. I suppose even things that are unconstitutional. I think that Eve Burns made a very interesting point. I think Congress has been very responsible in the last fifty years, even though Congress has made some changes in the law that I very strongly disagree with, that I would like to see repealed. I think in every case they took into account balanced pros and cons, of which there are many, on these difficult issues. I don't think any of us can say that Congress has to do exactly what we want or Congress is irresponsible. That's not a tenable position. But, on the other hand, apropos of what Eve said, I don't want to give the political structure more incentives to be irresponsible. That's the point I was making earlier. I think Congress has been responsible and I believe that social security is going to continue, as Bob Myers said. I think young people are going to get their benefits and I think the system is going to be solvent. I think there are going to be difficult financial problems, but I think, on the whole, with some exceptions, the Congress has been very, very responsible. But, again, I don't necessarily believe that every time the majority has elected somebody they have been right, so I think you have to have a philosophy about our constitutional system that takes into account that people can change their minds.

Burns: . . . or make mistakes.

Cohen: Yes.

Women in the Audience: Sir, we have a point of clarification for Wilbur Cohen. Are you saying that you agree with Mr. Myers that all social security benefits should be subject to the federal income tax?

Myers: No, 50 percent of it.

Cohen: He's saying 50 percent, but he was saying with no threshold. But keep in mind that if that threshold remains and we have 5 percent inflation a year and comparable wages that that will come in twenty or thirty years.

Myers: More than that.

Cohen: More than that. When it will be virtually complete, but then that depends on what the marginal tax rate is going to be and we're going through changes on that now. And wages. I think that's a separate issue for a future time.

Moderator: You.

Bustamente: My name is Becky Bustamante, and I'm with Senator Bingaman's office, but I've been working with social security and Senior Citizens for many years. What I would like to ask is what was the thinking on who should pay into the social security system? For instance, I think there are a lot of people who don't realize that many of the employees in the social security office have never paid into social security because prior to January of last year federal employees didn't have to participate. So what was your thinking in deciding who should participate in the social security system, who should pay into it? Thank you.

Myers: I think the thinking of the social security system experts, if I can use that bad word, has always been that all federal employees ought to have been in the system. But politically it just couldn't be achieved and it was quite a breakthrough that just the new hires were taken in last year, because, as you know, so many of the federal employee groups have always been opposed to coverage. This was largely on selfish grounds because in this way they could get two benefits. They'd get their civil service retirement benefits, and then by working elsewhere, as I have, for example, and my friend Wilbur has, they also qualify for a social security benefit. So it's been purely a political matter, not a theoretical matter, that federal employees haven't been covered right from the beginning.

Cohen: Mr. Myers and I have spent about twenty-five years trying to persuade federal employees, that like all other employees they should be covered under the basic floor protection of social security and have a supplementary system on top of it. I think that's what eventually is going to happen, but its not here yet.

Myers: It's always very embarassing when you go to a meeting, particularly as I have for members of Congress when I was with the Social Security Administration, and you say the system is a great system and so forth and somebody gets up from the audience and says, "Were you covered?" "No." "Well, you must know something we don't know, because it can't be such a great system as you say."

Eliot: There's someone over here on the right.

Moderator: Yes.

McBride: My name is Esther McBride. I'm a social worker. I'm an ex-student of Wilbur Cohen whom I salute as a very, very great teacher.

Cohen: Thank you.

McBride: I would like to address my question to Mr. Myers.
But first I want to say that as a social worker working with low income people it has been my experience that they are proud to pay a regressive tax if it's a program that they feel a part of. I think

they're proud to pay the social security tax, I think they're proud to pay a sales tax that goes for schools, for example, because they feel directly a part of those programs. I used to have my students at Tulane—I'm Tulane University's first early retiree—write a paper on a case for the regressive tax, and they were very perceptive and interesting papers. And many of them came from low income families.

Mr. Myers said that fifty years from now he expects 157 million covered workers. Did I get that right?

Myers: Yes.

McBride: And for the nonactuarial layperson, what sort of scares us, among a number of things, is automation. We look around and we see factories that used to employ seventy people now getting along with five. And that's kind of strange and you have a feeling that you're getting products without employing people. Therefore, what about something like figuring up a tax on the products produced without people. Are we really going to have 157 million working people fifty years from now? Now there have been some chilling articles in newspapers and magazines in the past year. I remember one especially in *Newsweek*, called "Blue Collar Blues," which said that steelworkers and the steel industry are gone if you ask Pueblo, Colorado. People that used to be making $30,000 a year in the steel mills are now down to $7,500. Their wives are out trying to cover the mortgage. They've given up buying homes. They've given up sending kids to college. This is really scary to your woman colleague up here. The level of living that we are willing to guarantee is very much on the minds of industrial workers.

The other thing I wanted to be sure that actuaries have in mind are things that are bugging some of the rest of us. For example, the proliferation of ex-wives. Yesterday I asked Mr. Rimlinger, "Do they do this in other countries, be so slap-happy about handing out benefits to ex-wives?" And he said "no," he said we were the only country that did that. He said that in Germany a woman can voluntarily contribute to be covered. I said I think that is true in Japan, they have an imputation system whereby a housewife can get covered either by paying in herself or her husband's employer doing it or whatever. And I said to him that it astonishes me that we are able to cover, in the United States, all of these multiple marriages, ex-wives, and all that stuff. And I said, "do you think we're okay to do that?" And he said, "we're doing it." Thank you.

Myers: Well, you raised several very good points. On the first one, I'm glad to hear you say that people want to pay the tax because they've a feeling of ownership. That's always been one of my arguments and I'm glad to hear it from somebody, you might say, on the firing line. It's really not a regressive tax, even though it may seem to be one. To your other point about whether we are going to have jobs for these 157 million people because of all the automation and so forth, I think the answer is yes. This is not my field of great expertise, but over the past history of the mechanization of the country whenever you create labor saving devices, you're creating more jobs, more production in the long run. There may be frictional problems at the moment when changes are made, but over the long run this results in a higher standard of living and greater production.

As to whether the system can afford benefits for ex-wives, for divorcees after ten years, I think there are various ways of handling this problem. I think the way we do it will work satisfactorily. Other countries may do it differently, but I think we have now worked out a system that creates proper equity between different spouses. And there's always, of course, the fact that a divorced spouse can only draw one benefit; one can't pile it up from several previous divorced spouses on top of their own. Rather, one always gets the larger of whatever benefits are available. So, from a cost standpoint this is no great problem.

Moderator: I think we have time for only one more question, and I see a hand up over there.

Randy: My name is John Randy and I'm a student at UNM. The other night on the news I saw that Congress guaranteed that Medicare is going to last until 1989. I'll probably start paying then. I was wondering, will I be able to get something when I turn sixty-five?

Myers: I'm sorry to take another question, but that's really an actuarial question.

First of all, you can't always believe what you hear on the radio and television. The lastest trustees' report, just issued yesterday is much more optimistic and says that the Medicare Hospital Insurance trust fund, according to the intermediate estimate, will hold out until the late 1990s. But, even so, that doesn't say that everything is set in concrete and nothing can change it. Just as changes for the cash benefits program were made in 1983 that put it in quite good shape, something will have to be done about the Medicare program in the future, and this is a problem that faces the whole nation. Health insurance plans for active workers are subject to severe financial pressures and the country will have to face up to just how medical services are to be furnished. And I think the country will have to recognize that if you want something you have to pay for it. So with increasing medical skill and increasing development of equipment and so forth, medical care is going to be more expensive. But if this is what people want—and I think they do want it—the country is going to have to pay for it and therefore the Medicare program will require additional financing. Of course, this is not to say that more and more should not be done to have greater efficiency in the medical care delivery system, but the fact that official actuarial estimates say that the system is going to go bankrupt doesn't mean that it is going to. It only means that it's a warning signal that tells the Congress they've got to do something about it. Some changes will have to be made either in outgo or income or both.

Moderator: I am sorry, but we must end now.

3 _____

Wilbur Cohen's Reflections on the First Half Century of Social Security

Moderator: We've heard a great deal from Wilbur Cohen, and I think we have seen many indications that we have barely scratched the surface. So we are very fortunate that Mr. Cohen was willing to step in, really at the last minute after Senator Domenici told us that he could not attend, and after Mr. Michael Carozzo, who was supposed to substitute for him, told us he could not be here. Mr. Carozzo is on the Senate Budget Committee staff and is responsible for Social Security.

We are extremely fortunate that in Mr. Cohen we have an individual who has had so many experiences and who is a marvelous teacher. A number of people have indicated that they have learned so much from him in class and outside of class. And, as I have just said, I think we still have so much to draw upon from Mr. Cohen's experiences, his observations, his own wide reading, that we could not do better than to turn the podium and microphone over to him for a few more minutes for some additional remarks. And so I am most pleased to introduce once again, Mr. Wilbur Cohen.

Cohen: I feel rather hesitant in speaking not only to a group that contains my distinguished colleagues that we have heard today, whom I respect for their contribution and their knowledge, but others who have been either my students, or my mentors, or my cooperators, or people that I've worked with in the Senate, like my good friend Fred Harris who I'm glad is here, in a number of different capacities.

Last night I prepared an outline for this discussion, but since about three-quarters of the items I was going to talk about came up this morning, I've had to revise my speech because there's no point in repeating what we've already talked about. I will deal with some of the things we didn't touch on. One other thing I want to say is that I am one of those people who has what I think of as a double life. If you come and take a course with me you will find me asking you as a student why a double-decker plan is a good plan; but if you hear me in a program like this, you will hear my personal views in which I will not agree it is a good plan. As a professor in a teaching capacity I ask my students to defend all of the things I don't necessarily agree with because I believe that one's role as a teacher is quite distinct from that of an advocate. And I try my best, and I want to make it clear in the university's position, that when I speak as an advocate that doesn't necessarily mean that if you took a course from me you'd find me expressing my own points of view. In fact, I've had students who say at the end of a course: "Gee the trouble with the course, Professor Cohen, is that I don't know what you think about these questions whatsoever." I say, "That's not the purpose in taking a course with me, to find out what I think. The purpose of a course in the university is to find out what you think. I'm not grading myself, I'm grading you." So I'd like to make that clear in connection with what I consider is a wonderful opportunity made possible by the University of New Mexico to give us this chance to be frank, to be controversial, to bring out ideas, because I think that's the function of a university. And I want to thank those who made this whole program possible because you've realized my dreams in having an opportunity to discuss these things. I'm going to be somewhat episodic today because I'm going to leave some things out that have already been talked about, and I'm going to include some things that we didn't talk about.

First point: How did social security get to be so ingrained in its acceptance by the American people? Why was it that other alternatives—double-decker, flat benefits, and other kinds of arrangements—were not accepted? And I think, here, to understand that, one must not only deal with the point that we talked about—about the impact of the Great Depression and the Townsend Plan and Huey Long—but rather an unusual sequence of events that occurred in American history and that changed the nature [of social security], part of which Ed Berkowitz has already touched on in his article in *Prologue* on the 1939 amendments. Have you published that anywhere else, Ed?

Berkowitz: Not yet.

Cohen: It is a very important article about the 1939 amendments. The importance of the 1939 amendments is that they came so quickly after the 1935 act, which no one could have predicted. Now all of you realize that the 1939 amendments—we'll just deal with the old-age insurance program—came shortly after the Supreme Court decisions upholding the constitutionality of the laws regarding unemployment insurance and old-age insurance. Then Senator [Arthur] Vandenberg*, a very conservative Republican, both with regard to foreign affairs and domestic affairs, raised the question about Bob Myers's forty-seven billion dollar estimate. At that particular moment in history, I forget exactly the number, but I think the gross national debt was about thirty-two billion dollars, or something in that neighborhood, anyway substantially less than forty-seven billion dollars. So Senator Vandenberg asked the question: What are you going to do when you have a reserve of forty-seven billion dollars invested in U.S. government bonds? Where are you going to put it if the national debt is only thirty or thirty-two billion dollars? And he said, "I can see only one alternative—you're going to spend fifteen billion dollars for something because that's the only way you can use the money, you have to invest in United States government bonds. And," he said, "I don't want to see Franklin D. Roosevelt and the New Deal go on that big spending spree, so we ought to have a reconsideration of social security."

What I'm trying to say is that Mr. Vandenberg didn't say, he had a different conception of social security, like Mr. Landon had in the 1936 campaign. He didn't say he saw a better way of doing it, he didn't say he thought there's a better substitute. All he could think

---

*Arthur Vandenberg (1884–1951) was an influential conservative Republican senator from Michigan.

of in his mind was that the New Deal was going to go on a big, vast spending spree during the next fifty years or so. Imagine, a reserve of forty-seven billion dollars in 1980 with a national debt of forty-seven billion dollars, an inconceivable, massive, gross national debt. And so he said "let's have a study." And Arthur Altmeyer, whom we haven't discussed today—I thought he was a very great statesman—said, "yes, I agree, let's have a study and we'll agree on an advisory committee to make the study." They both agreed on J. Douglas Brown of Princeton, whom we haven't really discussed fully today; he was one of the great people in this field who led the advisory council on which Bob Myers and I and other people in this room worked at the time.

Out of that consideration came many things—but I'm only going to discuss two—there came the idea of modifying the benefits structure in such a way that you would pay more currently and less later on with a roughly average cost to the system in perpetuity, about the same [cost] according to Bob Myers's data. In other words, and as it was frequently explained, it altered the teeter-totter. Mr. Altmeyer took Bob Myers's very complicated actuarial data and said that what the 1939 amendments did was to keep the cost of the system in perpetuity roughly the same, but changed the teeter-totter. In other words, by starting OAI benefits in 1940 rather than in 1942 we increased the costs to the social security system in the early years, but reduced them in later years.* Incidentally, that was probably the only time you could do it without any untoward efforts because no benefits had yet been paid. So we had an opportunity once in a lifetime, although we did it a little later in 1972 and 1977, but in a different way. But we did it without raising the question of whether we were giving people more or less, even

*Arthur Altmeyer and other social security policy makers hoped that these changes would satisfy both the advocates of increased benefits and the supporters of a smaller reserve fund. Altmeyer frequently used the analogy of the teeter-totter in his testimony before congressional committees. At one session, he explained the proposed changes as follows: "In other words, your present annual benefit cost goes up steeply, so that you have got one end of the teeter-totter way down and the other end of the teeter-totter way up, taking one end as 1940 and the other end as 1980. Our recommendation, in effect, raises the lower end. The increased benefits in the early years will be slightly more costly than the saving in the decreased benefits in the later years, so that your level premium cost will be a fraction more, but not much more." (Arthur J. Altmeyer, *The Formative Years of Social Security* Madison, Wisconsin, 1966, 101.)

though we were changing the whole structure. But since nobody was getting any benefits we didn't have any problem of taking them away from anybody who was actually getting them. Still we kept the overall cost of the system over many years roughly the same, raising the benefits immediately, getting the system started, and adding by a stroke of the pen as much life insurance for the people under social security as the total life insurance for all the private market. That's what Bob Myers's actuarial estimate resulted in. We were able to provide those people who were covered at that time with life insurance that, in effect, doubled the total quantity of life insurance to the American public. Then, in addition, and I think Bob will agree with me, that what it did was to introduce the idea (though it was not completely instituted until 1950) of the pay-as-you-go system. The inception of the pay-as-you-go system as against the reserve system was introduced in 1939 and then completed later on, in a sense with a small contingency reserve but not a partially reserve system.

Now what we didn't know at that time is that the war was going to break out, and what happened in effect was that you had a major, tremendously significant reform of social security. It was not viewed that way then because it was slightly before benefits came out and because it satisfied Vandenberg that the New Deal wouldn't be spending all this money in the future on reckless items. So it wasn't viewed as if it was a big reform; it was viewed as a reaffirmation and a continuation [of the original system]. But it broadened the benefits immediately and got the system started in an atmosphere of bipartisan support. Senator Vandenberg supported the legislation. The 1939 amendments went through. But, in effect, I recall there was no political debate. Once Vandenberg, and [Robert L.] Doughton, and [Byron Patton] Harrison, and all the conservative Southerners as well as the Republicans were for it, the thing passed—not in two years. It was introduced in 1939 and passed in 1939. And with the war breaking out then and when Roosevelt said, we're changing from "Mr. New Deal to Mr. Win the War"—that really meant that there was no effective legislation on social security from 1940 to 1950. Now the essence of what I'm trying to say is, to answer my own question, the happenstance of the Vandenberg interest in a relatively nonrelated benefit question—he was not questioning the fundamental structure—sort of instituted it in the fabric of legislation of that time. In my opinion, the 1935 Act, the 1937 constitutionality ruling, the 1939 amendments, the war coming out—all these together meant that when social security was up for reexamination in 1949 and 1950—that issue of changing the system to a double-decker and so on, although that was all in the ethos, never had any reality.

Now, the next time reform proposed was when Mrs. [Oveta Culp] Hobby was made secretary, the first secretary of HEW under Eisenhower, and she selected Nelson Rockefeller as the undersecretary. Rockefeller, I think, had a little bit more exposure to social security than Mrs. Hobby had. But the two of them agreed to a reexamination of social security in 1953 and ultimately came to the conclusion, despite tremendous pressure on them by Congressman [Carl] Curtis, later Senator Curtis,* from Nebraska, to go to a flat benefit. Mr. Curtis was in favor in 1953 of paying everybody $40 per month—I'm sure he would have negotiated to $42.50 or $45, or maybe $52.50 or $39.85 or some other figure. But as a rural Nebraskan he was the best exponent, with Sheridan Downey,† in 1940, of what I call the egalitarian approach, that is pay everybody the same. But pay them so little that they would really have to go out and scramble to have a decent level. And Congress couldn't see that, and it was not adopted. And when Mrs. Hobby recommended continuance of the existing plan, I'm sure President Eisenhower must have been startled. She came to agree that the Social Security program is best for our free market system because the benefits are related to wages and earnings, and the worker and employer have got to contribute; that was a better system than the one proposed by Congressman Curtis, who, by the way, was very influential in the Eisenhower administration. Charles [Schottland], you came in—in what year did you come, 1955?

Schottland: 1954

Cohen: Had that been completed by 1954?

*Carl Curtis was a very conservative Republican Congressman from Nebraska who had long opposed the social security system. In 1953, Curtis, who was then Chairman of the Social Security Subcommittee, aggressively pushed for the flat benefit plan, then supported by the U.S. Chamber of Commerce.

†Sheridan Downey (1884–1961) served as Democratic senator from California from 1939 to 1951. He was a strong advocate of old-age pensions.

Schottland: Yes.

Cohen: So you were the benefactor, in one sense, of all of this debate that had been heard, just previously to your becoming commissioner.

Schottland: You educated me a lot.

Cohen: I see. So the next point in my story is that it was Rockefeller, a wealthy individual and a man of great social consciousness, who preserved social security as it was. My view of Mr. Rockefeller at that time is that he had a more highly developed, Baptist philosophy of social consciousness as a wealthy man than had my friend Oveta Culp Hobby. While she had been the head of the WACS, I don't think she had the same kind of opportunity, later as a wealthy woman, to try to see what great responsibility in the social order wealth had. I think Nelson had some of that. Would you agree with that Charles?

Schottland: Yes, absolutely.

Cohen: And I think that, therefore, Rockefeller and Hobby put the last pin in the development of the acceptance of social security as part of the social fabric. Later on, then, we had the 1956 disability amendments, which came out of that, and in 1965 Medicare and you can keep on going. But, quite frankly in my opinion, with the Republicans and the Democrats during the 1935 period having blessed the system, including Vandenberg and the conservative Democrats from the South, Doughton and Harrison in 1935 and 1939, and then with the blessings of Hobby, Rockefeller, and Eisenhower in 1954, it was possible for the system to be sustained in 1981 and 1985, even though Mr. Reagan would have been very logically the one to try to make it a voluntary system because that was his point of view. Since the early fifties some people have sought to make the system voluntary, a point of view identified with the Goldwater/Reagan philosophy. And, although I think there are a lot of people in Mr. Reagan's personal staff and otherwise who still believe in a voluntary system, I just think that his not knowing that Vandenberg and Rockefeller and Eisenhower, and Nixon as well, all accepted the fundamental postulates of the contributory, wage-related social security system (whatever you want to call all this) made it impossible to change it. Mr. Reagan, despite what he said on May 12, 1981, when he recommended ten or eleven different substantive changes in social security, found that within twenty-four hours people of his own political party were not willing to cut benefits at age sixty-two, which was his number one priority, from 80 percent to 55 percent. He had to drop that. And then, of course, once he suggested he'd go along with the advisory council, and they were going to name Bob Myers the executive director, the fight was all over. Even though Mr. Greenspan was the chairman, Reagan didn't realize that by putting Claude Pepper,* and Bob Ball,† and the others on the Advisory Council who would know all this history, that they would be willing to continue the present system.

All right, that is the best I can do in disposing with the question I asked, why is social security a sacred cow? That's really the question that Joe Califano‡ used to ask me when I'd go in to see him. He'd say, "why can't we tinker with Social Security? Why is it a sacred cow? Why are you and Bob Myers and Bob Ball such high priests of Social Security," he would say. And I'd say, "well the only reason, Joe, I can offer is that Cohen was the high priest of Israel at least two thousand years ago, and I'm trying to continue it in 1980." So . . . Joe didn't think that was funny. [Laughter] He realized that since I had two thousand years ahead of him, he was foredoomed to failure on that issue.

Point number two is different but that builds on that: When is there going to be the next big development of social security? I'll tell you when its going to be—August 14, 1995. Why is that? Well, I'm a great believer in the Father Schlesinger and the Son Schlesinger* theory of the cyclical nature of politics. I believe there

---

*Claude Pepper, a Democratic Congressman from Florida, had formerly served in the Senate, 1936–1951. He is one of the staunchest defenders of social security.

†Robert M. Ball a leading expert and writer on social security, is currently Senior Scholar at the Center for Social Policy in Washington. He served as Commissioner of Social Security from 1962 to 1973.

‡Joseph Anthony Califano was Secretary of the Department of Health Education and Welfare, 1977–1979. Previously, he served as Special Assistant to President Lyndon B. Johnson, 1965–1969.

*Arthur M. Schlesinger was a distinguished historian who pioneered in American urban, social, and economic history. His more famous son, Arthur M. Schlesinger, Jr. was special assistant to President John F. Kennedy and briefly to President Lyndon B. Johnson. Arthur M. Schlesinger, Jr. is a leading historian in his own right who has written major studies on Andrew Jackson and Franklin D. Roosevelt.

is a generational attitude and politicians may have an impact on it. But I think when you really study things, what's important is the impact of different generations and different moods. Or to put it in some kind of a law of physics—if you're down low you're later going to go high, and if you're up high you're going to go down low. And I think the same is true in social reform. What do I mean by that? I mean that, perhaps in a better sense of physics, every action breeds a reaction—in politics and in social reform. Once you have a great surge of social reform, whether it's 1910 to 1914 (or 1916) under Wilson, you have the return to normalcy under Harding and Coolidge and Hoover. Once you have Franklin D. Roosevelt in 1933 to 1939, you have the reaction of the stability that people wanted under Eisenhower. Once you have the thrust of Kennedy and Johnson and the New Frontier and the Great Society, you had the wanting to cut back in the Ford and then ultimately the Reagan Administration.

I see this as a thirty year cycle. And what do I base it on? Very simple. In 1935 you had social security, in 1965 you had Medicare; just add another thirty years on—that's 1995. [Laughter] Now you might think that's awfully simplistic, and perhaps it is. But on the other hand I think there is a certain scheme of things that occurs beyond our understanding and our competence, in that five or ten years from now you will hear some young people at the University of New Mexico or the University of Texas say well we've got to strengthen the safety net, we've got to be more socially conscious about the needs of the poor or the indigent, or whatever it is.

Now in my opinion, that particular movement will not be so much on the cash benefit side, on old age, because if you read the Council on Economic Advisors' report this year you see the analysis that said that the last twenty-five to fifty years have been very favorable for the aged, that they are relatively as well off as other people. I believe that analysis overlooks many facts: there's 15–20 percent of the aged whose incomes are still below the cash poverty line; and there are many, maybe as many 25 to 35 percent, whose incomes are below a level that makes it possible for them to finance high cost medical care; and there are many who have other kinds of disabilities with high unemployment or sickness and other social problems, and that there needs to be more social services, support services, for people in this group. I think that's all overlooked, but, nevertheless, I think you can't deny the fact that we have in these last fifty years done a better job for the aged than we have for practically any other indigent group and that we ought to be doing some other things at the same time. And as I said earlier, I think it will come in some kind of consideration with regard to how to finance, administer, and develop access to a more comprehensive medical care system.

Now I don't want you to misunderstand me, as I think a couple of people did. One young man from the university here came up to me and said: "Why, why did you say you were in favor of nationalized, social medicine?" I said, "I don't think I said that, and if you think I did say it, I didn't mean it and I don't think I did imply it; I'm in favor of the nationalization of medicine," I said, "I think that's a different issue."

What kind of a financial mechanism to provide everybody with health insurance, or health coverage, or health protection are we going to have in 1995? I haven't got the slightest glimmer. I don't think its going to be like any of the other systems in any other of the countries of the world. Why? Because I have become convinced from studying social security, studying Medicare, studying SSI, studying AFDC—if fifty other countries did it in X manner, we're going to do it differently. Incidentally, you may think that's rather strange, but that strikes a very resonate cord in the body politic in the United States: that somehow or other, despite worldwide experience the ethos of the American spirit, the ethos of American creativity, will somehow produce something different—I think evidence would show that there's probably a good basis for it—that we can do it differently and we can do it better. Now you might not necessarily agree with that, but I think if you had been in the position that several of us have been in over the years of testifying before the Ways and Means Committee and the Senate Finance Committee, the question they don't ask is: Is this exactly the same way they do it in Germany? That's not the question they ask. [Laughter] They never have asked Bob Myers or me before a committee: Is this the way the Labor government does it in Britain, or the Conservatives? Nobody has even asked me whether Margaret Thatcher does it that way, much less the Labor government. The thing they want to know of us when we come there with a proposal is how does this fit into the American spirit of things, the American idea. I mean the emphasis is always on the fact that the United States experience is different from worldwide experience. So I would advise those of you who want to be the bearers of social policy in the future to keep this in mind. I guess if I were talking to a school of public affairs or a school of public policy I would emphasize it as follows: You've got to frame your proposal in a way that while based on world-wide experience adapts it to the American mentality, the American spirit, the American creativity, whatever you want to call it.

And so I believe that our next big social policy invention will be a health system that will probably have elements of the private enterprise system, the public role in it, some kind of combination that I think no one can possibly yet imagine. Just look what we had to do in Medicare to get it passed. We had a public responsibility for financing, but I recall being in the executive sessions of the Ways and Means Committee when I had to promise that the check that would go to the individual doctor would not be a government check. It would be a check that would come from Blue Cross or Aetna. The doctors felt that if they got the money directly from the government they would be contaminated. [Laughter] Keep in mind they wanted the money. [Laughter] They wanted the check. But the big reason we had to select a carrier or an intermediary is that the doctor could say, well, I didn't get it directly from the government. Now following what Eve Burns said the other day, that certainly would never have been a big issue in any of the foreign social security systems. But the American physician, and it was true of the hospitals as well, said if you will pay that check through Blue Cross it will be wonderful, and that's what we've done. We pay the check for Medicare through these intermediaries. Whether you want to call it the most efficient system is one thing. It's probably the most effective politically, and it has insulated things in a way that has created certain problems, but nevertheless that was part of what I call the American way of adapting a generalized principle from worldwide experience to the American situation. Now—how much more time are you going to give me?

Moderator: You have about ten to fifteen minutes.

Cohen: You know being a professor I can speak only in fifty minute units. [Laughter] Fred, have you gotten accustomed to that? [Laughter]

Harris: I'm Tuesday and Thursday, so we have an hour and fifteen minutes. [Laughter]

Cohen: I see. But having been a senator you were never subject to the five minute rule. [Laughter]

Harris: Here they walk out on us.

Cohen: Do they? [Laughter] I think it's very interesting. . . . Well, I should go back. As I said earlier, what Franklin D. Roosevelt did in 1935 was actually defend the federal-state system. I think Franklin Roosevelt could have suggested a national unemployment insurance system. I mean, theoretically. He had already decided in 1930 when he was governor not to favor a national system. But I'm saying within the theoretical confines of the alternatives, it was discussed. And Bryce Stewart* and all those people were for a national system. They couldn't persuade FDR or Altmeyer or Miss Perkins who had had state experience, but it was theoretically possible. I think you could have had a minimum national pension, but Roosevelt, Perkins, Altmeyer, [Paul] Raushenbush, [Elizabeth] Brandeis, the justice's daughter†, all were very state oriented. I think they really saved the federal-state system from virtual extinction. And I don't think you can find it acknowledged in historical analysis, in either public administration or public policy, that they really saved the state system. I want to make the point again, that it was virtually in collapse. The states didn't have the administrative function, they didn't have the money, and they didn't even have the psychological dynamism to take hold of it—it was given to them by Perkins and Roosevelt and Witte and Altmeyer. It wasn't taken away from, it was given to them. They were demoralized, as were the banks during that time. So if you're a believer in the radical philosophy, like a couple of the professors at Berkeley, and I think that quite rightly, if you believe that Roosevelt should have been more radical, he could have been more radical by nationalizing the banks, federalizing unemployment insurance and old-age assistance, and everything else. I think, by and large, he might have been able to get it but he didn't choose to do it.

So from 1935 until 1972 we had a federal-state system of old-age

---

*Bryce Stewart was a Canadian expert who worked on unemployment insurance for the Committee on Economic Security.

†Elizabeth Brandeis was a distinguished labor economist and disciple of John Commons. She taught for many years at the University of Wisconsin.

assistance and, of course, aid to the blind and aid to the disabled. Who federalized it? Who federalized these programs? The radicals? No. The Supplemental Security Income (SSI) system came into being in the Nixon administration. He enacted the SSI system, introduced the COLA, and federalized it. That's what I call the three radical things that Nixon did during his administration. He strongly suggested that we not have these ad hoc changes in social security any more, but that we just adjust it to the cost of living. Mills* was against it at the time. And I think Bob has recognized in his book that the ad hoc changes—except for maybe the 20 percent one— were an adjustment to the cost of living and the wage changes that had taken place, but mostly cost of living. Except we made an effort to which I was a party, and I think Bob was to some extent, to bring and rationalize a kind of quantum leap in the level of adequacy, with the 20 percent benefit increase, to put it up to some reasonable level before you tied it to a COLA.

But it was the SSI that came out of Nixon's family assistance program. The last thing, I think, Mr. Nixon, and Moynihan,† and Mel Laird,‡ and those people who were engineering the family assistance plan realized in 1969 was that what they were going to get out of it was not welfare reform but a minimum federal guarantee to the aged, the blind, and the disabled, which occurred in the Senate really, not in the House. I think the House bill passed a ninety dollar a month guarantee minimum. And then the Senate, under the influence of who? Huey Long's son—Russell Long—saw the opportunity to say: "Ah, we might not be able to make every man a king like my father promised, but we could make every aged person a queen." [Laughter] And Russell Long, I must say under a slight amount of prodding from someone who stands before you, said well, here's a chance for us to convert that system so the states don't have to bear even that cost to the aged. Obviously, I might say, that Oklahoma, Fred, was not opposed to that idea whatsoever at that

---

*Wilbur Mills, Democratic Congressman from Arkansas, was the powerful chairman of the House Ways and Means Committee.

†Daniel Patrick Moynihan, currently Democratic Senator from New York, served as urban affairs expert to Richard Nixon. He was the neoconservative architect of Nixon's ill-fated family assistance welfare proposal.

‡Melvin Laird served as Domestic Advisor to President Richard Nixon, 1973–1974. Earlier he was Secretary of Defense in the Nixon administration and a prominent Republican Congressman from Wisconsin.

time, because it fed right into what I call the Populist attitude, which was still there in 1972. I don't know whether that is true, but there was some remnant of it anyway. And it was adopted in the Senate and of course it was adopted in conference when the FAP program was decimated. So here again we have what I sometimes call the law of unintended consequences occurring, which I think political scientists ought to investigate to a greater degree. I mean, Mr. Nixon thought he was getting a welfare reform program, and what he got was a minimum income guarantee of a federalized program, which Franklin D. Roosevelt in 1935 would never have thought would have happened in his lifetime. Now that's the one big reform that has occurred. And, as a matter of fact, it would take just a little tinkering to raise the minimum amount on the single individual, to say the poverty level. We could take the—Bob I think you said it was 7 percent today, but I think if you add the blind and disabled on, I was taking just the aged, it's only about 5 or 6 percent anyway, isn't it?

Myers: No, it's 7 or 8 percent.

Cohen: 7 or 8 percent, well we're not far apart on that and we could look the figures up. But with a small amount of money, actually, you could have a system in this country in which every aged person did not fall below the poverty line, because we have the structure now in position. And I would think that is something that is likely to happen, I would say before 1995. It doesn't cost much more money, doesn't involve any new principle, and we have the administrative mechanism in place.

Now, for the historians who are here I'll take one other illustration, because I have several of my friends here who are much more interested in the welfare side. Let's go to ADC for a moment, which is very neglected in terms of historical and political analysis, except for people who are having discussions about welfare reform. How did the ADC program get into all of this? Well, it came into being because of Katherine Lenroot*, who was I think only the acting chief then, Tom. I don't know. Was she the chief by that time?

Eliot: Yes.

---

*Katherine Lenroot was a social worker who devoted virtually all of her career to service in the Children's Bureau, which she headed for many years.

Cohen: The chief of the Children's Bureau, Katherine Lenroot, was very much concerned during those times with the mothers' pension laws that had existed in this country since 1910. And she was influential in suggesting to Frances Perkins that we do something about these women with children whose husbands had died. High birth rates were also a factor because there were generally four children in the family at that time. There were high birth rates and high death rates, leaving vast numbers of children without a father, and that was the basis for the mothers' pension law. And Miss Perkins and Miss Lenroot were successful in persuading Mr. Witte, Mr. Altmeyer, and then Franklin D. Roosevelt to include that in the program. Roosevelt had no idea in 1930 or 1934 of including ADC. I must say, Tom, unless you tell me differently, I don't think he had any idea ADC was in it in 1935. I know that you had authorization to draft it, and it was in the report and all that.

But perhaps the best thing I can say about it is that Miss Lenroot and all the rest had no other idea but that this was a mothers' pension law that would help to bail out the states to provide more aid to these children where the mothers were indigent or poor because the father had died. Tuberculosis was still a very prevalent disease and, of course, if you have read *The Jungle* by Upton Sinclair, you know the high death rate in terms of industrialization was a real factor.

Miss Lenroot could have had no thought about teenage pregnancy, or the feminization of poverty, or what occurred in the fifties, sixties, and seventies. I don't know what she would have done if she had known it. The point I'm trying to make is that I don't think anybody, not anybody in 1934–35, gave any attention whatsoever to the long run consequences, or analysis and so on of what people now refer to as THE welfare program. When somebody asks me: What do you think about THE welfare program? I know exactly what they're talking about. They're talking about AFDC. They're not talking about subsidies for airports, you know as THE welfare program; they're not talking about subsidies for private pension plans or anything. When a person comes up to me and says: Now about THE welfare program? I immediately say, "yes, you're talking about aid to families with dependent children, aren't you?" "Oh yes, yes that's what I mean—that's the welfare program in the United States." Even though there are lots of other welfare programs that are not discussed, that one welfare program is very well known.

But the only point I'm making here is that really no consequences were discussed. And I'm not being critical. I don't think it was possible to have extrapolated from 1935 to 1980 what's happened with regard to the welfare program. I'm not being critical of anybody. I'm just again advancing my law of unintended consequences that occurs when you once put a program into operation and it changes with the times.

And if I had more time, I would then go on to the great contribution that Martha Eliot* made—another lady in the Children's Bureau, that created the Maternal and Child Health program. Now the reason I just say a few words about it though, is that the Maternal and Child Health program, which is rarely realized as having been instituted in connection with the Social Security Act of 1935, probably has been the most successful Social Security Act program, not withstanding the fact that I believe that social security which we call OASDI, is so successful. I think we probably have reached a very difficult time regarding welfare programs—part of that is due to teenage pregnancy, part of it is due to other factors in the change in the lifestyle, the feminization of poverty, and a lot of other factors. It's a big problem. Nevertheless, Martha Eliot's putting the Maternal and Child Health program into social security. . . . I think if you want to make an argument about cost benefit analysis with regard to social security—take the Maternal and Child Health program. It is one of the most successful. And last year, in the Reagan budget, they increased the money for it because it is a program which you can defend, you can explain, and it has got support in the country, and it's a very good program.

Now the interesting point for you historians and others here is to go back and see how that happened. The first important federal-state social welfare health program of any consequence was enacted in 1921, called the Sheppard-Towner Act. Senator Sheppard was from Texas, and he wrote into law over tremendous opposition of the AMA and others a small program that the Children's Bureau had developed for helping mothers and children to have a healthy start in life. It was attacked all through the twenties as socialized medicine and the invasion of the spinsters and the government into the internal affairs of children and mothers in the home; it was repealed

---

*Martha May Eliot was a physician who served for many years in the Children's Bureau. She directed the Division of Child and Maternal Health and in 1941 was appointed Associate Chief of the Children's Bureau.

in 1929, by inaction of the Congress. If you want to read about a controversial program, read the debate on the floor of the Senate in the twenties about the Infancy and Maternity Act. Yet in 1935, when it was reenacted in a more comprehensive form, it was accepted by the AMA and by the state health officers without any of the animosity, without any of the hostility, that had preceded the Maternal and Infancy Act of 1921 to 1929.

Now—hastening this process since it's getting late—this is again one of my examples that my students get of a program that is once vilified but may be the next program that is widely accepted. The AMA defeated it in 1929 but came out in favor of it in 1935. Why? Because they were so much against health insurance in 1935 that they had to figure out something that they were for. And so they said, my gosh here's something Tom Eliot had drafted in there, that Martha Eliot had done, we'd better be for that. Now they didn't go for it with any great enthusiasm—don't misunderstand me—they just had to say, "yes, it's all right." And they did, and it has been the most successful of programs. To me that indicates why in the American scene sometimes you see a program defeated, as Medicare was for fifteen years. And I guess I can draw this generalization from it— a program can be defeated many times, but all it has to do is win once and then it becomes enshrined as part of the American way of life. Maternal and Child Health, Social Security, unemployment insurance, and so on are all part of the American way of life.

I was chairman of the National Commission on Unemployment Compensation a couple of years ago and I was absolutely dumbfounded, when I was suggesting a whole series of reforms, that the employers—led by AT&T and the national concerns—came in and said, "Oh, Mr. Cohen we don't need any reform. We love unemployment insurance just the way it is. We think it's a wonderful program." I said, "but for the last twenty years you guys have been saying it was awful—you were saying terrible things about it." "Yeah, but rather than change it substantially, we would rather have it the way it is; we're willing to go along with it." So I've learned a very important lesson, which is that once these programs can last for more than one generation, the second generation comes around and forgets what the generation before them said, it then becomes a part of the American way of life.

And so ladies and gentlemen, today I think that you're witnessing us at a very important time. We're not going to see in the next year or two or three any monumental changes in social security. I don't think we're going to see such great setbacks either. There will be some further cutting or a little bit of tinkering here and there, but I think it is not possible, despite what people tell you, to reverse the welfare state as a global conception in a free market, capitalistic, American system that has both a public and private constituency or institutions. And the reason for it, I think, is more substantial than what we have talked about today. And I think there is a moral justification for a safety net. There also may be a political one, and I think there is. I think there is an ideological one, and there is a rational economic one, all subject to some kind of differences in opinion and intensity of debate. But I think that when reduced to its fundamentals, there is a consciousness of community, or what you said, Dr. Tomasson, in one of those questions, some kind of a sense of solidarity and community in the American system that we don't always talk about. That seems a little bit too too flaky—you know, to say that we believe in community, we believe in solidarity, we believe in social consciousness. But, you know, people do go to church on Sunday and say, yes, I am my brother's keeper. Of course Monday may be different. Monday may be different, but at least one out of seven days they may believe it. And my general idea about all this, if they believe it on two out of seven days we're on pretty good ground. I mean I don't try too much harder, but I do think there is a strong undercurrent in the Judeo-Christian philosophy of community, and family and social responsibility. That is what I think undergirds these programs. It may be inarticulate, it may be unspoken. It may be subject to controversy. We may have differences of how it ought to be financed or how far we ought to go. But fundamental to what we've been talking to today is a safety net that puts the human spirit ahead of everything else. And ladies and gentlemen I think that's what is great about the United States of America. Thank you very much.

Filing unemployment claims shortly after passage of the Social Security Act of 1935. *Sounce:* Franklin D. Roosevelt Library, Hyde Park, N.Y.

Edwin E. Witte of Wisconsin: Theorist of Social Security. *Source:* State Historical Society of Wisconsin.

Tenth Anniversary of the signing of the Social Security Act, August 14, 1945. Seated at center is Arthur J. Altmeyer, chair, Social Security Board, with staff. *Source:* State Historical Society of Wisconsin.

John R. Commons: Pioneer of social welfare economics (1937). *Source:* State Historical Society of Wisconsin.

First meeting of the Social Security Board, August 23, 1935. Left to Right: Arthur J. Altmeyer, John G. Winant (chair), Vincent M. Miles. *Source:* State Historical Society of Wisconsin.

Arthur J. Altmeyer on his last day as Commissioner of Social Security, April 10, 1953. *Source:* State Historical Society of Wisconsin.

Arthur J. Altmeyer (standing), chair of Social Security Board, 1938, with staff. *Source:* Franklin D. Roosevelt Library, Hyde Park, N.Y.

	INCOME (PER CAPITA) 1967	PHYSICIANS (PER 100,000 POPULATION) 1967	AFDC (MONTHLY PAYMENT PER RECIPIENT) DEC. 1967	SCHOOL EXPEDITURE (PER PUPIL) 1966-67
CO	$3865 (HIGHEST)	176.5	$54.50	$657
	$2993		4.80	$506
	(LOWEST)	72.7	$8.40	$335

Secretary of Health, Education, and Welfare Wilbur J. Cohen explaining workings of Social Security System, September 26, 1968. *Source:* Lyndon B. Johnson Library, Austin, Texas.

Secretary of Health, Education, and Welfare Wilbur J. Cohen at his desk, July 16, 1968. *Source:* Lyndon B. Johnson Library, Austin, Texas.

Attendees at the Social Security Symposium, 1985. Left to right: Wilbur J. Cohen, Thomas H. Eliot, Lois Eliot, Eveline M. Burns, Robert J. Myers, Rudy Myers.

PART II

General Studies

4

Introduction

In recent years, political leaders, the media, scholars, and special interest groups (representing beneficiaries, employers, and employees) have drawn attention to the crisis in the social welfare and social security systems in the United States and other industrialized nations. Few, if any of these systems face imminent bankruptcy; slight adjustments in benefits and small tax increases apparently can handle the short term difficulties. Nevertheless, long range problems do exist because of falling birthrates, the potential for intergenerational conflict, and lackluster economic growth. It is ironic that the very social insurance systems that were designed, in part, to provide social stability and serve broad national interests may, in the future, promote instability, divisiveness, and economic dislocation.

The existence of a crisis—real or perceived—frequently forces people to pause and reflect on the origins and subsequent development of the program or problem under scrutiny. Who was responsible for it? What were the motives and governing assumptions? What changes occurred and why? The opening session of the University of New Mexico's Conference on "Social Security: The First Half Century" focused directly on these fundamental questions and issues.

W. Andrew Achenbaum offered one approach by examining the history and contemporary crisis of social security in terms of three linked ideas—"risks, rights, and responsibility"—that have served as the foundation of American social insurance from the moment President Franklin D. Roosevelt directed the Commission on Economic Security to formulate a legislative package that would provide Americans with "security against several of the disturbing factors in life." For the past fifty years, Achenbaum argued, social security policymakers were remarkably successful in maintaining a balance among the admittedly ambiguous and perhaps intentionally imprecise concepts of risks, rights, and responsibilities; they were also strikingly consistent in "hewing to principles bravely enunciated in the depths of the Great Depression." The architects of American social insurance defined risks in narrow terms concerning specific conditions; they insisted that rights of beneficiaries were not contractual and could be changed or eliminated by Congress at any time; and they believed that social insurance embodied a commitment to "mutual responsibility" linked to the well-being of society. The last was the glue that held the entire system together, implying that solutions to any problems facing social security were as much moral as financial.

While social security policymakers have followed a coherent and consistent pattern of thought and action, politicians, the public, and the marketplace have changed their perception of social security's three r's—first in response to the significant expansion of social security's coverage and, recently, in reaction to the crisis in the system. Achenbaum warned that the "illusions" Americans harbor about social security's three r's may be more dangerous "than any economic downturns, demographic pressures, or intergenerational rifts within the electorate."

Is there a solution to this dilemma and to the present crisis in social security? Achenbaum did not find in the Supreme Court's narrow decisions any clear guidance. Nor did he believe that such writers as John Rawls and Robert Nozick have offered realistic answers. Instead, Achenbaum concluded that adherence to the three r's as defined by the pragmatic architects of social security provides a cornerstone for future initiatives. But, he added, Americans must be ready to modify the normative underpinnings of American social insurance in response to changes in a dynamic economy, a mobile society, and an aging population. Thus, for example, we may have to adjust age-based criteria in order to serve the needs of the broader community. Furthermore, we may have to correlate better the activities of a variety of American institutions that provide security. While he admitted that his optimism rested on the fragile basis of sense of "community" embodied in social security, he also saw no alternative. "We cannot depend on it," Achenbaum concluded, "yet we cannot live as a nation without it."

But who was really responsible for the creation and evolution of social security in the United States? Gary Freeman, attempted to answer this question by searching for an appropriate model to understand the origins, development, and dynamics of the social security system in the United States. Freeman approached the task by reviewing and analyzing the three main frameworks that scholars have utilized in their studies of social security. He first examined the three major expressions of the democratic political model: demand-side rational choice, the social democratic movement, and welfare capitalism. While considerations of voter preference and interest group pressures have occasionally impinged on the direction and expansion of social security, especially in the past decade, Freeman concluded that none of the demand side models offers a satisfactory explanation of the origins and subsequent development of social security.*

Instead, Freeman maintained that we need a supply side model. He found the bureaucratic model, which views the present social security system as a legacy of a small group of professional bureaucrats allied to and supported by academics and reformers, some of whom have moved in and out of government service, to be the one most consistent with the historical record. Still, Professor Freeman was critical of the way leading scholars of the bureaucratic

---

*Demand side models refer to the arguments made by scholars that the Social Security Act and its subsequent expansion resulted from the pressures mounted by individuals, organized interest groups, and reformers seeking to advance social welfare or social stability in the United States. Politicians, sensitive to these demands and desiring to secure reelection, thereupon voted to create and expand the social security system. Advocates of supply side models, on the other hand, believe that the beneficiaries and elected officials were negligible and largely passive factors in the development of social security legislation. Rather, they argue that the impetus has come from the bureaucracy and/or the state. For personal, national, or ideological reasons, they provided social security benefits that would fill the unmet needs of the citizenry.

school, notably Martha Derthick, Carolyn Weaver, and Jerry Cates, have treated social security policymaking.

Before he presented his own interpretation, Freeman evaluated the statist model, a supply approach that emphasizes the state as an active and creative factor. Such a perspective, Freeman noted, has seemingly been strengthened by the efforts of central state decision makers since 1972 to take over policymaking from the bureaucrats. But Freeman demonstrated that the involvement of the president and Congress has reduced rather than enhanced the autonomy of policymaking in the face of electoral pressures.

In conclusion, Freeman produced a modified bureaucratic interpretation which he integrated into the statist framework. Rather than being self-aggrandizing officials interested solely in advancing their own interests, American social security bureaucrats took advantage of the relative freedom they enjoyed to pursue goals that they sincerely believed served American society as a whole. However, the political entrepreneurs in the bureaucracy achieved their relative autonomy not by accident, but through creative statecraft that included the monopolization of expertise and astute public relations. Thus, Freeman added, "the social security bureaucrats, especially in the early days of the program, were not so much agents of a powerful and autonomous state able to act upon the society as they were part of a selfconscious elite intent upon building such a state."

While the first two papers focused exclusively on the United States, Gaston Rimlinger, reminded us that all of the industrialized nations are confronting similar crises in their social insurance systems. Furthermore, in the countries which he examined—Germany, France, Great Britain, and to a lesser extent the United States—he found that the problems are rooted in a common source. Professor Rimlinger argued that there has been a significant change in the objectives of the social security systems, from providing adequate minimum protection for those most at risk to maintaining a standard of relative comfort for all citizens. This fundamental shift subsequently undermined the original consensus that underlaid social insurance systems and, in the face of the economic slowdowns and high inflation of the 1970s and the demographic changes in the West, fostered severe political contests among competing economic groups.

Building on the thesis of Karl Polanyi, Rimlinger believed that social insurance schemes in the Western industrialized nations were originally designed to insure stability in the economic and political order. Differences in historical experience and national ideology required different rationalizations to legitimize state initiatives: paternalism in Germany, social solidarity in France, national efficiency in England, and self-help in the United States. Nevertheless, the various systems that evolved before the Second World War were based on collective interests and the common good.

However, a fundamental transformation occurred after the war that resulted in universal, comprehensive welfare systems for all citizens. Memories of economic suffering during the Great Depression and the hardships endured during the war years, combined with the growing acceptance of planned economies, encouraged the view that social insurance was an inherent individual social right. The prosperity of the 1950s and 1960s further enlarged the concept of social rights, while pay-as-you-go financing made the expansion of benefits relatively painless. But developments since the mid-1970s made it clear that there were limits to social protection and that industrialized societies had to make difficult choices regarding fairness of protection and the allocation of benefits and costs. Professor Rimlinger was concerned and somewhat pessimistic about the outcome of the debate. "The feelings of social solidarity that promoted social rights immediately after World War II," he concluded, "now seem to be crowded out by the political conflict over the distribution of rights and the allocation of burdens."

In his comments, Richard M. Coughlin, distilled four major points from the formal papers presented in this session. His observations touched on the key issues of the functional discontinuity between status equality and economic equality, the implication of the emphasis on the social rights of citizenship, and the concept of social control. In his concluding remarks, Coughlin asked whether the current debate over social security in the United States has not been overly preoccupied with the "upper limits" in the benefits social security can provide at the expense of the issue of how much misery Americans are willing to tolerate. The failure to address this question and the contemporary criticism of social insurance in general, he noted, reflects a utopian vision of the free market which forgets that the market mechanism may sometimes fail and cannot protect those in greatest need of the safety net.

Charles McClelland, concluded the session by addressing the

international and comparative context of social security. While social security has evolved into a vehicle for the welfare state, McClelland stressed that American social insurance still lacks a comprehensive medical care component and compares poorly in other ways to European systems. McClelland averred that the inclusion of medical coverage in other national systems may explain why they have been less open to criticism, even though social security taxes are higher and governments supplement them with general tax revenues. By comparing the historical experience in the United States and Germany, McClelland provided several insightful observations that center on the problem of creating an American consensus on social security.

These brief remarks only hint at the information, ideas, and insights found in the papers and comments that follow. In his own way, each contributor provides a perspective from which we can explore the contemporary debate on social security. More important, they underscore the fact that social insurance policy is a touchstone of how a society views itself and the vision it has of its future.

5

Social Security's Three R's

W. Andrew Achenbaum

Risks, Rights, and Responsibilities
under Social Security

On June 8, 1934, Franklin Delano Roosevelt announced his intention to "undertake the great task of furthering the security of the citizen and his family through social insurance." The President's simple, commonsensical language is as revealing in what it presumed and finessed as it is in what he actually said:

> I am looking for a sound means which I can recommend to provide at once security against several of the great disturbing factors in life—especially those which relate to unemployment and old age. I believe that there should be a maximum of cooperation between States and the Federal Government. . . . These three great objectives—the security of the home, the security of livelihood, and the security of social insurance—are, it seems to me, a minimum of the promise that we can offer to the American people. They constitute a right which belongs to every individual and every family willing to work. They are the essential fulfillment of measures already taken toward relief, recovery and reconstruction.[1]

The President never really defined "security"—though apparently a home, a job, and protection against the risks associated with unemployment and old age provide some of the means of achieving it. Furthermore, FDR was vague about who should have a "right" to such security. He referred to the right of "every family willing to work," but did he mean that all Americans would be eligible for benefits, or only those actually in the labor force, or some subset of the population in between? At this stage of program planning, the President left the decision up to his experts. Roosevelt definitely believed, however, that it was within Washington's power to ensure the public's well-being: "If, as our Constitution tells us, our Federal Government was established among other things 'to promote the general welfare,' it is our plain duty to provide for that security upon which welfare depends."[2] As a complement to the New Deal's more familiar three *rs* (relief, reform, and reconstruction), FDR added a second alliterative set. Building on themes and proposals that had been circulating in the United States since at least the Progressive era,[3] the President linked three ideas—"risks," "rights," and "responsibility"—in his vision of social insurance.

Maintaining a balance among risks, rights, and responsibilities has been a major concern among social security policymakers for fifty years. Social security's architects have been remarkably successful in hewing to principles bravely enunciated in the depths of the Great Depression. But there have been significant changes in the clusters of values and assumptions that surround such seemingly self-evident concepts in the political arena, in the marketplace, and in people's minds. Exploring how and why the meanings of these three terms have shifted illuminates prevailing themes, ambiguities, and contradictions in our way of thinking about the program's objectives and limitations in a dynamic and aging society. Over time, as social security has come of age, critics have assaulted its normative foundations. The political compact rests on philosophical and cultural tenets whose salience and perdurance the public accepts nervously on blind faith. The illusions Americans harbor concerning the meaning of risks, rights, and responsibility under social security, in my opinion, may pose greater concern than any economic downturns, demographic pressures, or intergenerational rifts within the electorate.

The Meanings of Risks, Rights, and Responsibility in the Formative Years of Social Security

Policymakers basically agreed about the principal causes of "insecurity" afflicting Americans in the 1930s: "They are unemployment, dependency in old age, loss of the wage earner of the family, and illness."[4] Far from being isolated phenomena, these "major hazards of life" were considered unfortunate "risks" that directly or indirectly affected people at critical junctures in their lives. The economic vicissitudes of late life clearly evoked great sympathy. "Old-age dependency is definitely and positively one of the great tragedies of modern economic progress. . . . The only way [the elderly] can subsist and save themselves from penury, hunger, and want is to join the great caravan that finally wends its way over the hill to the poorhouse."[5]

How many elderly Americans actually needed assistance? The Committee on Economic Security assumed that at least fifty percent of the population over sixty-five was "dependent," a figure accepted by the seventy-fourth Congress.[6] The number of older people unable to find work and maintain their previous standard of living was expected to continue growing even after prosperity returned to the land. Commentators at the time pointed out, moreover, that young as well as old workers needed some assurance that their old age would not be troubled financially.[7] Hence lawmakers thought it necessary to address the future as well as the current dimensions of old-age dependency. The views of William Green, president of the American Federation of Labor, were representative of the times: unlike the threat of unemployment, Green observed in congressional hearings, *all* workers risked financial insecurity in their later years.

The original measure was designed to protect Americans against the threat of dependency. Title I made old-age assistance a right that could be legally enforced. Title II created a mechanism to enable the aging to reduce the likelihood that they would become impoverished through no fault of their own. As the chairman of the Senate Finance Committee pointed out during deliberations, old-age insurance "comports better than any substitute we have discovered with the American concept that free men want to earn their security and not ask for doles—that what is due as a matter of earned right is far better than a gratuity. . . . Social Security is not a handout; it is not charity; it is not relief."[8] Benefits were tied to cumulative wages (although not proportionately so) on which contributions were paid. Thus were both blue-collar and white-collar earners to be assured that no one was abandoning the nation's traditional reliance on self-help. Old-fashioned values could be preserved in new ways: America's social insurance program, according to this view, was helping workers help themselves.

Nonetheless, legislators noted that whatever rights to social security benefits workers had "earned," their benefits were neither contractual nor transferable. "It must be remembered that this effort to create an old-age reserve account to take care of all persons in the future is not a contract that can be enforced by anybody. What we do here is merely to pass an act of Congress, which may be changed by any Congress in the future, and has in it nothing upon which American citizens can depend."[9] From the start, therefore, Congress was identified as the ultimate arbiter determining whether a person's "right" to social security constituted an enforceable claim. Yet the distinction being drawn between *political* rights enjoyed by all citizens and *contractual* rights guaranteed to people whose needs fell into certain categories was murky—especially to ordinary citizens who were not conversant in administrative jargon and procedures. "Bureaucracy is probably the most important of our negative symbols," observed Thurman W. Arnold at the time. "It does not hold up an ideal. Instead, it pictures a vague terror."[10]

Under these circumstances, then, why should the federal government, rather than (say) a private insurance company, have taken the lead in this endeavor? Only Washington, policymakers believed, had the requisite powers to influence and direct the American people to do what was in their individual and collective best interests. The rationale offered by Representative David J. Lewis was indicative of the arguments made by those most committed to the idea of social insurance: "It is the question of faith. It is the controlling element in our conditions. Now, the Government supplies that element of faith. The private company has to face a wall of distrust and break through it. . . . The Government has no wall of distrust to meet. It can educate the public."[11] States-rights advocates, conservatives, and some lobbyists for corporate interests tried to expose holes in this line of reasoning. They pointed out that such rhetoric could not wholly mask the federal government's own bid for power in the political arena.[12] In response, advocates of the new social security legislation simply advanced to higher ground. Federal intervention, they argued, was reinforcing a longstanding American commitment to the ideal of mutual responsibility. Social security, declared Congressman Wolverton during the House debate, "recognizes the principle that, 'We are our brother's keeper.' The mere recognition of this great fundamental principle is in itself an outstanding victory."[13]

It was under the banner of promoting "mutual responsibility" that the creators of the 1935 legislation hoped to win their campaign. This commitment had profound policy consequences. Nowadays, we tend to think of social security as an old-folks' institution. We too often lose sight of the *transgenerational* nature of economic transfers envisioned by the program's architects. By coordinating the old-age insurance program with a system of old-age assistance, the federal government was adopting a plan that "amounts to having each generation pay for the support of the people then living who are old."[14] Assuming that the relationship worked as the experts anticipated, Titles I and II could serve as vital precedents for creating a "safety net" for all age groups. In the meantime, however, lawmakers hardly ignored the plight of younger Americans. The original Act allocated funds for establishing state unemployment insurance programs (Title III), aid for dependent mothers and orphans (Title IV), and for the blind (Title X); money was appropriated to provide better public health services to children and their guardians.[15] In this way, American legislators demonstrated concern for some of the poorest segments of the population. The 1939 amendments to the Social Security Act went even farther in promoting the concept of "adequacy" under the social insurance umbrella—despite the racist and sexist biases that were introduced into the policy debate and ultimately affected the scope of provisions.[16]

Lest such sentiments strike the present-day reader as excessively pious, hopelessly naive, or calculatingly oblivious to the possible abuse of federal power, I hasten to add that the creators of the Social Security Act acknowledged that pragmatic calculations informed their humanitarian impulses. "The vast amount of human suffering and the enormous relief costs, which inevitably will result in increased taxes, show conclusively the folly of failure to give thought to the security of men, women, and children."[17] Since taxpaying citizens could not "escape from the costs of old age," social security offered a "dignified and intelligent solution." Given the magnitude of the funds being committed in this initiative, it made sense to have federal officials assume ultimate responsibility for the program's direction. But no one presumed Titles I and II to be a *complete* solution. Social insurance addressed existing woes and immediate hazards. It did not try to solve the underlying causes of structural unemployment or old-age pauperism. Not only did policymakers emphasize the limited nature of the protection being afforded by social security, but they also were quite explicit about the narrowly circumscribed nature of potential beneficiaries' "rights." Social security neither relieved the individual of primary responsibility for his or her well-being nor diminished the importance of family members' duty to one another. What should be underscored, therefore, is the caution with which lawmakers at the federal level tried to deal with hazards of modern life.

Risks, Rights, and Responsibilities under Social Security, 1940–1972

Over time, federal officials endeavored to increase the range and level of protection against major risks that threatened the financial well-being of most American individuals and households. Edwin E. Witte envisioned a social insurance system that "would provide 'cradle-to-grave' security, but in amounts not so large as to discourage industry and initiative, providing only a floor below which Americans would not fall whatever catastrophe might strike them."[18] The original old-age insurance scheme (Title II) gradually evolved into old-age, survivors, disability, and hospital insurance (OASDHI). The administratively complex federal-state method of relieving the aged poor, blind, and disabled was replaced in the 1970s with a Supplemental Security Income (SSI) program exclusively financed by Washington.

As social security grew in scope, the differences between social insurance and other types of protection became more apparent. Unlike private insurance, benefits were not based exclusively on prior financial contributions adjusted for actuarial factors, administrative costs, and changing personnel priorities. Unlike most public assistance schemes, officials had little discretionary power in determining a person's eligibility or imputed need for entitlements. "Social insurance must implement the concept of adequacy in the prevention of hardship, not by some single arbitrary estimate of need, but by relating a standard schedule of events that disturb the normal status and create a need."[19] More than any other program, social security provisions were centered around specific "risks" such as disability, old-age dependency, and acute-care hospitalization. Because these hazards normally struck at certain intervals in the life course, chronological age increasingly demarked the schedule for allocating benefits under separate titles of the Act. Yet age-based eligibility criteria created holes in coverage. An age-specific set of categories could not fully insure people throughout their lives. The boundaries established for social security programs were fuzzier than the printed rules suggested: often they were an artifact of some political compromise or administrative convenience rather than a decision based on some hard empirical reality. Extending the scope of social insurance in an incremental manner in keeping with a risk-oriented focus made it difficult to achieve the ultimate goal of assuring continuous protection from womb to tomb.[20]

In large part, given the manner in which federal officials designed the initial social security bill and later sought to liberalize its scope, a gap in coverage could not be avoided. Social security's architects wanted to maintain some correlation between the risks covered by the system and the basis upon which an individual was entitled to benefits. Social insurance was intended to protect workers and their dependents from the loss of wages by providing a deferred "living wage" in time of need. The payroll tax thus linked *risks* and *rights*. "Social insurance is predicated on the assumption that the risks derivative from the system of production should be protected chiefly by a charge on that production."[21] Requiring employees and employers to make payroll contributions placed most of the financial responsibility for the social security program directly on the productive enterprise. In addition, relating benefits to prior contributions afforded a reasonable and acceptable method for establishing the extent of one's "entitlement." Because of prevailing financial arrangements, however, social insurance experts were confident that existing deficiencies were remediable. By making social security a universal program, policymakers hoped that *all* workers ultimately would be protected against certain specific but ubiquitous risks. By augmenting benefits in tandem with increased revenues, the societal costs of such insurance could be prudently managed in ways that satisfied the liberals' objectives and allayed the conservatives' fears.

Just as the range and nature of risks alleviated through social security expanded after World War II, so too one can trace the evolution of more and more elastic definitions of citizens' *rights* to governmental income transfers. Politicians reiterated the goals of universal and comprehensive coverage enunciated by Lord Beveridge in his report on *Social Insurance and Allied Services* (1942–

43) and President Roosevelt in his so-called second bill of rights as they grappled with reconstructing a new world order amid postwar realities. Members of the Organization of American States in 1948 unanimously adopted in its "Declaration on the Rights and Duties of Man" the principle that "every person has the right to work [and] to social security which will protect him from the consequences of unemployment, old age and disabilities arising from causes beyond his control."[22] The Universal Declaration of Human Rights passed by the United Nations General Assembly in December 1948 included entitlement to social security among its catalog of basic "social and economic rights." These declarations were intended to be something more than a utopian manifesto. But it quickly became apparent that different countries would interpret them in accordance with their own economic priorities, political systems and foreign policy goals. The United States was no exception.

"The guiding idea in American social insurance is that the *individual earns* the right to benefit through payment of contributions by himself and on his behalf," observed economist Gaston Rimlinger in 1961. "Nevertheless, the act of contributing, while it has important political advantages, can only bind the government morally, rather than legally, to render specified benefits."[23] The notion of "contract" under social security, Rimlinger pointed out, had ideological rather than legal standing—as the Supreme Court held in the landmark case of *Flemming v. Nestor* (1960). In February 1960, the nation's highest tribunal considered the request of Ephram Nestor to have his social security benefits reinstated. Nestor, who had emigrated from Bulgaria in 1913, began to contribute to the social security system in January 1937; he received his first old-age retirement benefit in 1955. In July 1956, Nestor was deported from America for having been a Communist from 1933 to 1939. The government thereupon notified Nestor's wife (who had remained behind) that his benefits had been cut and that no further payments would be made. To justify its action, the Social Security Administration cited a 1954 law, which expressly declared that any person deported because of past Communist membership should be wholly cut off from any benefits to which he or she had contributed. In a 5–4 decision, the Supreme Court ruled against Nestor on June 20, 1960.

At first glance, Nestor and his wife appear to be minor victims in a larger Cold War drama: Communists simply should not be allowed to enjoy the fruits of the American way of life. But the significance of *Flemming v. Nestor* goes beyond the question of whether Nestor was treated unfairly in the post-McCarthy years because of his prior party affiliations. What makes this case so important in the history of social security is the manner in which the Court defined "entitlements." In stating the majority opinion, Mr. Justice Harlan argued that "to engraft upon the social security system a concept of 'accrued property rights' would deprive it of the flexibility and boldness in adjustment to ever-changing conditions which it demands."[24] Harlan thus extended the Court's line of reasoning in *Helvering v. Davis* (1937) by reaffirming Congress's right to exercise its power— and specifically to determine the precise nature of governmental entitlements under social security—as long as the legislative body operated within constitutional bounds. Significantly, Mr. Justice Black accepted this argument in delivering his dissenting opinion: "It is true, as the Court says, that the original Act contained a clause, still in force, that expressly reserves to Congress '[t]he right to alter, amend, or repeal any provision' of the Act. . . . It could repeal the Act so as to cease to operate its old-age insurance activities for the future. This means that it could stop covering new people, and even stop increasing its obligations to its old contributors."[25] Social security entitlements, in short, never were, and had not become, inviolable property rights. According to the Supreme Court, current and future beneficiaries are entitled to receive whatever Congress decides it can afford to pay them in light of prevailing social, economic, and political realities. To some, *Flemming v. Nestor* revealed the dark side of permitting an enlightened state to gain so much power that it could legitimately disregard individual rights under the seemingly benign rubric of "the public interest."[26]

Paradoxically, the Supreme Court's ruling occurred at a time in which scholars and public officials were taking another look at the socioeconomic obstacles and philosophical-legal justifications for taking rights seriously. Liberals tried to respond to and capitalize on the civil rights movement sweeping the land. "An age attuned to the idea that a government has vast responsibilities for the material welfare and human rights of citizens can hardly share the founders' fear of strong national government."[27] Not since the New Deal had the broad powers of the central government been called upon—and utilized—to promote the "rights" of individuals to participate and prosper in the American way of life regardless of race, geography, education, or age. Especially in the 1960s, older Americans became "entitled" to basic social and health-care services and more generous income-maintenance support.[28]

By extension, if Washington were really serious about advancing the rights of older Americans through congressional action and judicial intervention, then a new basis for understanding *rights* in our society was taking shape. The nature of the national polity itself was being transvalued. "The national idea means something more than mere centralization of power," Harvard political scientist Samuel Beer declared. "As the principle of community, it provides, along with the democratic idea, one of the standards by which governmental unification can be justified and by which it should be controlled and guided."[29] Far from threatening individual freedom, the increasing concentration of power in the federal government seemed to Beer among others to be the best way to sustain democratic ideals and advance individual rights. Even though the precise nature of rights and entitlements remained a matter for Congress to debate and the courts to adjudicate, these political and constitutional facts of life did not relieve public officials of the need to look out for the interests of the poorest and least articulate members of society. Thus, there arose a flurry of scholarly interest in delineating and guaranteeing the rights of welfare recipients to public benefits.[30]

Court decisions often helped to sharpen thinking. Perhaps the most significant Supreme Court case affecting the nature of rights under social security since *Nestor v. Flemming* was *Goldberg v. Kelly* (1970), which involved the case of a person whose AFDC benefits were terminated without giving the plaintiff the chance to appeal the decision. In this case, the Supreme Court held that "welfare benefits are a matter of statutory entitlement for persons qualified to receive them and procedural due process is applicable to their termination."[31] A fairly subtle but straightforward line of reasoning thus emerges from opinions rendered in these two cases at either end of the volatile 1960s. While the actual benefits under Title II of social security are not contractual, a citizen *is* guaranteed the right to due process—that is, to a hearing before his or her welfare benefits under Title IV can be terminated. Courts, it seemed, offered citizens the greatest protection of their rights in cases of suspension or revocation, but even then, that protection extended mainly to a consideration of whether or not the legal *process* had been observed. The right to a standard of living that was adequate on the basis of any objective criteria had not been made a constitutional issue or even a matter to be formalized in public law. Nonetheless, established and reasonable bureaucratic guidelines, far from being *negative* symbols of government's clout, could be used to generate positive and constructive results.

In the 1960s, the judicial, legislative, and executive branches paid unprecedented attention to the rights of the low-income elderly and welfare recipients under social security. Their efforts on behalf of the disadvantaged helps us to understand the legal, economic, and political status of rights under various programs of social security during a period in which the system's growth was so dynamic. New policy initiatives, such as the Job Corps, VISTA, and community action programs which were operated by the Office of Economic Opportunity, to be sure, attracted far greater attention and criticism. Furthermore, officials in competing bureaucracies often espoused views that made social security administrators seem staid. The Bureau of Labor Statistics, for instance, had devised a poverty index which counted greater numbers of needy Americans than did Orshansky's measure. Daniel Patrick Moynihan wrote his controversial report on *The Negro Family* while serving as assistant secretary of labor.[32]

And yet, as the nation's commitment to building a Great Society began to falter after 1966, daring experiments and innovations were rejected—especially if they required new bureaucratic structures and large amounts of revenue in order to be implemented. In this suddenly changed climate, social security's incremental approach to the problems of inequality ironically made it the most appropriate vehicle for social reform. Wilbur J. Cohen, who became secretary of HEW in 1968, unveiled "A Ten-Point Program to Abolish Poverty." He called for an end to racial discrimination in jobs and education as well as an overhaul of the federal government's public welfare, health care, and social insurance programs. Cohen's proposal specified six changes in social security intended to ensure that the program was *the* basic system of income security in America.[33]

Serving the interests of middle America, in other words, provided undeniable political opportunities for those who wanted to wage a "war on poverty." After all, a major reason why the social insurance program was so enormously popular in the 1950s and 1960s was that it worked so well for middle-class Americans. In the words of that eminent economist Paul Samuelson: "Often, government is one of the 'cheapest' ways of providing insurance against important risks."[34] Social security worked because individuals benefitted from participating in a system of mutual responsibility. That operating a system in this way made sense was rarely questioned— mainly because it did work and seemed to conform to quintessential American values.

J. Douglas Brown, from the very beginning one of social security's most thoughtful and eloquent defenders, realized that the notion of "mutual responsibility" being applied to the principle of social insurance had thus far eluded systematic examination. Yet he thought the system was supported by a venerable, covenantal tradition:

> The strongest support for the indefinite continuance of the transfer of funds . . . is the sense of mutual responsibility deep in the minds of people. The tradition of mutual responsibility has long been a cohesive force among industrial workers. It was exemplified in the first mutual aid societies, which later evolved into governmentally established contributory social insurance systems. Such systems embodied a covenant between the young and old, the gainfully employed and the dependents of those who die, and the strong and disabled. The covenant is not a legal entity but it has a subtle and powerful force in a democracy, in which the government must reflect a general consensus of its citizens. . . . History is on the side of those who believe that the covenant between those who contribute and those who need help will continue.[35]

To Brown, the soundness of social security was not really a question of demographic ratios or the proper ratio between contributions and disbursements. Ultimately, the only issue that truly mattered was whether or not government had the capacity to fulfill the promises of its intergenerational covenant. If it could, its ability to honor basic commitments made in the name of all citizens corroborated continued faith in the American system. If social security were to become vulnerable in the long run, its "bankruptcy" would have to be addressed in moral as well as financial terms. This possibility soon loomed as a haunting prospect.

Sobering Thoughts about Risks, Rights, and Responsibilities under Social Security since 1972

During the past decade, the types of risks covered under social security have changed very little. Yet the cumulative impact of expanding social security coverage and increasing benefits has encouraged the American people to demand less risk and greater protection from their public and private institutions. After World War II, American lawmakers with overwhelming popular support have treated the problem of economic insecurity as if it were some disease that could be cured and possibly even conquered—if only the right combination of medications were prescribed and conscientiously administered. Since the 1970s, however, the very engine that fueled the politics of incrementalism in an age of affluence suddenly made social security's premises and operations vulnerable to attack amid a shaky economy and new political realities.

Through an increasing welter of government programs, Washington has become involved in sharing the burden of risk associated with an extraordinary variety of likely natural and man-made disasters, ranging from guarantees to federal assistance in the wake of earthquakes and floods to quality-control standards in the marketplace and intricate safety regulations in the workplace. "The welfare state has been turned into an insurance state, as all individuals are protected against a whole array of risks by shifting the burden of their consequences to a larger group or the whole community or simply by eliminating them," Yair Aharoni declared in *The No-Risk Society* (1981). "The movement is away from a reliance on the rational individual as a decision maker and a bearer of the consequences of his choice to a socially determined allocation and distribution of resources, much of which is designed to shift the responsibility for both new and existing risks from individual to society."[36] Aharoni has identified an important trend, but he misses the irony implicit in his terminology. In the 1930s, even mildly welfarist objectives had to be sanitized by demonstrating their compatibility with time-tested American insurance principles.[37] Now Americans can admit that it is in the interest of their welfare to underwrite risk-centered insurance programs as a necessary part of public policy.

The expansion of the social insurance programs, especially at the federal level, nurtured the belief that full protection against the hazards of contemporary life were genuinely possible. Large private institutions, in response to public pressure and their own organizational requirements, have also allocated greater portions of their capital and resources after World War II in order to complement and expand the coverage against "risk." Most corporations now offer their workers supplemental wages, health-care, and retirement benefits that enable them to maintain their standard of living during temporary layoffs, long-term illness, and in their later years. It is not by accident that many of these corporate and union policies were designed to dovetail with existing governmental programs.[38] Paradoxically, however, heightened expectations about the degree to which a risk-free society could be achieved inexorably fueled unrealistic demands on our socioeconomic and political institutions. It quickly proved difficult to sustain the momentum of translating greater expectations into better protection. Skepticism about the efficacy of such initiatives mounted amid new economic uncertainties.

> The reaction against the mass sufferings of [the depression] years moved people to build fortifications against any recurrence. Few ideas have animated so much subsequent history as the quest for security. It conceived Big Government and tamed the worst aspects of unrestrained capitalism. . . . So today's new insecurities exist along with a gut appreciation that the urge for absolute security may be futile and, more than that, responsible for some of the present predicament. The attempt to satisfy everyone's desire for job security and rising living standards led to inflationary policies and, in particular, to inflationary money growth. . . . What emerges is a pervasive confusion with everyone professing allegiance to yesterday's ideals while trying to cope with today's realities. . . . All this marks a continuing eclipse of Depression-era psychology and politics.[39]

At one end of the political spectrum, conservatives bemoaned the dire consequences and emphasized the hidden (and wasteful) costs of pursuing the chimera of a risk-free society. "The riskless society, with all its misallocation of resources, regimentation, and erosion of individual freedom, is evolving rapidly. . . . Unless its nature is recognized and appreciated, there is little reason to believe that this trend will be reversed."[40] Writers emphasized that government must regulate itself, and correct its own excesses by cutting back and eliminating those programs that squander valuable resources and fuel cynicism by promising far more than they can possibly deliver.

Elaborating this viewpoint, reformers on the right recommended shifting some of the burden for underwriting protection against major risks back to individuals. Social security became a prime target for their attack. "Social security now departs so widely from any recognizable principle of insurance that the 'social insurance' mythology surrounding it ought to be discarded once and for all," David A. Stockman wrote in 1975. "Conservative duplicity and liberal ideology both contribute to the dynamics and durability of the social pork barrel."[41] If more and more people acknowledged there is no such thing as a free lunch, the so-called neo-conservatives fervently believed, middle-class individuals would recognize that it was in their best interest to behave in a more prudent manner in order to eliminate unnecessary expenses and keep costs down.

Thus far, the liberal camp's response to such arguments has been to defend the status quo, contending that the remedies proposed are more pernicious than the problem posed by sustaining the image of a riskless society. The cost of *not* attempting to address the risks of old-age dependency, broken homes, unemployment, and disability through social insurance far exceed the net outlays of helping individuals help themselves. Indeed, many policymakers remain certain that administering programs on the basis of age entails less invidious criteria than a means-tested index. The aged are different from the rest of us, the public largely still believes, and thus deserve and need categorical assistance. The best available data and scholarly studies, however, have begun to undermine the credibility of this position.

In recent years, it has become increasingly apparent that age-based criteria do not meet the needs of large segments of the population. "A case can be made that at the same time that age itself is becoming less relevant in the society, legislators and administrators have been proliferating laws and regulations that are age based."[42] Age-specific assistance and protection may have the ironic effect of denying services to those older persons who need the most help. It is possible, moreover, that age has become a less valid predictor than gender, race, income, education, or employment status in determining need. Those over sixty-five as a group, after all, are healthier, wealthier, and better educated than any comparable cohort in American history. The men and women in this age group who need the most help typically suffer from some long-term disadvantage, often exacerbated by sexism, nativism, or racism. Thus what strategy best addresses the "fact" that most poor older Americans are women—making the problem a "women's issue" or dealing with it as a special feature of the economics of late life? Might it not make more sense to tackle the racism that is endemic in our culture than focussing on the specific woes of elderly minorities?

The trouble with posing questions in this manner has been that it lulls policy analysts and the American people to miss a critical point about the interconnections among risks, rights, and mutual responsibility under social security. Rather than trying to isolate the effects of age and need in any choosing how to proceed, it might be wiser to remind ourselves that the purpose of social insurance was to protect a majority of *citizens* against well-known risks. In putting the matter this way, we quickly realize that in analyzing the nature of "risks," we must reconsider *who* is at risk and *who* deserves some measure of protection through social insurance. Discussing "risks" from this perspective leads us at once into the equally problematic question of "rights."

In a series of cases involving eligibility for social security benefits during the 1970s, the Supreme Court often placed itself in the position of having to decide whether rights should be differentiated on the basis of gender, need, or some other criterion. A review of recent decisions leads to two conclusions. On the one hand, the Court succeeded in drawing finer lines in determining the constitutional basis for "entitlements" under social security. On the other hand, it hardly resolved the question of *what* rights were at stake.

In *Weinberger v. Wiesenfeld* (1975), for instance, the Court overturned a gender-based distinction between widows' and widowers' benefits by declaring that whatever was provided for a surviving mother must also be granted to an eligible surviving father.[43] Feminists and supporters of children's rights hailed the decision. Yet two years later in *Mathews v. DeCastro*, the Court ruled against a divorcee with a minor to support (who had been married for more than twenty years to a retired contributor) who claimed to have the same right to benefits as did the wife of a retired or disabled worker who had a child to support.[44] The Court did not believe that due process was being violated in this case, because divorced persons typically choose to live lives independent from their previous spouses. Such reasoning, however, leaves moot the question of whether divorced parents have also severed their family responsibilities. Insofar as promoting the welfare of children was—and remains—a major rationale for sponsoring social insurance provisions, then it indeed is quite pertinent that child-support payments tend to be low and irregularly paid. So did the decision rendered in *Mathews v. De Castro* advance rights or subject them to further adjudication? Grappling with such questions ensured that the issue of women's rights under social security would continue to be a lively topic of debate.

Similarly, the Court continued to be sensitive to the *procedural* contexts in which rights to benefits are determined and terminated. Here too, distinctions were drawn on very technical grounds. In *Mathews v. Eldridge* (1976), the Court ruled that an "evidentiary hearing" was not required prior to terminating disability benefits as long as the beneficiary was notified beforehand of the proposed action and had the right to review his or her file and supply additional evidence. In reaching this verdict, the Court relied heavily on the fact that disability benefits under Title II, unlike AFDC payments, under social security were not based on need: "The private interest that will be adversely affected by an erroneous termination of benefits is likely to be less in the case of a disabled worker than in the case of a welfare recipient."[45] Apparently the question of need did, under certain circumstances, influence the Supreme Court's thinking about due process. No wonder defining "rights" under the law was so perplexing. Besides such familiar categories as "privileges" and "claims," legal scholars had to distinguish among procedural, administrative, statutory, and contractual rights, and even then, they had not exhausted the possible ways to define the basis of "entitlements" to social security benefits. The Court typically refined constitutional precedents in a highly pragmatic style: case by case, they opted for drawing finely spun, context-bound distinctions rather than asserting any deeply seated vision of "rights."[46]

Indeed, the most important effort to redefine the basis of "rights" in modern America during the 1970s probably took place in halls of philosophy rather than in courts of justice. The study of public ethics was reinvigorated by the publication of several brilliant monographs and the exchange of ideas disseminated in such prestigious magazines and journals such as *The Public Interest, The New York Review,* and *Philosophy and Public Affairs.* Determining the nature of rights under social security was not the primary issue preoccupying public philosophers, but much that was written about justice, liberalism, and equality has a direct bearing on this subject.

John Rawls's seminal *A Theory of Justice* (1971) elevated the debate over individual rights and entitlements to a new level, and remained the work most regularly cited and attacked for the rest of the decade. If a society truly wishes to be *just,* in Rawls's view, it must protect the fundamental rights of the least fortunate members of society.[47] Under Rawls's concept of justice, the redistributive features of social security's benefit structure should afford the poorest members of society a truly acceptable "minimal" standard of living.[48] Robert Nozick presented quite a different philosophical basis for promoting individual rights in *Anarchy, State and Utopia* (1974). Whereas Rawls presumes that conforming to the principles of just distribution sets limits to the possible extent of legitimate acquisition and entitlement, in Nozick's view, sanctioning acquisition and protecting entitlement constrains governmental action in the area of redistributive justice: a person is "justly" entitled to social security benefits to the extent that he or she "owns" them as property—that is, through legitimate acquisition or earning them as a right. As long as a beneficiary can claim proper title to those benefits, no one can legitimately take them away.[49]

For all their differences, Rawls and Nozick share certain assumptions about how the debate over the meaning of rights should proceed. But the manner in which they couch critical issues makes it difficult to link their ideas to the concerns expressed by social security loyalists, critics, and reformers. Both have adopted the economist's view of modern man in order to facilitate their efforts to discuss ways that people can maximize and preserve the attainment of desired and desirable goals.[50] And both have taken individual rights *so* seriously that they tend to ignore or at least minimize the extent to which unpredictable historical factors and dysfunctional societal norms and structures confound personal options even as they shape individual's choices. "Society" operates like a utopia in both scholars' books. Rawls takes for granted that a "well-ordered" society is stable, homogeneous, and smoothly functioning, and regulated by a clear sense of "justice."[51] Nozick's "minimal state" similarly has no life independent of what it can do for individuals:

"Treating us with respect by respecting our rights, it allows us, individually or with whom we choose, to choose our life and to realize our ends and our conception of ourselves, insofar as we can. . . . How *dare* any state or group of individuals do more. Or less."[52]

It is doubtful that sociopolitical arrangements envisioned by Rawls and Nozick are possible anywhere save in a utopia: none has yet been discovered by historians. Political commentators and public philosophers have long emphasized the extent to which societal values and structures influence our thinking about individual rights. "What marks . . . a community is not merely a spirit of benevolence, or the prevalence of communitarian values, or even certain 'shared final ends' alone, but a common vocabulary of discourse and a background of implicit practices and understandings within which the opacity of the participants is reduced if never finally dissolved."[53] The current meaning of "mutual responsibility," accordingly, must also be probed in terms of recent national experiences.

Just as recent events and scholarly inquiries have exposed illusions in our understanding of "risks" and contrarieties in our definition and application of "rights," so too a new—and not terribly comforting—perspective on the meaning of "responsibility" is being formulated in analyses of the contemporary American polity. For openers, students of American civilization have demonstrated that puncturing myths about the Republic's covenant with Nature's God has been a central motif in the writing of American history since at least the 1830s: "The covenant . . . was broken almost as soon as it was made. For a long time Americans were able to hide from that fact, to deny the brokenness. Today the broken covenant is visible to all."[54] Hence covenant does not accurately describe the pact between generations that is manifest in social security's operations.

If we cannot reasonably draw analogies between social security and some American covenant, does the principle of mutual responsibility rest on the system's *intergenerational* features? Probably not. Less clear-cut than the distinction between parent and child, the term *generation* might refer with equal plausibility to all people between certain ages, to progenitors of any age (as opposed to their progeny), and/or to people who lived through a monumental experience (such as the Great Depression). The very ambiguity of meaning makes it hard to know who is precisely included or excluded in a definition. Worse, referring to people as being of a certain generation attributes to them characteristics that they may or may not possess.[55]

Even if the exact meaning of *generation* in the social security context were perfectly clear, some commentators question the legitimacy of claiming that the system's intergenerational income transfer is based on the *moral* responsibilities that children owe their parents *as* parents. Peter Laslett, an eminent British social historian and political philosopher, frames the issue this way: "Duties go forward in time, but rights go backwards. . . . A crude metaphor would be that of a chain made out of hooks and eyes, where hooks have all to lie one way, and at the point where the chain stops a hook without an eye is always hanging forward."[56] Laslett does not mean to say that children have *no* responsibilities to their parents. Natural esteem, historical precedent, and common law do combine to reinforce reciprocal care and concern. Nevertheless, whereas parents provide for their children spontaneously through love, affection, and identity, "the duties of children towards parents, in later life at least, must be looked on as predominantly social or even political in character—as instances in fact of the universal obligation we all have towards contemporaries in need—rather than as generational."[57] The younger (working) generation's responsibilities to their (retired) elders is similarly based on a compact that is political, not demographic, in nature.

Justifying social security's modus operandi in *political* terms, alas, offers no firmer basis for confidence than does invoking the image of a covenant or taking refuge in the murkiness of the idea of generation. Paradoxically, as we have become more and more concerned with our individual rights and the possibilities of distributive justice, we have been less inclined to talk about what we owe one another as members of a democracy. "Our sense of citizenship, of social warmth and a shared fate, has become thin gruel."[58] In part, this reflects the loss of a common vocabulary with which to discuss the nature and meaning of such basic elements of a polity as rights, justice, virtue, and responsibility. "In any society where government does not express or represent the moral community of the citizens, but is instead a set of institutional arrangements for imposing a bureaucratised unity on a society which lacks genuine moral consensus, the nature of political obligation becomes systematically unclear."[59] Thurman Arnold's astute observation about a bureaucratic world's "negative" symbols comes back to haunt us: We lack a clear sense of both the locus and focus of mutual responsibility. For this reason, we debate but never really quite know what guidance we can derive from the ethical foundations that presumably are embedded into our country's political fabric.

It appears, then, that we the elders of the twenty-first century must hang our chances for getting social security when we reach sixty-five (or sixty-seven or whatever the normal retirement age is then) on one of two hooks, to use Laslett's metaphor. We can hope that the dynamics of bureaucratic inertia and special-interest-group politics will continue to fuel the pay-as-you-go system of social insurance contributions and benefits indefinitely.[60] Or we can pin our confidence on faith in America's long-term prospects, and assume that an eleventh-hour solution to Social Security's immediate difficulties—such as the one that became the basis for the 1983 amendments—can be achieved whenever necessary. Is it possible that I have painted too grim a picture? Does a third option exist?

Coda

By way of conclusion, let me address this last question by recasting the evidence presented thus far in a different manner. Consider, for the moment, simply the definitions of "risk," "rights," and "responsibility" used by the architects of social security and those charged with monitoring its operations and ensuring that it can meets its future obligations and objectives. There has been very little change in the basic stance taken by social security policymakers over time. The program's creators and protectors have consistently defined "risk" in narrow, condition-oriented terms. Furthermore, they have continually reiterated that the "rights" beneficiaries could claim under social security were not contractual. This meant, among other things, that current benefits could be altered in light of changing economic conditions, Congressional vote, and judicial wisdom. And this, from the perspective of seasoned experts, was how the system *should* operate, because social insurance embodied a commitment to "mutual responsibility" that was intimately linked to the well-being of society as a whole.

And yet, when we put official definitions of risks, rights, and responsibility into a broader perspective—that is, when we consider how changes in American society and culture have affected the meanings of these three terms—a different picture emerges. When times were good, when the economy was booming and public confidence in government was high, people expressed little concern about the *limits* to broadening rights and expanding benefits. The need and the capacity of the public sector to foster mutual responsibility was considered a self-evident truth, particularly since it did not cost too much or jeopardize the economic prospects of the middle class. Such a felicitous set of circumstances could not last forever. Indeed, they were never expected. The program's creators fully recognized that as the system matured, adjustments would have to be made in its financing and operating principles. They could not have foreseen, however, that after more than thirty-five years of relatively painless growth, social security would enter a critical transitional period that coincided with a decade of serious economic dislocation, political upheaval, and social unrest. Far from reversing the historical tide of recent years, the economic policies and public philosophy embodied in Reaganomics vindicates the proposition that "affluence strains resources for enlightened compassion."[61] The future of social security hangs in the balance: We are less confident than before about what risks average Americans have a right to expect their government to take responsibility for underwriting. This stance is probably more intellectually honest than the half-truths and misconceptions that surround social security, but it is hardly a palliative for the despair and dubiety expressed by the system's friends and foes.

I believe that we should draw two fundamental lessons from past experiences. First, we should use the bureaucrats' definitions of social security's three r's as the basis for our future discussions: they constitute a reasonable and consistent starting point for discussions. They offer well established categories and rules—criteria for making informed judgments in a disorderly and ever-changing political arena. The 1983 amendments to the Social Security Act, after all, were justified in terms of their success in reaffirming the traditional functions of social insurance. Indeed, policymakers took special pains to emphasize the soundness of the structural and normative foundations that had long girded the system. Thus in presenting its findings to the president and Congress, the National Commission on Social Security Reform declared that "Congress, in its deliberations on financing proposals, should not alter the fundamental structure of the Social Security program or undermine its fundamental principles."[62] That such a recommendation was unanimously endorsed, at a time when various experts and critics were urging that social security be converted into a strict annuity program or welfare scheme, underscores the depth of support for maintaining social security in its present form as far as practicable. This theme reemerged in both House and Senate debates. Whatever the system becomes, it will be no less than it already is. But this observation quickly leads us to a second point.

Even if we believe that the rationale articulated by the first generation of social security's policymakers should remain the cornerstone of all future initiatives, we must acknowledge that major changes nonetheless are inevitable. The social security program that presently exists could not have been foreseen fifty years ago. Nor will it resemble in 2035 what it has become today—though I suspect that its basic structure will not be radically transformed. The society that has sustained its evolution continues to undergo profound transformations. Consequently, we must be ready to modify the normative underpinnings of America's social insurance program if it is to meet the challenges and opportunities of an aging population.

In this regard, the words of Thomas Jefferson, invoked by Jennings Randolph during the recent congressional debate are illuminating:

> Some men look at constitutions with sanctimonious reverence, and deem them like the ark of the covenant, too sacred to be touched. They ascribe to the men of the preceding age a wisdom more than human, and suppose what they did to be beyond amendment. I knew that age well. . . . It was very like the present; and forty years of experience in government is worth a century of bookreading; and this they would say themselves, were they to rise from the dead. . . . Laws and institutions must go hand in hand with the progress of the human mind. As that becomes more developed, more enlightened, as new discoveries are made, new truths disclosed, and manners and opinions change with the change of circumstances, institutions must advance also, and keep pace with the times.[63]

Jefferson lived long enough to see a rising generation of Americans reform and re-form institutions that he and the Republic's other Founding Fathers had designed to serve as the foundation for "the new order of the ages." We find ourselves in a somewhat similar situation today. Because so many people have a stake in social security, it is politically tempting to treat the program as a "covenant, too sacred to be touched." And yet, social security has proved to be an enduring institution despite—and largely because of—its sensitivity to short-term changes in the political economy. The issues raised in the depths of the Great Depression remain salient today even though the times bear little resemblance. What this suggests is that social security has been reasonably well served by a mode of policymaking that is intelligently present-minded. In weighing current options, it has been essential all along to understand the logic and constraints that influenced past decisions. No policymaker has been able to predict the future, but failing to consider the consequences of reforms has always been irresponsible. Social security's history demonstrates that the institution is malleable: by capitalizing on popular support and administrative adaptability, its overarching objectives and functions have remained central amid ever-changing realities. Hence we should reconsider anew how (and how far) we intend to go about protecting Americans against the risks of contemporary life as well as what we *want* to mean today by individual rights and mutual responsibility under social security. A continuing and constructive debate over the meanings of simple words that form the basis of economic well-being in aging America is not only essential; it is unavoidable.

Accordingly, in dealing with "risks" under social security in the future, we would do well to remember that from the start policymakers intended that social insurance afford protection against specific hazards associated with successive stages of life. Roosevelt and his advisors concentrated on the plight of the aged poor, because in the 1930s old-age dependency was a major problem inadequately addressed by existing programs. In selling a program that was unfamiliar and untested on American soil, however, they emphasized that this risk was shared by all age groups. Thus even age-specific measures were designed to appeal beyond chronological boundaries. Citizens of all ages, not just the aged, had a vested interest in programs for the aging. And ultimately, the New Dealers expected their program to provide cradle-to-grave coverage and benefits.

In its main lines, this line of reasoning still makes sense, but certain anomalies must be redressed. Social security remains older

Americans' most important source of economic support, but the old are not the only people who benefit from social insurance. This fact needs to be emphasized. And if intergenerational tensions do not abate, policymakers surely will want to rethink ways to better serve children and the middle-aged through this program. Nor is social security the only means of support for most middle-class senior citizens. Many neo-liberals and neo-conservative critics—who are in the vanguard of the baby-boom birth cohort—are suggesting that it is now politically and economically feasible to reduce the relative importance of federal expenditures for old-age and survivors insurance. I think that such a tack is possible, *but* only if it is implemented *while* increasing pension coverage and average retirement benefits under other retirement resources in the private and public sectors. Whatever "savings" are ultimately realized in the area of income maintenance, moreover, should be used to cover other social insurance expenditures, especially those related to the health-care needs of Americans over seventy-five.

There are more compelling reasons to put greater stress on the cross-generational features of social security than at any earlier phase of the system's development. We live in a society in which the life cycle has become fluid. Age-specific norms have less and less basis in reality. Becoming sixty-five no longer conjures up the image of obsolescence that once prevailed. Indeed, in an *aging* society— one in which two-thirds of all the changes in life expectancy at birth and gains in adult longevity have taken place in this century—the future needs of the aged can most effectively be addressed by taking steps to enhance people's opportunities at earlier stages in their lives. Demographic trends are not the only factor at play here. During the past fifty years, the labor force has become more heterogeneous. Talking about differences between blue-collar vs. white-collar workers has become anachronistic; the distinction between the public and private sectors of employment has grown shadowy. Nowadays, working men and women of different races, ages, and educational attainments face very different problems. To hew to a definition of "risk" that deals with "normal" hazards of our existing modes of production makes little sense unless that definition takes account of such diversity. For this reason, the goal of social insurance demonstrably must be to provide economic security—"a living wage"—for people who find themselves in very different circumstances at various stages of life.

Similarly, in establishing "rights" under social insurance, we must bear in mind that social insurance is risk-conditioned: it properly deals with the setting of human life rather than presuming *either* that Government knows (best) how individuals choose to live their lives, *or* that Government does best when it encourages Americans to think of themselves as a crowd of individuals competing for spoils in a free market. "It is easy—too easy—to plan for abstract aggregates of *individuals*, regarded for planning purposes as so many arithmetically equal units composed of identical drives and needs," observed the sociologist Robert Nisbet more than twenty years ago. "It is far more difficult to plan for, to legislate for, *persons* who live not in simple economic or political perspectives but in complex associative and normative systems that are the product of tradition and custom."[64] To my mind, the distinction Nisbet makes between "individuals" and "persons" has special pertinence for social security planning. In making successive changes in the Social Security Act, Congress has reserved "the right to alter, amend or repeal any provision"—a *right* no Supreme Court ruling has ever challenged. Rather than bemoan this historical truth, we should take advantage of it. Recognizing that social security is not the only way to provide for the vicissitudes of life means that we simply cannot afford to discuss the program's scope and financing as if they operated in a vacuum. We must take a broad view. Policymakers must take account of the role that other institutions in American life—the family, the church, voluntary organizations, private companies—play in contemporary life. We must remember that these mediating institutions facilitate our individual and collective efforts to attain a measure of security from the risks of modern times. They afford the average American an extraordinary range of options and thereby promote individual choice. What we need is better—and sometimes indirect—coordination among these various institutions to fill in gaps and correct inequities in existing programs.

Does such a stance imply, at bottom, that the role of social insurance in American society should be minimized? Does it mean that the principle of "mutual responsibility" long associated with social insurance should be played down, or discarded as chimerical? Not at all. Neo-liberals and neo-conservatives alike should take their cue from Sen. Bill Bradley who in the midst of the debates over the 1983 amendments noted that "social security is the best expression of community that we have in this country today."[65] Ironically, the challenge before us is to turn Thurman Arnold's aphorism on its head: we have to demonstrate to a skeptical and scared public that a bureaucratic institution really is a vital symbol of modern American society.

Viewing social security as neither covenant nor contract, but as an expression of community reaffirms some of the program's most important traditional values. It enhances the familiar claim that all Americans have a stake in the program. It underscores the system's central role in American life: no other bureaucracy is so well positioned to assure everyone regardless of race, gender, or age the financial wherewithal necessary for a minimal standard of living. At the same time, it sets an agenda which acknowledges that sustaining mutual interdependence in the American community presupposes both a shared past and a common future. For if a major function of social insurance is to promote flexibility and to maximize each person's options in a highly fluid, uncertain and technocratically driven society, social security bears major responsibility for ensuring that fundamental protection is afforded across the public and private sectors.

The meaning of community embodied in social security is fragile indeed. We cannot depend on it, yet we cannot live as a nation without it. As a people, we must constantly renew our affirmation to longstanding American values while we reshape this vital public policy to meet basic national objectives. How we treat our fellow citizens and our future selves under the principle of social insurance thus mirrors, for better and for worse, what we take to be the essential quality and tenor of American life.

Notes

1. Franklin Delano Roosevelt, "Objectives of the Administration," June 8, 1934 in *The Public Papers and Addresses of Franklin Delano Roosevelt*, 13 vols. comp. by Samuel I. Rosenman (New York: Random House, 1938), Ill: 291–92.

2. Ibid., p. 291.

3. See Theda Skocpol and John Ikenberry, "The Political Formation of the American Welfare State," in Richard F. Tomasson, ed., *Comparative Social Research*, vol. 6 (1983), pp. 187–214.

4. U.S. Senate, 74th Cong., 1st sess. (1935), Report of the Senate Finance Committee, No. 628: The Social Security Bill, p. 2.

5. *Congressional Record*, April 16, 1935, p. 5789.

6. Social Security Board, *Social Security in America* (Washington, D.C.: Government Printing Office, 1937, pp. 149, 154.

7. Henry J. Pratt, *The Gray Lobby* (Chicago: University of Chicago Press, 1976), ch. 2; W. Andrew Achenbaum, *Old Age in the New Land* (Baltimore: Johns Hopkins University Press, 1978), ch. 6–7; Carole Haber, *Beyond Sixty-Five* (New York: Cambridge University Press, 1983).

8. *Congressional Record*, vol 102 (May 17, 1935), p. 15110. See also, J. Douglas Brown, *Essays on Social Security* (Princeton University: Industrial Relations Section, 1977), pp. 28–31; Edwin E. Witte, "Old-Age Security in the Social Security Act" (1937) in *Social Security Perspectives: Essays by Edwin E. Witte*, ed. Robert J. Lampman (Madison: University of Wisconsin Press, 1962), p. 146.

9. *Congressional Record, Senate*, June 17, 1935, p. 9419. See also, sections 208 and 1104 of the Social Security Act.

10. T. W. Arnold, *The Symbols of Government* (New Haven: Yale University Press, 1935), p. 209.

11. *Congressional Record*, June 19, 1935, pp. 9636–37.

12. Jill S. Quadagno, "Welfare Capitalism and the Social Security Act of 1935," *American Sociological Review*, vol. 49 (October 1984): 632–47.

13. *Congressional Record*, April 19, 1935, p. 6070. For a contemporary analysis indicating the ominous relationship between ethics and power in the political marketplace being espoused by *all* interested parties, see Reinhold Niebuhr, *Moral Man and Immoral Society* (New York: Scribner's, 1932).

14. U.S., Senate, 74th Congress, 1st sess. (1935), *Economic Security Act*, Hearings before the Senate Committee on Finance, p. 1337.

15. W. Andrew Achenbaum, "Stitching a Safety Net," *The Wilson Quarterly*, vol. 9 (New Year's 1985): 132–33.

16. See Edward D. Berkowitz, "The First Social Security Crisis," *Prologue*, vol. 15 (Fall 1983): 133–49.

17. U.S. Senate Finance Committee, *Social Security Bill*, p. 27. The phrases quoted in the next sentence comes from S. 1130 (The Economic Security Act) (1935), p. 1338.

18. Edwin E. Witte, "Social Security-1948" in *Social Security Perspectives*, p. 31. Witte reiterated in this theme in a 1955 essay, "Changing Roles in the Quest for Security." See *op. cit.* p. 77. See also, Eveline M. Burns, *The American Social Security System* (Boston: Houghton Mifflin, 1949).

19. Brown, *Essays*, p. 20.

20. See Deborah A. Stone, *The Disabled State* (Philadelphia: Temple University Press, 1984); and Jerry L. Mashaw, *The Bureaucratic State* (New Haven: Yale University Press, 1983). I develop this theme more fully

in ch. 2 of my Twentieth Century Fund study, *Social Security: Visions and Revisions*. (New York: Cambridge University Press, 1986).

21. Elizabeth Wickenden, "Social Welfare Law: The Concept of Risk and Entitlement," *University of Detroit Law Journal*, vol. 43 (July 1966): 528.

22. Tom J. Farer, "Human Rights and Human Welfare in Latin America," *Daedalus*, vol. 112 (Fall 1983): 166.

23. Gaston V. Rimlinger, "Social Security, Incentives, and Controls in the U.S. and U.S.S.R.," *Comparative Studies in Society and History*, vol. 4 (1961–62): 108–9. For the difference between the American approach and tacks adopted elsewhere, see *idem.*, "Capitalism and Human Rights," *Daedalus*, vol. 112 (Fall 1983): 51–79; Guy Perrin, "Reflections on Fifty Years of Social Security," *International Labour Review*, vol. 99 (March 1969): 249–92.

24. Flemming v. Nestor, *80 Supreme Court Reporter* 1367. Justice Harlan's remarks appear on p. 1372.

25. Justice Black's remarks appear at *ibid.*, para. 624, p. 1380.

26. Charles A. Reich, "The New Property," *The Public Interest*, no. 3 (Spring 1966): 86.

27. Archibald Cox, "The Supreme Court—Foreword," *Harvard Law Review*, vol. 80 (November 1966): 119.

28. For views on this development that span the political spectrum, see Robert M. Ball, *Social Security: Today and Tomorrow* (New York: Columbia University Press, 1978); Martha Derthick, *Policymaking for Social Security* (Washington, D.C.: Brookings Institution, 1979); Robert J. Myers, *Social Security*, 3rd ed. (Homewood, Ill.: R. D. Irwin, 1985); Carolyn Weaver, *The Crisis in Social Security* (Durham: Duke Policy Studies, 1982); and W. Andrew Achenbaum, *Shades of Gray* (Boston: Little, Brown and Co., 1983).

29. Samuel H. Beer, "Liberalism and the National Idea," *The Public Interest*, no. 5 (Spring 1966): 82, but see also pp. 78–80.

30. For an influential and prophetic essay representative of the genre, see Charles A. Reich, "Individual Rights and Social Welfare: The Emerging Legal Issues," *Yale Law Journal*, vol. 74 (June 1965): 1245–59.

31. 397 U.S. 254 (1970).

32. Daniel Patrick Moynihan, *The Negro Family: The Case for National Action* (Washington, D.C.: Department of Labor, 1965). From the start, Moynihan's data and interpretations were challenged (and ultimately discredited) by social scientists, historians, and policy analysts. For our purposes, it is worth noting that Moynihan's defenders often accused his critics (especially in the Department of Health, Education and Welfare) of opposing the report in order to protect their own vested interests. See Lee

Rainwater and William L. Yancy, *The Moynihan Report: The Politics of Controversy* (Cambridge, Mass.: M.I.T. Press, 1967).

33. Wilbur J. Cohen, "A Ten-Point Program to Abolish Poverty," *Social Security Bulletin*, vol. 31 (December 1968): 3, 13. Cohen's social security proposals appear on pp. 7–8.

34. Paul A. Samuelson, "Social Insurance," *American Economic Review* vol. 54 (May 1964): 95.

35. Brown, *Essays*, pp. 31–32.

36. Yair Aharoni, *The No-Risk Society* (Chatham, N.J.: Chatham House Publishers, Inc., 1981), pp. 1–2.

37. Jerry R. Cates, *Insuring Inequality* (Ann Arbor: University of Michigan Press, 1983), esp. pp. 29–35; Andrew Hacker, "'Welfare': The Future of an Illusion," *New York Review*, vol. 32 (February 28, 1985): 37–38.

38. Peter F. Drucker, *The Unseen Revolution* (New York: Harper & Row, 1976); and John Myles, *Old Age in the Welfare State* (Boston: Little, Brown and Co., 1984).

39. Robert J. Samuelson, "Social Insecurity," *National Journal*, vol. 14 (May 29, 1982): 965. I have reversed the sentence order in the original.

40. James L. Athearn, "The Riskless Society," *The Journal of Risk and Insurance*, vol. 45 (December 1978): 573; See also, Aharoni, pp. 35–36, 207.

41. David A. Stockman, "The Social Pork Barrel," *The Public Interest*, vol. 39 (Spring 1975): 16, 30.

42. Bernice L. Neugarten, "Policy for the 1980s," in *Age or Need?*, ed. Bernice L. Neugarten (Beverly Hills: Sage Publications, 1982), p. 25.

43. In order to ensure equal protection under the Due Process Clause of the Fifth Amendment, the Court ordered that a father with children be paid a benefit equal to 75 percent of the disability benefit which the deceased wife would have received if disabled rather than dying. The classification discriminates among surviving children solely on the basis of the sex of the surviving parent. See *Weinberger v. Wiesenfeld*, 420 U.S. 651.

44. *Mathews v. DeCastro*, 429 U.S. 181, 185–57. Subsequent amendments to the Social Security Act have rendered this case moot, since the present law now provides benefits in such instances.

45. *Mathews v. Eldridge*, 424 U.S. 319, esp. pp. 321, 340–41. See also, Lawrence H. Tribe, "Unraveling *National League of Cities*: The New Federalism and Affirmative Rights to Essential Governmental Services," *Harvard Law Review*, vol. 90 (April 1977): 1080–81; and Melvin Aron Eisenberg, "Participation, Responsiveness and the Consultative Process," *op. cit.*, vol. 92 (December 1978): 421.

46. For a fine summary of the literature and issues that it raises for

constitutional law, see Peter Weston, "The Empty Idea of Equality," *Harvard Law Review*, vol. 95 (January 1982): esp. 540–41.

47. John Rawls, *A Theory of Justice* (Cambridge, Mass.: Harvard University Press, 1971), p. 303.

48. Such a strategy, critics charged however, might overstep Washington's range of powers. See Marc Plattner, "The Welfare State vs. The Redistributive State," *Public Interest*, no. 55 (Spring 1979): 47–48; and Frank I. Michelman, "In Pursuit of Constitutional Welfare Rights: One View of Rawls's Theory of Justice," *University of Pennsylvania Law Review*, vol. 121 (1973): esp. 1002–3.

49. Robert Nozick, *Anarchy, State, and Utopia* (New York: Basic Books, 1974), p. 153. At present, there is no constitutional basis for sustaining Nozick's position: the Supreme Court repeatedly has held that social security benefits are not accrued property rights.

50. Alasdair MacIntyre, *After Virtue* (Notre Dame: University of Notre Dame Press, 1981), p. 231.

51. See John Rawls, "A Well-Ordered Society," in *Philosophy, Politics & Society*, 5th series, ed. Peter Laslett and James Fishkin (New Haven: Yale University Press, 1979), pp. 6–9.

52. Nozick, *Anarchy, State, and Utopia*, pp. 333–334.

53. Michael Sandel, *Liberalism and the Limits of Justice* (Cambridge: Cambridge University Press, 1982), pp. 172–73.

54. Robert N. Bellah, *The Broken Covenant* (New York: The Seabury Press, 1975), p. 139; see also, Paul Nagel, *This Sacred Trust* (New York: Oxford University Press, 1971).

55. For more on the difficulties with the concept, see the argument and notes in chapter one of Robert Wohl's *The Generation of 1914* (Cambridge, Mass.: Harvard University Press, 1979). See also, S. N. Eisenstadt, *From Generation to Generation* (Glencoe: Free Press, 1956); Edward Shils, *Tradition* (Chicago: University of Chicago Press, 1981), pp. 35–37.

56. Peter Laslett, "The Conversation Between the Generations," in *Philosophy, Politics and Society*, 5th series, ed. Peter Laslett and James Fishkin (New Haven: Yale University Press, 1979), p. 48.

57. *Ibid.*, p. 51. See also, Kingsley Davis and Pietronella von den Oever, "Age Relations and Public Policy in Advanced Industrial Societies," *Population and Development Review*, vol. 7 (March 1981): 5. For a good introduction to the literature on intergenerational inequalities and tensions, see Nancy Foner, *Ages in Conflict* (New York: Columbia University Press, 1984).

58. George F. Will, *Statecraft as Soulcraft* (New York: Simon and Schuster, 1983), p. 45. See also, Morris Janowitz, *The Reconstruction of Patriotism* (Chicago: University of Chicago Press, 1983).

59. MacIntyre, *After Virtue*, p. 236.

60. In theory, this has been the way social security financing has operated since the 1940s. As a result of the 1983 amendments, however, a large trust fund will be built up between 1990 and 2040, and then dissipated as the baby-boom generation collects retirement benefits. It is quite possible, in an era of rising federal deficits, that this large trust fund will tempt "reformers" on both the left and right to raid this source of income to underwrite their political objectives.

61. John Kenneth Galbraith, "The Heartless Society," *The New York Times Magazine*, September 2, 1984, p. 44.

62. *Report of the National Commission on Social Security Reform* (Washington, D.C.: Government Printing Office, 1983), p. 2-2. To underline the significance of this decision, the panel went on to say that it had "considered, but rejected, proposals to make the Social Security program a voluntary one, or to transform it into a program under which benefits are a product exclusively of the contributions paid, or to change it to a program under which benefits are conditioned on the showing of financial need."

63. See *Congressional Record*, March 21, 1983, p. S3488. For the full text, see Letter from Thomas Jefferson to Samuel Kercheval, July 12, 1816, in *The Writings of Thomas Jefferson*, ed. Albert Ellery Bergh (Washington, D.C.: The Thomas Jefferson Memorial Association, 1907), vol. 15, pp. 40–41.

64. Robert A. Nisbet, *Community and Power* (New York: Oxford University Press, 1962), p. 272.

65. *Congressional Record*, vol. 129 (March 24, 1983): S4098.

6

Voters, Bureaucrats, and the State: On the Autonomy of Social Security Policymaking

Gary P. Freeman

Until recently, the politics of social security was almost universally ignored by American political scientists. The absence of much scholarship on what was already by the 1950s fast becoming our largest domestic program is itself an interesting indicator of the consensualism and passivity associated with the evolution of social security. There was no literature on the politics of social security because, most seemed to believe, there was very little "politics" around the program; certainly none of the rancorous and partisan conflict that made public assistance or medical care such inviting targets for social scientists. [1] The increasingly bitter conflict over the future of social security that has unfolded in the last decade has eliminated any lingering doubts that the program is intensely political. The changed climate of social security policy poses an analytical challenge to political scientists and invites a critical reassessment of existing interpretations of the emergence and maturation of the American public retirement system.

A number of theoretical and analytical frameworks, explicit or implicit, have been employed by scholars to account for the dynamics of American pension politics. The literature may be usefully divided into three categories. What I will call the Democratic

Politics Model explains the introduction and expansion of the social security system in terms of the social forces at work in a representative democracy. Depending on the viewpoint of the author, these social forces may be individual voters or coalitions of voters seeking to maximize their preferences, politicians seeking to maximize their votes, businessmen attempting to increase productivity and ensure social stability, or reformers with a social democratic orientation. In any case, social security policy is seen, in this model, as primarily a response to pressures exerted on the public sector by private actors.

Perhaps the dominant interpretation of American social security rejects the centrality of societal forces and focuses instead on the role of a small set of reformers and civil servants acting, at times, at least more or less independently of outside pressure. I will call this the Bureaucratic Politics Model. Proponents of this interpretation, while agreeing that one need not resort to the activities of voters, interest groups, or broad popular movements to account for the emergence, growth, and character of the American retirement system, disagree sharply over the precise motives of bureaucratic decisionmakers and of the consequences of their dominance over policymaking. For some the bureaucrats are the solution to the puzzle of how a country that lacks an articulate and consistent voice for the working class and the poor could nevertheless develop a massive and surprisingly generous pension system. For others, the role of the bureaucrats has been to deflect genuine and often radical popular preferences into "safe" programmatic channels.

A third and recent contribution to the discussion comes from those who employ a Statist Model of social welfare development. These analysts shift the focus from the demands or "inputs" from society to the internal dynamics of the state itself, conceived either as an actor in its own right, with strategic capability, or as a vital institutional-structural framework that decisively shapes political culture, popular opinion, and political possibilities.

I will argue that each of the three theoretical models makes important contributions to our understanding of the politics of social security. The evidence to be considered indicates, however, that explanations like the Democratic Politics Model that stress demand-side variables are widely off the mark. Social security requires a supply-side model. The issue is whether a Bureaucratic or Statist framework is superior.

The Democratic Politics Model

This term refers broadly to explanations of social security development that emphasize the role of societal forces such as public opinion, parties, electoral competition, and class conflict. What holds these otherwise disparate theories together is their common acceptance of the origins of public policy among private societal actors rather than among public officials. They agree on little else as we shall see. This discussion will proceed under two headings: (1) demand side rational choice models based on an individualist conception of voters and politicians in a majority-rule electoral system, and (2) group or class-based models that focus on the primacy of either social democratic or capitalist interests.

Demand-Side Rational Choice Explanations

Rational choice analysts of social security have generally been motivated by a desire to understand how the system got to be so large. They take the program's popularity for granted, but find it problematic since it violates the market values most rational choice theorists explicitly endorse. A central thesis of the demand side rational choice interpretation of social security is that "perverse" political forces lead voters to "favor a larger system than they would if they understood its true consequences."[2] There are, in this view, at least four related characteristics of the social security program that, when placed in the context of a majoritarian political system, encourage "irrational" voter decisions and lead to the inefficient "overexpansion" of the program.

The prohibition against the provision of alternatives by private insurance carriers makes the average citizen incapable of evaluating the *relative* return he receives or can expect to receive on payroll tax contributions.[3] The decision to adopt pay-as-you-go financing sacrificed the built-in fiscal restraints of a fully funded system so that "the rate of return on social security payments would be determined after 1939 by the relatively unconstrained operation of majority rule."[4] The absence of funding meant that contributions would be misleadingly low, seducing large numbers of people to believe social security was a better deal than it was. This misperception, it is argued, was encouraged by the program's creators who deliberately fostered a "fiscal illusion."[5] Finally, social security "created an apparatus through which coalitions of voters could potentially vote for transfers to themselves to be made good by claims on other workers' incomes."[6] The key to understanding this process is the impact of an individual's position in the age distribution on his preferred social security tax rate. From the public choice perspective, social security politics is a process by which older voters appropriate the income of younger voters—it is the politics of intergenerational conflict.

Although the argument can be laid out in formal language, the essence can be stated in three general propositions:

1. The older the voter, the higher the preferred social security tax, both because he will have to pay it for a shorter period and because it will finance higher benefits that he hopes to enjoy.[7]
2. Younger worker-taxpayers acquiesce in the continuation of the program because they hope to become beneficiaries eventually and because they have already invested in the program through their payroll taxes.[8]
3. Worker-taxpayers accept higher social security taxes than they should in strict utility-maximizing terms because of their "rational ignorance" about the true costs and benefits.[9]

These characteristics specific to social security interact with a political decision process based on majority rule. Tufte, Keech, and others have tried to generalize about the connection between social security policy decisions and the timing of elections. They suggest the following propositions:

1. Political parties pursue policies on social security based on their desire to win elections.[10]
2. Politicians have incentives to increase cash benefits paid to voters immediately before elections.[11]
3. Likewise, they have incentives to avoid tax increases altogether and, when that is impossible, to put them into effect only after elections.[12]
4. The impact of the electoral cycle will be to encourage social security benefit expansions and to discourage payroll tax increases to pay for them.

Taken together, the incentives of *voters* to increase their present or anticipated social security benefits and displace their costs onto future generations and the incentives of *politicians* to distribute benefits to voters and avoid imposing costs appear to be a recipe for expansionary policy. This model provides a compelling account of the dynamics of fiscal illusion and plausible reasons for expecting an electoral cycle for social security policy. There are, nevertheless, a number of serious problems with the attribution of social security growth to the democratic expression of individual voter's preferences.

The heart of the model as it relates to voters consists of its assertions about the age-related proclivities of citizens with respect to unfunded public pensions and the impact of these on policy. There can be little doubt that, *other things being equal*, the older an individual, the higher his preferred payroll tax rate. If these preferences are expressed through a majority-rule decision process, a tax rate higher than the life-time tax preferred by voters when they enter the program will be chosen.[13] But the value of this proposition lies in its ability to predict the behavior of voters in the political system as it actually operates, not in an ideal-typical democratic state. It ought to be noted that no rational choice theorist, so far as I am aware, has actually attempted through empirical or experimental means to test the claims of the model with respect to voters' behavior. Rather they have been content to establish the surface consistency of the model with the general evolution of the program. By taking this stance, scholars such as Browning and Mitchell have skirted two difficult questions; one having to do with what voters actually prefer and how they express those preferences with their ballots, the second having to do with the real links between voters' preferences and social security policy.

Support for the expansion of social security as well as confidence in the program is positively associated with age.[14] Still, in 1978, Binstock concluded that "the most important general assertion to be made about the contemporary electoral power of the aged is that there is no 'aging vote'."[15] It is likely that as the elderly population becomes better educated and as the salience of social security increases, the elderly will play a more important role. Interest associations of the elderly have devoted considerable resources to monitoring social security in the past [16] and are even stronger today. The age-based claims of the rational choice model are likely to be more valid as a predictor of the future, then, than as an explanation of the past.

Even then, however, it is highly doubtful that the straightforward, utility-maximizing behavior predicted by the model would actually take place. The direst predictions of the model require us to believe that as voters approach and experience retirement, they will militantly support confiscatory payroll taxes and exorbitant pension benefits even if such policies wreak havoc on the American economy, the federal budget, and the average taxpayer. This is highly unlikely, not only because it dismisses the possibility that retirees can distinguish between their short and long-term interests as well as between their interests as individuals and as members of the society. Such a stance also neglects the obvious fact that the taxpayers being bilked by the elderly in this scenario are their own children and grandchildren. To suggest that parents would cold-bloodedly drive their children into personal and national bankruptcy strains one's credulity and amply illustrates the alarmingly counterintuitive conclusions toward which a theorist armed with a few seemingly harmless premises may be driven.

Leaving aside its predictive capability, the model is prey to a serious problem as an explanatory framework. Rational choice models tend to take voter preferences for granted. Even though analysts such as Browning fully appreciate the way the structure of the social security program affects the capacity of voters to develop "rational" preferences on the issue, they still tend to locate the chief source of support for the program in the mass public. As we shall see in the discussion of the Bureaucratic and Statist models, this is largely misleading. It obscures the extent to which the structure of the program and the bureaucrats who have run it have gone beyond simply disrupting the accurate expression of voter preferences by decisively affecting the content of those preferences in the first place. Moreover, to say this does not require one to endorse a conspiracy theory. In the rational choice model voters hold essentially "natural" preferences about retirement arrangements in the free market and the state intervenes to distort the process by which those preferences are expressed. This cannot be true because it implies that voters' preferences could be formed outside the context of alternatives created by some kind of political system, democratic or otherwise, that establishes a framework of law and property rights. Retirement is itself a social artifact arising out of a particular mode of political economy[17] and the various ways by which it can be satisfied have no meaning outside a historically-specific political system.

Turning to the process by which voters' preferences are translated into policy, Browning himself admits that social security policy is not made by "simple majority voting."[18] We can say much more. National elections are a poor means by which the electorate can express its views on social security. No election has ever been fought primarily on the issue of social insurance, and the political parties have not consistently offered the voters fundamentally contrasting opinions on the issues.[19] One is hard-pressed to argue that any election in the period after 1936 until 1980 had more than the most indirect implications for social security policy. The last two are a different story. Social security was clearly a major concern in 1980 and 1984 and though the candidates in each tried to make political gains by attacking each other's record or intentions with respect to the program, all of them were united in their rhetorical commitment to protect it at all costs. That this would be true in a period of budget austerity and program financial stress does suggest that the threat of punishment by the voters for tampering with the program was perceived to be severe. The validity of the rational choice model must be tested over the whole period of the program's existence, however.

Several analysts have investigated the role of public officials in manipulating social security spending and taxing for the purpose of maximizing electoral outcomes. Tufte has made the strongest and most plausible case for an electoral cycle of social security taxes and benefits.[20] Keech, in a careful reassessment of this argument, finds less impressive confirmation of Tufte's thesis. He shows that in the thirteen election years between 1950 and 1974, there were only seven in which social security benefits were increased; only five in which they were boosted within six months of polling day. There were, furthermore, benefits increases in three off years. In addition, Keech finds that during the same period Congress increased social security taxes six times during election years as opposed to seven times in off years. He concludes that with respect neither to benefits nor taxes is Tufte's argument strongly confirmed.[21]

We can bring this argument up to date. As Keech points out, it makes little sense to discuss general benefits levels after 1975 when they were automatically indexed to the cost of living. On the other hand, the indexing formula itself has been modified, the date at which inflation adjustments go into effect has been changed, the inflation threshold that triggers benefits increases has been manipulated, and there has been a series of unprecedented benefits reductions. Moreover, since 1974 there has been one massive payroll tax increase and a decision to move up scheduled increases. The timing of these actions does appear to have been strongly affected by electoral considerations.

In 1976 President Ford proposed modest payroll tax increases to take effect only after the midterm elections, but Congress failed to act. The two occasions when Congress has either raised the payroll tax (1977) or moved up the dates at which increases are to take effect (1983) were in off years. The change in the indexing formula also occurred in 1977. By choosing a wage-indexing basis instead of a price-indexing formula, Congress selected the most generous of the two principal alternatives, although the new method does significantly reduce the long-term benefits that some individuals can anticipate.[22] During the 1984 presidential campaign Ronald Reagan proposed that basic benefits be adjusted for inflation even if the annual rate of inflation in the previous year did not meet the required 3 percent. More important are the benefits reductions. These were enacted in off year 1981 in Reagan's first budget and in 1983 following the report of the bipartisan commission on social security that issued its recommendations only after the 1982 midterm elections had safely passed.[23] In the heat of the 1984 campaign, President Reagan responded to attacks from Walter Mondale by issuing a sweeping promise not to propose cuts in social benefits for present or future retirees in his second term. In sum, events since 1974 indicate a close relationship between elections and the timing of changes in the social security program.

The rational choice model rightly draws our attention to key features of an unfunded public pension system that induce somnolence among the majority and provide concrete incentives for the mobilization of an intense minority. Such a model is helpful in understanding the absence of a more vociferous politics of social security in its early stages. The recent intensity of conflict over the program can also be seen as bearing out certain of the model's claims as it has occurred after the true costs of the program have become much more visible. Its chief weaknesses are these: it falls short as an account of the introduction of social security, concentrating as it does on the public's response to the program once it was established, and it insufficiently answers the puzzle of the source of public preferences. The model shows why the public went along, but it does not really address the issue of who was playing the leading role in creating the alternatives to which the public was asked to respond.

The Social Democratic Model

The rational choice model as it has been employed by the scholars considered here reduces society to an amalgam of utility-maximizing individuals. The only systematic division in the society that is relevant to social security is that between the old and the young. The remaining studies to be considered under the Democratic Politics rubric reject this individualist bias, identifying the origins of social security policy in the conflict between capital and labor.

Michael Shalev has written of the "emergence during the 1970s of a 'social democratic model' of welfare state development in capitalist democracies. . . . The leading hypothesis of this model is that the bulk of the observable variation in welfare state emergence and growth in the western nations can be accounted for by the strength—especially in government—of social democratic labor movements."[24] Shalev presents a detailed critique of this thesis, but finds an impressive accumulation of evidence that supports it in its most general terms. I do not wish to evaluate the social democratic model as a whole; instead, I will enquire only into its utility with respect to the American social security experience.

We have to begin by recognizing that many interpretations of the American case are consistent with the model insofar as the absence or weakness of social democratic institutions is thought to explain its relative backwardness in welfare matters. A number of studies have documented the weakness of social democratic or "corporatist" forces in the United States—the low percentage of workers belonging to unions; the weak, decentralized structure of union federations; the inability of socialist candidates and parties to gain votes; the moderation of the Democratic party which is the only viable "left" party in the country.[25] A general inspection of the American welfare state apparatus—the relatively small share of GNP devoted to social programs, the extensive reliance on means tests, and the absence of national healthcare—provides evidence not simply of a slow start or laggardliness, but of a structurally conservative and often punitive system of social benefits. Even if we restrict the discussion to the old-age pension system, the evidence seems consistent with the social democratic model. Among the alternatives that were available, the founders of the program put in place a system of conservative, contributory, insurance-paying, earnings-related benefits. The state had no obligation to subsidize benefits out of general revenues. Benefits were not universal rights of citizenship but entitlements earned by participation in the labor force.

There is, therefore, a strong surface consistency between the American case and the social democratic hypothesis. There is an undeniable correlation between a weak social democratic tradition and a weak welfare state. Whether we should leap from the recognition of this association to impute a causal connection is not exactly clear. There are several ways one might approach an explanation of this relationship. The first is to conclude that the social democratic model is confirmed. This would imply, of course, that the major proponents of the welfare state are to be found among labor unions and working-class political organizations. The shape of the American welfare system, then, would be determined in political conflicts in which these actors lost decisive battles because of their lack of resources or numbers. The empirical question really becomes whether the primary or initial pressure for the welfare state came from what may be labeled social democratic elements in the society. A second line of explanation would be to turn the problem, in a sense, on its head. If the frailty of social democracy in the United States is the source of the slowness of welfare state development, then we might want to spend our resources investigating the actors who *were* strong, the groups that won the arguments over social policy. Especially if we follow the social democratic model's assumption that the welfare state is about class conflict, then we ought to turn our attention in the American case to the activities of representatives of capitalist interests.

In order to assess the validity of the first notion, that weak social democratic organization in America led directly to a late and poorly developed American welfare state, it may be necessary to distinguish between the timing of welfare program introduction and the pattern of subsequent development.[26] As Shalev employs it, the social democratic model may be too general because it is taken to account at once for the emergence, growth, and structure of welfare programs. The empirical questions for the student of American social security, therefore, are whether social democratic pressures were crucial to the introduction of social security in 1935, and whether they played a significant role in the subsequent evolution of the program. The answer given to the first question does not necessarily determine that to the second.

Limitations of space do not permit an extensive consideration of these issues. A fair summary would be that the overwhelming weight of scholarly opinion is that social democratic interests were not crucial to the formulation of social security in 1935 and that they were even less significant in the later phases of the program. This may seem surprising, particularly if one considers the New Deal origins of the public pension system. There can be no doubt, for example, that the formation of the coalition of interests that produced Democratic party majorities in 1932 and after led to a massive expansion of the role of the federal government and to the creation of a fledgling welfare state. Skocpol and Ikenberry make a persuasive case, however, that it is misleading to interpret the politics of the New Deal, and more specifically the politics of the Social Security Act, as either a victory of social democratic forces or as a direct concession to them by the state. In their words, "New Deal social-welfare innovations cannot be understood as straightforward products of popular pressures, demands, or political support."[27] They note that the Democratic party was not committed to any recognizable political program, certainly not a social democratic program, and was only partly rooted in the industrial working class. The truly radical proposals and movements in the thirties such as the Townsend Plan and the Lundeen Bill were generated outside the framework of the Democratic party and were decisively rejected by its leaders. The Democratic party was not committed to social democracy and there were few if any social democratic elements within it pressing for their agenda. Organized labor was itself divided and in any case was preoccupied with matters more central to its interests than social welfare policy.

On the other hand, the general conditions of mass unemployment and political unrest reflected in such phenomena as Townsendism, clearly created an environment in which social reform was both necessary and possible. In their influential book, *Regulating the Poor*,[28] Piven and Cloward attribute social policy advances in the thirties to the threat of mass turmoil. Even if this interpretation could be sustained (and it cannot),[29] it would not be consistent with the social democratic model. Mass disorder arises out of the weakness rather than the strength of social institutions. Skocpol and Ikenberry conclude that mass political pressures had cross-cutting effects on the shape of the New Deal. It both spurred the Roosevelt administration to consider social reforms and, at the same time, heightened its concern that those reforms be "cautious" in order to avoid creating "public programs that might result in politically uncontrollable, easily expandable 'handouts' from the public treasury to masses of individual citizens."[30] Social democratic pressures, therefore, at best created a context in which a public retirement system of some kind could be adopted, they were not decisive either for the actual timing of adoption or for the shape the program initially took.

Much of the data presented in the discussion of the rational choice model is pertinent to the question of the connection between social democracy and the incremental expansion of the program after 1935, especially that dealing with the minimal impact of electoral politics on social security policy changes. Moreover, close students of the expansionary period have demonstrated, on the one hand, the secondary role played by organized labor, and, on the other hand, the great lengths to which program advocates went to distance it from social democratic language and ideology. The conservative social insurance model was emphasized for the clear purpose of accommodating the program to the values of the market, and redistributive elements of the system were both consciously limited and downplayed in administrative rhetoric.[31] The activities and demands of groups that might reasonably be called social democratic had, therefore, an ironic effect on American social security. Too weak to win decisive battles over the structure of the program, the alternative they proposed was sufficiently threatening to administrators to push them to develop a program even more conservative than might otherwise have been chosen. The general conclusion one is forced to draw is that social security was not a social democratic reform either when viewed from the perspective of the characteristics of the groups and individuals primarily responsible for its adoption or from the perspective of the characteristics of the program itself. If we are interested in locating the persons who animated social security reform, we will have to look elsewhere.

Welfare Capitalism

It would appear logical to turn our attention to the role of business. As I have suggested, the very weakness of social democracy in

America seems to have reduced the need for representatives of corporate capitalism to block radically redistributive social welfare proposals. Capital's direct role in the development of the American welfare state may have been less in its resistance to leftist pressure than in its efforts to bring about gradual reforms compatible with its own interests. What of the role of the "enlightened" capitalist, the corporate liberal who has loomed so large in revisionist historiography?

Such individuals were undeniably significant to the early stages of the social security program. Indeed, Berkowitz and McQuaid have argued that they were central to the emergence of the entire welfare state. They contend that throughout the 1920s a welfare capitalist ideology dominated discussion of social policy. Welfare capitalism was founded on a consensus that the private business corporation ought to be the basic unit of social welfare policy and that economic efficiency could and should be the ultimate goal of social reforms. Social policy was, therefore, ancillary to the market. The onset of the Great Depression disrupted this consensus, however. Many businessmen turned against welfare reform altogether, especially insofar as it entailed federal government intervention into the activities of corporations. A small minority of executives— men like Henry S. Denison, Gerard Swope, Edward A. Filene, and Owen D. Young—continued to believe in the merits of business-government cooperation and exerted a profound influence on the Roosevelt administration. They preferred, according to Berkowitz and McQuaid, a social policy model with a substantial federal role for setting standards, but one that left administration firmly in the hands of private employers. Numerous corporate liberals were given seats on the Business Advisory Council of the Commerce Department which became "an institutional bridge between the welfare capitalism of the 1920s and the New Deal."[32] Referring specifically to the Social Security Act, they argue that "the old-age insurance program, despite its unprecedented grant of federal power, represented the acceptance of approaches to social welfare that private businessmen, not government bureaucrats, had created."[33]

There are two major empirical challenges that this interpretation must meet. The first is to show that the principal ideas that were incorporated into the Social Security Act, especially in its old-age pension and unemployment insurance provisions, can trace their lineage to welfare capitalism. The second is to demonstrate that individual welfare capitalists intervened decisively in the policy process by which the bill was formulated and finally enacted. Berkowitz and McQuaid make both of these claims, as we have seen, but their evidence is relatively thin. They imply that of the two leading alternatives for unemployment insurance considered by the President's Committee on Economic Security, the Wisconsin and Ohio models, the former was most compatible with the business view because it stressed the administrative role of employers, the predominance of the states over the federal government, and because it exhibited more affinities to private insurance.[34]

Ikenberry and Skocpol contend, however, that "the lineage of progressive capitalist experiments with intracorporate employee welfare programs was not the primary stream of policy intelligence and programmatic experimentation that fed into the formation of the Social Security Act."[35] They suggest instead that "policy ideas that would ultimately be used . . . in the New Deal's Social Security system were generated in, and at the intersections among, academic and professional organizations, reform associations, and governments, especially state governments" (6). They also point out what they see as the "central paradox" of the Social Security Act, that it required *less* national uniformity than leading welfare capitalists had urged (7). As to the actual role of these individuals in the formulation of the bill, Berkowitz and McQuaid seem content to assume influence rather than to demonstrate it. The role of business in the creation of the Social Security Act is, to summarize, at the very least highly controversial. The linkages between the Wisconsin plan and the final bill deserve more intensive exploration than they have received, but available evidence does not support a claim that corporate liberals were central to the process.

As was the case in our discussion of organized labor, it is even less plausible that corporate liberals were decisive in the expansionary period of the program. The most comprehensive study of that era, Martha Derthick's *Policymaking for Social Security*, produces two inescapable conclusions. The first is that the Advisory Councils that were set up, initially in an ad hoc fashion but eventually on a permanent footing, to oversee social security policy, and which were the major institutional conduit for the participation of leading businessmen, were effectively dominated by social security administrators. As she puts it,

Advisory Councils composed of "outsiders" reinforced rather than compromised the program-oriented character of policymaking. The outsiders tended to become insiders. . . . Leadership, membership, staffing, and the definition of the agenda all combined to preclude consideration of alternatives that were in conflict with program maintenance, and to assure recommendations falling within a range that program executives would find acceptable.[36]

The second point is that what little there was of a conservative resistance was vitiated by their "political ambivalence" and by the program's "political ambiguity," leaving program administrators with "room for maneuver and choice" (156–57).

This review of various Democratic Politics interpretations of social security leads to the conclusion that for all their ingenuity, insight, and plausibility, they fail to produce intellectually or empirically compelling accounts. All three versions tend to exaggerate the extent to which social security policy was the product of societal political pressures. They either overstate the degree and clarity of public opinion in favor of specific programs, oversimplify the process by which such preferences can be translated into a policy mandate, or overemphasize the roles particular sectors of the public have actually played.

It is important to grasp, however, the distinction between political *demands* and *needs*. The Democratic Politics Model deals only with the former, with the concrete expression of preferences in the political arena, and has nothing directly to say about needs. There may be a wide disjuncture between needs and demands in any political system because certain sectors are much better situated than others to transform their perceived needs into demands. To deny that demand-side models are satisfactory as an account of social security politics is to make no claims whatsoever as to whether the program was a response to the needs of American society or some part of it, however those needs might be measured.

The Bureaucratic Politics Model

The most fundamental point of disagreement between the Bureaucratic and Democratic Politics approaches is the significance assigned to popular political forces. Bureaucratic Politics interpretations present a supply-side version of social policy development. Proponents of this view argue that though there was a general demand for some kind of income protection for the elderly during the depression, the president and his advisors exercised considerable discretion in fashioning the particular response. Moreover, public officials took the lead in shaping social security over the years.

This section will consider three important studies of the development of social security that focus on the central role of the bureaucracy.[37] All three sharply depart from the Democratic Politics Model, demonstrating that social security administrators exercised broad autonomy during both the founding and evolution of the nation's public retirement system. They differ markedly, however, in their assessment of the limits of that autonomy, of the motives of the bureaucratic actors, and of the consequences of their behavior.

Derthick concludes that through most of its history the policymaking system for social security was very small. The central actors were the bureaucrats at the Social Security Administration, whom Derthick calls program executives or "proprietors"; a small group of political executives, including the president and officials appointed by him; and the congressional committees with jurisdiction over the program. Within this triangulated policy system, the program executives were dominant and relatively autonomous in two important senses: they operated largely unconstrained by mass pressures and they managed, usually, to have their way with other governmental actors or to reach some kind of suitable accommodation.

Why were they successful? Most important, perhaps, is that the program executives had an agenda. Derthick maintains that they had, from 1935 on, a clear and elaborate plan for a comprehensive system of social insurance, but were sufficiently pragmatic and politically astute to take one step at a time. They were greatly aided in their quest by the longevity of a few key individuals who had helped design the program in the thirties and then stayed on to run it for several decades. What is more, they deliberately constructed the program to make it ideologically ambiguous, to ensure that its expenditures were "uncontrollable," and to limit the ability of Congress to determine its fate.[38]

Carolyn Weaver covers much of the same ground as Derthick and draws congruent conclusions, but her explanatory apparatus is more systematic. Drawing on the public choice theory of bureaucratic behavior,[39] she sees program bureaucrats and their "reformer-zealot" allies as utility maximizers. Their preferences with regard to the mode of retirement income provision—whether it should be through public or private means, whether the federal program should be compulsory and enjoy a monopoly, whether it should be independent or under the authority of a cabinet-level office—were guided by their rational calculations of their interests. These might include an ideological component, to be sure, as most program bureaucrats favored government action to regulate the market and supported redistributive policies, or they might be very narrowly related to individual interests, but in either case they entailed pursuing agency autonomy, resources, and growth (7–9). Weaver's account of social security is for her but one chapter of a more general interpretation of the sources of government growth. She sees self-interested bureaucrats taking steps to create, protect, and extend the monopoly status of their public bureaus.

One of the strengths of Weaver's analysis is that she attempts to integrate the demand and supply-side public choice models into a perspective that sees public programs as moving from demand-side origins to supply-side control. In Weaver's analysis "new programs and their bureaucratic apparatus emerge in response to broadly based changes in citizen demands, but the detailed institutional features of programs—which are critical to the bureau's survival, growth, and redirection—are deduced mainly from the interests of the new bureaucracy and only in part from citizen demands" (12). Furthermore, she construes the term bureaucrat broadly: it includes private citizens playing at times the role of "reformer-zealots," at others "advocate-experts," as well as the actual holders of public positions. Indeed, a central premise of her argument is that the two sets of actors tend necessarily to overlap (13).

In his analysis of the activities of the Social Security Board/Administration between 1935 and 1952, Jerry Cates lays out a scenario that shares a number of important features with those of Derthick and Weaver. He agrees, for example, that policy has been dominated by those who have administered the program and he recounts the various ways in which they sought to preserve the prerogatives of the agency against critics, internal or external. But Cates presents a profoundly different interpretation of his subject. Whereas both Derthick and Weaver are preoccupied with trying to understand how the social security program got so big, so successful, and so generous and redistributive in spite of the conservative and market-oriented society out of which it emerged, Cates is at pains to show that the program is fundamentally conservative. Furthermore, his book seeks to document the ways in which program administrators worked hard to keep it that way. This is not simply a matter of different perceptions arising out of the ideological proclivities of the analysts. It is an empirical matter whether the program administrators devoted more energy to staving off conservative attacks on the program or to short-circuiting expansionist pressure.

Cates attempts to make his case by showing, first of all, that the reformer-bureaucrats who served on the Committee for Economic Security strongly preferred the "conservative social insurance" model of the Wisconsin unemployment insurance plan to the more redistributionist Ohio plan. On this point, his study reinforces other interpretations of that crucial choice. Where Cates breaks new ground is in his painstaking documentation of the efforts of the social security bureaucrats, especially Arthur J. Altmeyer, to contain pressures for expansion and redistribution after 1935 and, in general, to resist efforts to reduce the "anti-poor bias" of the program.

The principal threats to conservative social insurance, especially from 1935–1945, were a variety of liberal flat-rate benefits plans (50–70), the movement to violate the insurance rhetoric by "blanketing-in" those persons already too old in 1935 to accumulate sufficient credits to receive benefits (70–85), efforts to upgrade benefits beyond 80 percent of previous income for certain categories of recipients, and attempts by state governments to raise public assistance benefit levels and ease eligibility criteria (104–135). Social security administrators, according to Cates, vigorously opposed all of these pressures, making the program less redistributive and more conservative than political forces in the states and in the congress seemed to prefer. They also, to be sure, fought off conservative Republican attempts to change the program. Nonetheless, the chief value of Cates's book from the analytical perspective of this chapter is that it underlines liberal threats to the program and casts doubt on an interpretation of program administrators as hell-bent for expansion. Where Derthick and Weaver chronicle the efforts of bureaucrats to monopolize information and control the legislative agenda in order to expand the program, Cates provides numerous examples of deliberate bureaucratic distortion of the "facts" in order to prevent improvements in public assistance and in its basic benefit levels because they were believed to threaten the long-run prospects of social insurance (61–70; 109–118).

In an important sense, Cates's book goes beyond one of the chief features of what I have called the Bureaucratic Politics model. His central argument is that the conservative role of bureaucrats was not an "unintended" outcome resulting from the dynamics of bureaucratic organizations (what he calls the goal drift model (10–13). Instead he claims that the best explanation of the behavior of the social security bureaucrats is a combination of their commitment to a conservative social insurance *ideology* and their adoption of *strategic* decisions to advance, implement, or defend that ideology (143). The conservatism of policy was intentional, therefore, not accidental. This puts him, however, squarely in the camp with Weaver and Derthick since despite their disagreements over the consequences of bureaucratic behavior, they all agree that the bureaucrats were the chief source of social security policy.

Of the interpretations I have surveyed, the Bureaucratic Politics model is the most compelling and the most consistent with the facts. It shifts our attention away from those arenas where not much was happening to where the action was. It identifies a core of individuals who clearly were crucial to the story we are following. Nonetheless, there is something unsatisfying about these accounts. All three scholars treat bureaucrats as active shapers of their political environment rather than passive recipients of demands and pressures. Yet, what have they given us but another version of the politics of pluralism? This time the political system, as represented by civil servants, political executives, and legislators, is itself a collection of groups pursuing private interests through politics. That this is the position of the scholars considered here is obvious from the normative stances they take vis-a-vis the bureaucrats who are the protagonists of their tales. Weaver makes no effort to conceal her venom for these "zealots" who substituted their own preferences and welfare for the dictates of the market. Derthick tries to remain neutral but ends up indicting program executives for squelching debate, manipulating the agenda, and "cooking" the books. Cates is even more forthright: if for Derthick bureaucrats can be seen as self-ascribed but ultimately misguided conspirators in the public interest, for

Cates they are more old-fashioned conspirators who work to prevent a radical or redistributive transformation of government policy.

In other words, all the proponents of Bureaucratic Politics assert that the administrators substituted their own agenda for that which would have been produced by the market. Hence, their analyses are not really consistent with a demand-side framework. Yet none of the authors go beyond the conceptual plane of group politics. They reduce the behavior of program executives and other public officials to the simple politics of private interest. The public interest plays no role in these books beyond serving as a cynical and illegitimate rhetorical cover for the self-aggrandizement of bureaucrats. The only thing that distinguishes the latter from other interest groups is that they happen to occupy official positions.

The model to be considered in the next section takes the official nature of bureaucratic roles as problematic, considers the idea that public policy is guided by conceptions of the public interest as at least as intuitively plausible as the idea that it is solely the outcome of the clash of private interests, and explores systematically the question of just how independent program administrators were, and under what conditions.

Statist Models

A recent review argues that the two most promising perspectives on the role of the state are (1) that which sees it as a purposive, goal-seeking actor and (2) that which views it as an institutional framework having a decisive impact on the structure of politics in a society.[40] No one has produced a fully developed interpretation of the politics of American social security from either of these perspectives, although bits and pieces of relevant work are beginning to appear.[41] The purposive or strategic model of the state makes the most ambitious claims and sets the statist framework apart from its alternatives most clearly. Furthermore, the question of whether the state has goals and can pursue them seems crucial to settling many of the controversies in the literature that I have described. I intend, therefore, to deal almost exclusively with the issues of whether the state can be seen as having goals in the social security sphere and whether or not it has been capable of achieving them. Toward this end, I will draw on several attempts to develop the state concept from an actor perspective and see if it can account for some of the most important aspects of the social security case.

Stephen Krasner conceives of the state "as a set of roles and institutions having peculiar drives, compulsions, and aims that are separate and distinct from the interests of any particular societal group."[42] The state, for Krasner, exists independently of society and is a unitary and "autonomous" actor (1). The goals of the state depend on the central decisionmakers dominant in specific issue-areas and in order for a statist approach to be plausible the goals of the state must be "related to general societal goals, persist over time, and have a consistent ranking and importance" (13). He calls such goals the "national interest" (11–13). Empirically, the test of the utility of the framework resides in demonstrating that central decisionmakers have such a set of goals and are able to pursue them "against resistance from international and domestic actors" (10–11).

Krasner's operationalization of the concept of state goals is especially pertinent to the present discussion. What we want to do is establish some criteria for distinguishing between the personal goals of bureaucrats, the particularistic goals of individual agencies or programs, and the goals of the state proper. Krasner's notion of durable, hierarchically ranked goals related to general societal interests is a place to begin. His identification of the state with central decisionmakers dominant in a given area is less satisfactory. He assumes that the identities of these decisionmakers can and will change from issue to issue and at least implies that some set of central decisionmakers will be dominant. This, of course, is just what we wish to determine through empirical investigation and is not a matter that may be asserted. Moreover, Krasner provides few if any guidelines for determining who are central and who are peripheral policymakers. The domination of social security through much of its history by what are arguably peripheral bureaucrats causes one to doubt the accuracy of a statist interpretation in the first place.

No conception of the state will be sufficient if it does not allow for a degree of disaggregation. At the very least we need to be able to distinguish between the bureaucratic apparatus and the temporary government that supposedly controls it.[43] The necessity of such an approach for the United States is clear. The American state developed slowly and erratically and as the bureaucracy evolved, it tended to be closely tied to large, organized private interests.[44] The essential characteristic of the American state is its fragmented structure, both because of the constitutional principles of separation of powers and federalism and because of the historical tendency to give agencies substantial formal independence from both the executive and the legislature. It appears at times, furthermore, as if no government can be said to exist (common parlance refers to presidential administrations rather than to governments). Executive-congressional division and conflict, the absence of cohesive political parties, and the decentralized authority structure of the Congress all serve to constrain the ability of a government (those occupying the formal positions of leadership and authority in the political executive and the Congress) to direct the activities of the bureaucratic apparatus. Indeed, this is precisely why scholars have for so long been skeptical of the utility of the statist approach to American public policy. Apart from the foreign policy arena, few would argue that the American state is either unified or oriented toward the realization of a set of clear and consistent goals.

The existence of division within the state will normally limit its autonomy. In the absence of cohesion in the state apparatus, the domination of the rest by one part of it is essential for it to operate autonomously.[45] This implies that unless one can demonstrate the existence of a relatively cohesive state elite (or a dominant state institution) little is to be gained by introducing the state as a concept. But once the existence of intrastate conflict and a multiplicity of state goals is admitted, one is perilously close to the sort of interpretation based on bureaucratic pluralism and interbranch competition that the statist model sets out to reject. While I view this as a danger, it seems to me to be an open question whether division and fragmentation within the state render the explanatory power of the concept useless. Nonetheless, if the state model is worth the acquisition of a new terminology, it must be able to alter substantially the significance attached to bureaucratic politics and executive-legislative conflict, even when no cohesive state preferences or policy are evident. State theory ought, in other words, to provide just as useful an explanatory framework in societies with weak states as in those dominated by strong states.

Apart from locating state actors and describing their goals, it is necessary to assess whether they are able to pursue them successfully. Nordlinger[46] identifies three conditions for state autonomy depending on the divergence or coincidence of state and societal preferences and the convergence or divergence of state preferences and authoritative state actions. Type I state autonomy occurs when state-society preferences diverge but the state pursues authoritative actions consistent with its own preferences anyway (I will call this Non-Consensual Autonomy). Type II autonomy occurs when state-society preferences are initially divergent but public officials engineer a shift in societal preferences to make them congruent with their own, and then take authoritative actions consistent with these now consonant preferences (I will call this Quasi-Consensual Autonomy). Awareness of the possibility of this type of autonomy allows the analyst to avoid falling into the trap of mistaking a "circularity" of opinion for popular sovereignty.[47] Type III autonomy occurs when state-society preferences are nondivergent and the state acts on its own preferences (I will label this Consensual Autonomy). When the state follows societal preferences, Nordlinger suggests that one is dealing with cases of "societal constraint" (27–31).

This framework needs to be elaborated to take into account the possibility of state-government conflict. The meaning one attributes to each of these situations depends on the divergence or convergence of bureaucratic and governmental preferences and on the particular characteristics of the bureaucracy in question. Bureaucratic autonomy can be interpreted as state autonomy if, and only if, one of the following conditions prevails:

1. A cohesive bureaucracy is the dominant state institution and acts autonomously in the face of weak, divided, or unstable governments; or

2. Within its limited sphere, a particular fraction of the bureaucracy achieves autonomy over a sub-set of policies, is able to carry them out over the objections of the government, or can win the government over to its viewpoint, and pursues a set of cohesive, ordered objectives related to general societal interests.

If, on the other hand, the bureaucracy is not the dominant institution of the state as a whole, does not pursue general societal goals, or exercises only limited autonomy within its sphere, being checked periodically at the boundaries by the government, then we have bureaucratic pluralism or sub-system politics of the type described by Derthick and Weaver. The issue in this case would become whether or not the assertion of ultimate control by the government over the bureaucracy is a manifestation of the autonomy of the state as a whole or, being a response to electoral or interest group pressure, is an instance of societal constraint. In sum, we need not only to clarify whether the bureaucracy or the government is in control, and under what conditions, we need also to demonstrate that these institutions are expressing a state or general societal interest.

We can dismiss out of hand the possibility of a cohesive bureaucracy that dominates the government over the whole range of public issues. Such bureaucracies dominate states in other countries, but the American bureaucracy is much too fragmented, too little guided by a cohesive higher civil service, and too closely allied to important private interests to play such a general role. On the other hand, it is possible that some portion of the bureaucracy can come to exercise hegemony over an aspect of public policy. As scholars have amply illustrated, there is strong evidence that this is the case with social security. Our task is first to understand how this situation came about and what, if anything, it tells us about the autonomy of the American state.

I believe the evidence supports the conclusion that the social security bureaucracy had clearly articulated goals, that these were transitively ordered (the compulsory and contributory aspects of the program were much more important than its redistributive impact), and that these were related to general societal interests (the creation and nurturing of a conservative social insurance system, the protection of the long-run stability of the political system as a whole). The uncritical acceptance of the idea that the administrators were unswerving expansionists has led some scholars to conclude that their activities are explicable largely in terms of personal or bureaucratic utility maximization. Cates demonstrates, on the contrary, that ideological preferences led them to oppose steps that would have expanded both their personal power and agency resources. It seems reasonable that they held such views because they were convinced that they were in the long-term interests of the society—that is, that they believed themselves to be the vehicle for the realization of the public interest. Whether they were in fact such a vehicle is an important but secondary question in the present context. I am interested in identifying durable, transitively ordered ideas that are plausibly connected to general societal goals and that are associated with institutionalized *roles* rather than particular individuals.

In this light the ideas of the social security bureaucracy may reasonably be labeled "state goals." If they were realized in spite of societal and governmental opposition, this ought to be called "state autonomy." Although the data that have been reviewed in previous sections are not without some ambiguity, it seems evident that the social security bureaucracy has exercised over most of its life a substantial autonomy from societal pressures. Bureaucratic autonomy from societal interests was, as has been shown, the result of the administrative structure of the social security program and of the dynamics of an unfunded public pension system. The program's administrators skillfully exploited these characteristics to enhance their autonomy from societal pressures. There are numerous examples that testify to the success of such efforts.

With respect to economically powerful interests, for example, the ability of the staff of the Committee on Economic Security (CES) to help kill the Clark Amendment that would have permitted private employers to contract out of the old-age insurance system was absolutely essential for the future of the program.[48] That business was not powerless is seen in the defeat in 1935 of the proposal to allow the federal government to sell voluntary annuities, but latent business opposition was effectively silenced in the years following through the device of the Advisory Councils and was in any case vitiated by divisions within the business community.[49] Autonomy is perhaps even more apparent with respect to mass pressures. The bureaucracy succeeded in forging its conservative social insurance model against more popular versions, managed to delay the beginning of payment of benefits, and kept them relatively modest.

If defeating the Clark Amendment and flat-rate plans are examples of Non-Consensual Autonomy, the coincidence of much of the agency's activities with public opinion in the long period between 1940 and 1972 is plausibly an example of Quasi-Consensual Autonomy. Although it is impossible to answer such questions definitively, public support of the program was probably as much a response to agency policy as a cause of it. Program executives were not free to ignore public opinion, of course, and the evidence suggests they were very sensitive to it. Nonetheless, within its broad confines they were able to give the program its peculiar shape. They played a key role in creating a program (both in its structure and size) that the public did not, strictly speaking, prefer. In doing so, the bureaucracy mediated social conflicts and demonstrated independence from social pressures.

Numerous features of agency and program structure contributed to the arsenal of weapons bureaucrats had at their disposal to enhance their independence from successive governments as well.

1. The original Social Security Board, though appointed by the president, was granted formal independence and when it was integrated into the Federal Security Agency in 1953, it had already developed a tradition of self-government that was not effectively challenged by departmental secretaries until at least 1981.

2. The payroll tax made the program self-financing and put it outside the normal budget process.[50]

3. More than is the case with most public programs, the agency exercised a monopoly over technical aspects of policy planning and enjoyed a reputation for skill and honesty.[51]

4. Finally, because of the unusual role played by certain members of the staff of the Committee on Economic Security in planning, setting up, and then running the program for many years, the program's administrators had both an unusually coherent set of policy goals and an unparalleled opportunity to realize them.

Instances of autonomy of the bureaucracy vis-a-vis the government need to be explored in three varieties: those circumstances in which the bureaucracy prevailed because of governmental apathy or inactivity, those in which it prevailed by setting the agenda for the government, and those in which it prevailed in spite of governmental opposition. There can be no doubt that there are numerous instances of bureaucratic autonomy that fit the first two circumstances. These, in fact, may be said to be the dominant modes of policymaking for social security, especially between 1940 and 1972. Very often central political executives, especially the president but sometimes even HEW secretaries, paid little or no attention to social security issues. At most, it was far down their list of domestic priorities. Whether this indifference stemmed from a vague satisfaction with what was going on is hard to say given the gross disparity between the rhetoric of the bureaucrats and the long-term implications of their actions, implications the bureaucrats, if no one else, fully appreciated. It is easier to point to numerous instances in which agency officials had their way with the government because they set the agenda and controlled relevant information.[52]

It is the final category that is most problematic. Could the bureaucrats win in head-to-head conflict with the political officials in the White House and the Congress? While there are instances which suggest that they could, I believe the brunt of the evidence is negative. We can organize the cases to illuminate certain general conditions under which the government prevailed over the bureaucracy.

The government could and did defeat the bureaucracy, at least temporarily, when fundamental questions, or what Derthick calls "boundary issues" were at stake. These involved significant program additions (disability and Medicare) and other fundamental structural matters (the use of general revenues). In each of these cases, the government seized control of policy development (general revenues) or greatly affected the speed and ultimate shape of policy (disability and Medicare). These three cases are good tests of the ability of political officials to curb the bureaucracy because they involve sharp differences of opinion between the two. There are other instances, however, in which either congress or the president set policy not by a reversal of bureaucratic preferences but a too rapid movement in the direction the bureaucrats preferred. Political officials repeatedly intervened either to raise benefits faster than the agency had requested (1972 is the most extreme case) or to delay the coming to force of taxes already enacted. These latter episodes are critical, for they shed light on what is the final analytical puzzle this section of the chapter will address. When the government intervened, was it to assert the autonomy of the state as a whole over a particularistic bureaucratic agency, or was it to respond to societal pressures? That is, do the victories of the central executive over the program bureaucrats represent an instance of state autonomy or do they indicate the vulnerability of elected officials to public opinion?

I believe the evidence suggests the latter. Disability and Medicare are the clearest instances. In both, presidential and congressional sensitivity to organized interests (employers and health care professionals) set them at odds with the agency.[53] The case of general revenues is slightly more complicated. When in 1935 FDR and the Congress insisted that the new program be self-financing, they were under heavy pressure from private business and its foremost representative in the government, Treasury Secretary Morgenthau. Resistance to general revenues in more recent times has been fueled by concern over budget deficits and taxation levels.

This is at least consistent with a view that the government was imposing discipline on a run-away agency in the interest of overall state goals.

Much more crucial for our purposes is the entire period since 1972 in which we have witnessed a gradual but uninterrupted decline of bureaucratic autonomy. Under the administration of Ronald Reagan, much of the leadership of SSA was placed in the hands of political appointees from outside the social security family and policymaking was wrested from its traditional agency-congressional subsystem and inserted directly into the budget process on the one hand, and deferred to a bipartisan commission, on the other. It is tempting to argue that this period illustrates the ability of central executive decisionmakers to reassert their control over a specific program in order to achieve national budget and economic policy goals. There is ample evidence that participants in the governments of Ford, Carter, and Reagan sought to do just this, and many of the social security reforms enacted during each of these administrations, especially that of Reagan, are consistent with such a view.

Nonetheless, a thorough review of events since 1972 leads to a very different interpretation. There have been forceful proponents of modifications of the program to more closely tie it to the macroeconomic policy goals of savings, capital formation, and budgetary stability. These views are most common among central executive officials at the Council of Economic Advisers, Office of Management and Budget, the Treasury, and among the staffs of congressional committees and the Congressional Budget Office. From time to time presidents have endorsed such proposals and a few have been adopted, especially in Reagan's first budget.[54] On the whole, however, such attempts have failed. Even a president as committed to budget reductions and tax cuts as Ronald Reagan was unable to alter substantially the largest federal entitlement program. Confronted with growing congressional opposition to his cost-saving measures, he resorted to a bipartisan panel that presented a compromise package designed to keep the system in the black but that did not achieve the most fundamental reforms advocated by critics of the system. Social security policy since 1972 is not so much an example of central state decisionmakers coordinating subsystem programs as it is an example of a thoroughly heteronomous government dealing with a crisis under intense, even unprecedented, political pressure. The entrance of the president onto the scene reduced, rather than enhanced, the autonomy of policy.

This brief excursion into a Statist interpretation of social security politics produces very mixed results. Bureaucrats did pursue goals that were coherent, transitively ordered, and related to general societal interests. It makes as much sense, maybe more, to think of these as "state" goals as to consider them the product of calculations of personal or agency interests. But by the other two tests of the state autonomy thesis, the agency bureaucrats fail. They were not part of a cohesive civil service that exercised dominance over the whole range of state policies. Moreover, program bureaucrats were unable, ultimately, to prevail over the elected officials who make up the government. What is more telling, when central government decisionmakers intervened, especially in the period since 1972, it was to impose what can be seen as politically necessary restraints on the activities of program advocates. In other words, presidential and congressional interventions illustrate the inability of the state to act autonomously with regard to electoral pressures.

Conclusion

The extreme fragmentation, decentralization, and weakness of the American state produce a policymaking process characterized by bargaining, compromise, logrolling, and coalition building. This process, in turn, tends to be dominated by powerfully organized and narrowly based interest groups. Recognition of these facts has led most analysts of American politics to develop demand-side interpretations of the origins and growth of public programs. The evidence we have considered regarding the social security program is inconsistent with such a view. Social security is probably the most striking example of a supply-side domestic policy in the American political system. It is not that demand-side pressures have been totally absent. They were considerable during the thirties when the system was forged and they have reappeared with a vengeance since 1972. But public opinion, interest group pressure, and political party preferences on social security have seldom produced a cohesive and organized majority view. More surprisingly, intensely motivated and influential minorities have failed to materialize as well, except over the Medicare issue. Demand-side pressures have created a large envelope within which public officials could act. To understand social security we clearly need a supply-side model. The decisive players in this game were public officials, and of these the program executives were indisputably the most important. But what kind of supply-side interpretation will do?

I believe the social security case reveals a number of important aspects about the American political system and suggests how phenomena that are typically attributed to simple bureaucratic politics may need to be integrated into a statist framework. This case shows that bureaucratic autonomy can be (though it is not necessarily or normally) an instance of state autonomy. In doing so it illustrates one process by which the American state itself has developed.

The discussion of the Statist framework shows pretty conclusively that strong claims about the role of the state in the evolution of social security cannot be sustained. It is difficult to attribute the introduction and growth of the program to the autonomous efforts of central executive decisionmakers (the president, his personal staff, and executive appointees). Moreover, in recent months as such officials have moved to exert control over the program the result has been to intensify rather than reduce the impact of popular pressures on policy. In the context of the balkanized and weak American state, autonomy over domestic policy is not likely to be achieved by the central executive. These officials are ultimately too vulnerable to electoral constraints and interest-group influence and they are forced to share power with the legislature and the courts. Autonomous decisionmaking can be created only by establishing policymaking *enclaves* tucked away here and there in the sprawling federal bureaucracy. Indeed, the very dispersal of power and authority in the American state encourages such enclaves of bureaucratic dominance, especially when the issues involved are of limited general interest. Normally, however, these enclaves are autonomous only vis-a-vis the executive, readily falling prey to organized interest groups and their congressional allies. Moreover, their outlook is usually exceptionally narrow and self-interested. Such enclaves represent, in other words, not state autonomy but the very limited sub-system autonomy that is well described by the Bureaucratic Politics model.

The social security experience suggests, however, that under certain conditions bureaucratic autonomy can serve more general purposes than those of the bureaucrats, the agency, or affiliated organized interests. Whether it does or not depends on the motives and behavior of the bureaucrats, the structure of the agency, and the characteristics of the program it oversees. The evidence presented in this chapter suggests that the social security bureaucrats cannot fairly be seen as self-aggrandizing officials busily verifying Parkinson's Law,[55] nor as another interest group playing the politics of pluralism, as various versions of the Bureaucratic Politics Model would have it. They were not directly linked to any identifiable, tightly organized, private interest, even less were they manipulated by such interests. Nor did they administer a program delivering concentrated benefits to a discrete minority of the population. The conditions, in other words, that typically produce interest-group dominated subsystem politics in other arenas of American politics were missing. As I have argued, the bureaucrats took advantage of their relative freedom to pursue goals that they believed were in the long-run interest of the society as a whole. They were less pushed by popular demands, organized groups, or their own interests than they were pulled by a conception of social needs and the possibilities of responding to them through public policies.

Toward this end, administrators worked actively to shape the program in order to create and sustain public support, to ensure an institutional basis for independent decisionmaking, and to close off challenges and alternatives from the private sector. The autonomy of social security policymaking was not, in sum, merely the fortuitous outcome of a set of favorable circumstances. It was statecraft, the creative handiwork of a small number of political entrepreneurs. In light of this, to ask, as I have done, whether the politics of social security needs to be understood by means of a model of the American state may appear to have put the cart before the horse. Along with the military establishment, the IRS, and the courts, the social security program is today one of the central pillars of the American national state. To deny the relevance of a Statist Model to an analysis of the role of social security in the modern American political economy would be a serious error. Nonetheless, the social security bureaucrats, especially in the early days of the program, were not so much agents of a powerful and autonomous state able to act upon the society as they were part of a self-conscious elite intent on building such a state.

Notes

1. Gilbert Steiner, *Social Insecurity: The Politics of Welfare* (Chicago: Rand McNally, 1966); *The State of Welfare* (Washington, D.C.: The Brookings Institution, 1971); Theodore Marmor, *The Politics of Medicare* (Chicago: Aldine, 1970); Robert R. Alford, *Health Care Politics* (Chicago: The University of Chicago Press, 1975).

2. Edgar K. Browning, "The Politics of Social Security Reform," in Colin D. Campbell, ed. *Financing Social Security* (Washington, D.C.: American Enterprise Institute, 1979), 197.

3. Carolyn L. Weaver, "Social Security: Has the Crisis Passed?" *Policy Report* 1:1 (1979):3.

4. Ibid.

5. William C. Mitchell, *The Popularity of Social Security: A Paradox of Public Choice* (Washington, D.C.: American Enterprise Institute, 1977).

6. Weaver, "Social Security," 3.

7. See Browning, "Politics of Social Security Reform," 1979; "Why the Social Insurance Budget is Too Large in a Democracy," *Economic Inquiry* 13 (1975):373–88; "Social Insurance: The Constitutional Perspective," *Economic Inquiry* 15 (1977):455–57; Weaver, "Social Security"; "Competition in the Provision of Social Security: An Old Idea Revisited," in Gordon Tullock and Richard E. Wagner, eds., *Policy Analysis and Deductive Reasoning* (Lexington, Mass.: D. C. Heath, 1978): 93–110; and *The Crisis in Social Security: Economic and Political Origins* (Durham, N.C.: Duke Press Policy Studies, 1982).

8. James M. Buchanan, "Social Insurance in a Growing Economy: A Proposal for Radical Reform," *National Tax Journal* 21 (1968):388–89.

9. See note 7 for works by Browning and Weaver; Mitchell, "The Popularity of Social Security"; Anthony Downs, *An Economic Theory of Democracy* (New York: Harper and Row, 1957); and Downs, "Why the Government Budget is Too Small in a Democracy," *World Politics* 12 (1960):541–64.

10. William R. Keech, "Elections and U.S. Public Policy: A Working Paper." Delivered at Workshop on the Politics of Inflation, Unemployment and Growth, University of Bonn, West Germany, 1979; Downs, "Why the Government Budget is Too Small."

11. Edward R. Tufte, *Political Control of the Economy* (Princeton: Princeton University Press, 1978).

12. Ibid.

13. Browning, "Why the Social Insurance Budget is Too Large."

14. Neal E. Cutler, "Demographic, Social-Psychological, and Political Factors in the Politics of Aging: A Foundation for Research in 'Political Gerontology'," *American Political Science Review* 71 (1977):1011–25; Laurily Keir Epstein and William P. Browne, "Public Opinion and the El-

derly," delivered at the Annual Meeting of the American Political Science Association, Chicago, 1979; Paul Light, *Artful Politics* (New York: Random House, 1984), 66.

15. Robert H. Binstock, "Aging and the Future of American Politics," *The Annals* 415 (1974):202.

16. Henry J. Pratt, *The Gray Lobby* (Chicago: University of Chicago Press, 1977); Roy Lubove, *The Struggle for Social Security* (Cambridge: Harvard University Press, 1968).

17. William Graebner, *A History of Retirement* (New Haven: Yale University Press, 1980); John Myles, *Old Age in the Welfare State: The Political Economy of Public Pensions* (Boston: Little, Brown, 1984).

18. Browning, "The Politics of Social Security Reform," 387.

19. John P. Bradley, "Party Platforms and Party Performance Concerning Social Security," *Polity* 1 (1969):337–58; Martha Derthick, *Policymaking for Social Security* (Washington, D.C.: The Brookings Institution, 1979).

20. Tufte, *Political Control of the Economy.*

21. Keech, "Elections and U.S. Public Policy," 11–15.

22. Colin D. Campbell, *The 1977 Amendments to the Social Security Act* (Washington, D.C.: American Enterprise Institute, 1978).

23. Light, *Artful Politics*; John A. Svahn and Mary Ross, "Social Security Amendments of 1983: Legislative History and Summary of Provisions," *Social Security Bulletin* 46 (July):3–48.

24. Michael Shalev, "The Social Democratic Model and Beyond: Two 'Generations' of Comparative Research on the Welfare State," in Richard F. Tomasson, ed., *Comparative Social Research* 6 (1983):316.

25. Robert H. Salisbury, "Why No Corporatism in America?" Presented to the Annual Meeting of the APSA, New York, 1978; Louis Hartz, *The Liberal Tradition in America* (New York: Harcourt, Brace, and World, 1955).

26. Charles Lockhart, "Explaining Social Policy Differences Among Advanced Industrial Societies," *Comparative Politics* 16 (1984):335–50.

27. Theda Skocpol and John Ikenberry, "The Political Formation of the American Welfare State in Historical and Comparative Perspective," in Richard F. Tomasson, ed., *Comparative Social Research* 6 (1983), 121.

28. Frances Fox Piven and Richard A. Cloward, *Regulating the Poor* (New York: Vintage Books, 1971).

29. R. B. Albritton, "Social Amelioration Through Mass Insurgency? A Reexamination of the Piven and Cloward Thesis," *American Political Science Review* 73 (1979):1003–1011; John Myles, *Old Age in the Welfare State.*

30. Theda Skocpol and John Ikenberry, "The Political Formation of the American Welfare State," 124.

31. Martha Derthick, *Policymaking for Social Security* (Washington,

D.C.: Brookings Institution, 1979). Jerry R. Cates, *Insuring Inequality: Administrative Leadership in Social Security, 1935–54* (Ann Arbor: University of Michigan Press, 1983).

32. Edward Berkowitz and Kim McQuaid, *Creating the Welfare State: The Political Economy of Twentieth-Century Reform* (New York: Praeger, 1980), 85.

33. Ibid., 103.

34. Ibid., 98–101.

35. John Ikenberry and Theda Skocpol, "From Patronage Democracy to Social Security: The Shaping of Public Social Provision in the United States." Draft manuscript, 6.

36. Derthick, *Policymaking for Social Security*, 109.

37. Derthick, *Policymaking for Social Security*; Weaver, *The Crisis in Social Security*; Cates, *Insuring Inequality*.

38. Derthick, 17–37.

39. William A. Niskanen, *Bureaucracy and Representative Government* (New York: Aldine Atherton, 1971); Gordon Tullock, *The Politics of Bureaucracy* (Washington, D.C.: Public Affairs Press, 1965).

40. Theda Skocpol, "Bringing the State Back In: Strategies of Analysis in Current Research." In Peter Evans, et al., eds. *Bringing the State Back In* (Cambridge: Cambridge University Press, 1985).

41. James Malloy, "Statescraft and Social Insurance Policy in Latin America and the United States," in Carmelo Mesa-Lago, ed., *The Crisis of Social Security and Health Care: Latin American Experiences and Lessons* (Pittsburgh: Center for Latin American Studies, University of Pittsburgh, 1985); Laura Katz Olson, *The Political Economy of Aging: The State, Private Power and Social Welfare* (New York: Columbia University Press, 1982); John Myles, *Old Age in the Welfare State*; and Skocpol and Ikenberry, "The Political Formation of the American Welfare State."

42. Stephen Krasner, *Defending the National Interest: Raw Materials Investments and U.S. Foreign Policy* (Princeton: Princeton University Press, 1979).

43. Nora Hamilton, *The Limits of State Autonomy: Post-Revolutionary Mexico* (Princeton: Princeton University Press, 1982), 73.

44. Grant McConnell, *Private Power and American Democracy* (New York: Vintage Books, 1966); Theodore J. Lowi, *The End of Liberalism* (New York: Norton, 1968); Stephen Skowronek, *Building a New American State: The Expansion of National Administrative Capacities, 1877–1920* (Cambridge: Cambridge University Press, 1981).

45. Hamilton, *The Limits of State Autonomy*, 15.

46. Eric F. Nordlinger, *On the Autonomy of the Democratic State* (Cambridge: Harvard University Press, 1981).

47. Charles E. Lindblom, *Politics and Markets* (New York: Basic Books, 1977), 201–21.

48. Weaver, *The Crisis in Social Security*, 89–92.

49. Derthick, *Policymaking for Social Security*, 132–57.

50. Gary Freeman, "Presidents, Pensions, and Fiscal Policy," in James Pfiffner, ed., *Presidents and Economic Policy* (Philadelphia: ISHI Press, 1985).

51. Gary Freeman and Paul Adams, "Ideology and Analysis in American Social Security Policymaking," *Journal of Social Policy* 12 (1981):75–95.

52. Cates, *Insuring Inequality*, 86–103; Derthick, *Policymaking for Social Security*, 206–10.

53. Theodore Marmor, *The Politics of Medicare*; Derthick, 295–315.

54. For an analysis of these see Freeman, "Presidents, Pensions and Fiscal Policy;" and Freeman and Adams, "Ideology and Analysis in Social Security Policymaking."

55. Parkinson's Law, which states that "work expands so as to fill the time available for its completion," explains government growth as the product of bureaucratic interest. See C. Northcote Parkinson, *Parkinson's Law and Other Studies in Administration* (Boston: Houghton Mifflin Co., 1957).

7

Social Security in Trouble

A World View

Gaston V. Rimlinger

I. Introduction

The 1980s is the decade for social security anniversaries. In 1981 the Max Planck institute organized a series of conferences in Berlin to commemorate the 100th anniversary of the Kaiser's message to the Reichstag calling for the creation of social insurance in Germany. The occasion for the present conference is the fiftieth anniversary of the U.S. social security system. It seems appropriate at this occasion to look back at the evolution of social security over the last hundred years. The disturbing fact is that although social security has always been a controversial subject, it seems to arouse more criticism today than ever before. Widespread demands for retrenchment and reform are an indication that social security has lost much of its legitimacy. A common criticism is that, while the burden of modern welfare policies has become very heavy, the policies in place fail to protect those most in need while they provide extensive protection where it is least needed. Instead of providing a solid floor of protection against extreme economic inequality, modern social security programs often seem to insure inequality. Some critics argue also that modern social policies contribute to social instability instead of preventing it.[1] Old-age pensions are said to undermine economic growth by reducing the labor supply and the rate of capital accumulation. Health insurance leads to runaway cost inflation, and unemployment insurance is seen as the cause of higher unemployment rates.

I shall return later to an examination of the post World War II evaluation which has led to this troubling perception. Before doing that, it may be useful to look back at the earlier history of social security in order to explore whether there have been any fundamental shifts in the social foundations of support. The central theme of this paper is that there have been some fundamental shifts in the objectives of social security systems in the industrialized countries. The chief goal is still protection against interruption of income from work, but the original aim of providing a more or less adequate minimum of protection for wage and salaried workers has everywhere evolved into a system which aims at the maintenance of standards of living achieved through work for all citizens. The erosion of national consensus on social security seems to be related to this shift in goals and its economic and social implications. The early concensus on minimal social protection could draw on traditional values as well as collective interests. The attempt to secure differential standards of living invariably led to political contests among competing interest groups.

II. Legitimizing the Birth of Social Insurance

In *The Great Transformation*, Karl Polanyi argued that societies have a natural tendency to develop protective institutions when they feel threatened. "If market economy was a threat to the human and natural components of the social fabric, as we insisted, what else would one expect than an urge on the part of a great variety of people to press for some sort of protection."[2] The emergence of social insurance in industrialized countries certainly seems to be one of the main protective measures that fits Polanyi's historical hypothesis. It implies that social insurance was initially legitimized not with reference to the economic or social rights of any particular group, but with reference to the threatened stability of the social or political order. In this section I want to examine how the creation of social insurance was legitimized in the leading Western industrial countries.

It was no historical accident that Germany, a relative latecomer to industrialization, became the pioneer of modern social insurance. In Germany the transition to industrialism occurred in a social and political setting which was still marked by strong vestiges of feudal attitudes. A rapidly growing wage-earning class was concentrated in industrial centers but largely denied effective methods of organized self-help through strong unions. The working class shared the attitude of other major social groups—big industry, the agrarians, the churches, and the intellectuals—that it was the duty of the ruling classes, through the state, to protect the workers against the most serious economic hazards of industrial society. These attitudes were consistent with the paternalistic tradition of German rulers and reflected the historical weakness of German liberalism. To be sure, some German employers feared that the burdens imposed by compulsory state insurance would weaken the international competitiveness of German industry. But the grounds for such fears were rather weak since Bismarck aimed merely at alleviating the major economic risks in the workers' existence. He was anxious to leave employers an otherwise free hand in the treatment of their workers and was quite conscious of the cost element.

The fundamental logic of the Bismarckian system was clear: the industrial workers were defenseless against the serious economic risks generated by industrialization and urbanization; they had a legitimate claim to protection, and it was the duty of the state to provide this protection; if the state were to fail in its duty, the workers would be driven to subversion and revolution, and the security of the state would be endangered. Although a general consensus on this reasoning provided the necessary legitimacy for the social insurance program, its enactment was still controversial. The essence of the controversy was related to Bismarck's endeavors to use social insurance for partisan political purposes. He was not content with providing a basic sense of security to the workers. His aim was to undermine the growing influence of socialism and to bind the workers to the monarchical state. He wanted workers to feel that their economic security was dependent on the security of the state. This objective naturally aroused the hostility of Socialists and labor leaders. It generated resistance also among other political groups in the parliament and even within the bureaucracy. This resistance forced Bismarck to accept compromises that weakened his political objectives to the point where he almost lost interest in social insurance. Even though Bismarck failed in his objective to destroy socialism, the German social insurance system provided an important element of industrial stability and may have helped to turn German socialism from revolution to revision.

In France, the parliamentary debate over social insurance began in 1880, at about the same time as in Germany, but the birth pains were much more prolonged, and by 1914 the policy achievements much more modest than in Germany. Classic liberalism was deeply rooted in France and had been sanctioned by the Great Revolution. The revolution had abolished the old system of feudal reciprocities and enthroned individual liberty based on private property. The working classes had no special claim to protection, nor did the ruling classes have any obligation to provide it. The duty of the state was to provide security and equality before the law. French liberals argued vehemently, and for a long time successfully, against any kind of law which would impose compulsory insurance. French liberal lawmakers and jurists argued that acceptance by the state of the obligation to assist the poor would necessarily involve income redistribution and hence a violation of property rights, which were the foundation of modern civilization.[3] Workers who would have to contribute to compulsory programs, the argument ran, would be less able to accumulate capital to acquire land or a small shop of their own. Such acquisitions, in a country characterized by small property holdings and artisan shops, was judged to be a preferable way to insure economic security as well as family solidarity. The liberals recognized that individuals had a moral duty to assist the destitute, but this duty should never be translated into a formal obligation of the state and even less into a right of the poor.

At the left wing of the French political spectrum, the Revolutionary Syndicalists who led the labor movement made extravagant demands for social protection of the workers while at the same time rejecting every form of collaboration with the bourgeois government. They distrusted the government. Like the German Socialists, they were contemptuous of what they considered the pitiful benefits envisaged by the legislators. They vehemently denounced the notion that workers should have to pay contributions to be eligible for protection when their insecurity was the consequence of exploitation by the existing social and economic system.

French employers had a more ambiguous attitude toward social protection of the workers. As in other countries, the larger employers often favored wage supplements, in a spirit which combined paternalism and self-interest. The most conspicuous manifestation of this spirit was the growth of family allowances in the late nineteenth century. But employers generally approved of such benefits only so long as they were voluntary.

Given the widespread hostility and indifference toward social legislation, we must ask where the driving power and the legitimizing force for social insurance was to be found. In contrast to Germany, it was very difficult in France to use the notion of dependency of the working class as a basis for a claim for protection from above. A society which stresses private property, individual liberty and self-dependence cannot legitimize protection on the basis of social dependence. Some other rationale had to be formulated which could be shared by those people who held the middle ground between libertarianism and syndicalism. It had to be a rationale which did not affront the dominant individualistic ideology, yet provided a justification for collective action. Such an eclectic philosophy emerged around the turn of the century under the label of *solidarity*.[4] The central idea, as formulated by Léon Bourgeois, was that in addition to the private contract which regulates exchange, social relations involve also a "social quasi-contract." The social quasi-contract was a recognition of the interdependence of modern society as a means of legitimizing collective action for the common good. It offered a model of social relations that allowed collective action within a framework of social equality and thus differed sharply from the dependence model, which was an expression of inequality. It was a rejection of both individualistic laissez-faire and state paternalism.

The standard bearers of this social solidarity ideology were mainly Radical Republicans and independent Socialists in Parliament and the bureaucracy, men like Millerand and Paul-Boncour. Their ultimate concern was not logically different from that of Bismarck. They also wanted to safeguard the country's fundamental political institutions against subversion. In their case the institutions were democratic and republican. The threats to the Third Republic were real, both from the extreme right, from monarchists, as well as from the extreme left, from Revolutionary Syndicalists. Social legislation inspired by the ideals of solidarity was intended to provide social stability as well as legitimacy to the still fragile democratic institutions of the Third Republic. As a social philosophy, Solidarity was itself hardly robust. The achievements of French social legislation before World War I remained limited. The debates which led to the 1897 workmen's compensation act, the 1905 public assistance act and the 1910 old-age pension act took decades and still failed to generate broad popular support.

In Great Britain, another bastion of classical liberalism, conditions in the late nineteenth century were more favorable than in France for the enactment of social security legislation. The free market tradition was offset to some extent by the traditions of Benthamism and of Tory paternalism. When the Victorian conscience was shocked by the revelation of widespread abject poverty through the social investigations of Booth and Rowntree, many voices called for remedial action by the state. Clearly, the free market system had failed in a major way. The conditions of the poor as well as the demands from workers for social reforms and the readiness of many employers to accept reforms presented an objective situation that was favorable to the enactment of social legislation. Oddly enough, the decisive thrust behind the emergence of the British welfare state was neither the needs of the poor nor the reform demands of workers, but the perceived vulnerability of the British Empire. By the turn of the century Great Britain was becoming conscious that she was falling behind as an economic power. Britain was being surpassed by newly emerging industrial states, such as the United States and Germany. Serious doubts were raised whether Britain still had the economic vitality to defend the interests of a world wide empire. Recruiting during the Boer War demonstrated an unsuspected poor physical condition of the working classes. The degradation of the health of the working population was seen as a fundamental cause of national economic debility, especially when contrasted with German vitality. This concern added momentum to the drive for greater national efficiency which swept the country around the turn of the century. It was precisely this "quest for national efficiency" as Bently Gilbert noted, that "gave social reform what it had not had before—the status of a respectable political question."[5] As I have pointed out elsewhere, "national efficiency became a novel way of legitimizing protection of the lower order."[6] It contrasted with German paternalism as well as with the French appeal to social solidarity. It had the support of Conservatives who worried about the empire as well as Socialists, like the Webbs, for whom efficiency was a prime social objective. It was an argument that appealed to men like Winston Churchill,

Lloyd George, and the higher civil servants who shaped the social security legislation of 1908 and 1911.

Turning now briefly to the emergence of social security in the United States, there is no need to belabor the crisis circumstances which afflicted the country fifty years ago. The historical circumstances were different, but the pressures for action were similar to those that led to the enactment of social security in the other countries. The Great Depression dramatically demonstrated the inadequacy of voluntary efforts and individual state actions. Nevertheless, to make a compulsory social insurance system acceptable in the U.S., it had to be as free as possible from overtones of state paternalism as well as from any socialist ideologies of redistribution. The American tradition was that neither society nor the wealthy classes had any responsibility to protect the worker. The role of the government was to help the workers to help themselves. As J. Douglas Brown explained: "We wanted our government to provide a mechanism whereby the individual could prevent dependency through his own efforts."[7] Such mechanisms existed, of course, in the private market economy, but it was evident that the voluntary approach had failed to prevent widespread dependency in old age. State intervention became necessary, just as in other industrialized countries, because without it there was a serious potential threat to social and political stability. If the government did not act in time, pressures from organizations like the Townsend Movement might some day force it to establish programs that were less compatible with traditional institutions and values.

The American social security system was legitimized by stressing self-help and compatibility with market principles. There was no emphasis on social contract or solidarity, but on private contract between the individual and the state. The right to unemployment compensation was earned as part of a "fair labor contract." The right to old-age pensions was earned through contribution. As Brown testified before the House Ways and Means Committee: ". . . by contributing the individual worker established an earned contractual right to his annuity through his own thrift."[8] This ideological emphasis on equity implied a benefit structure which minimized redistribution. Furthermore, only benefits providing a basic floor of protection were compatible with the tradition of self-help, but they were applicable to all citizens, which made American social insurance an innovator of the universalist approach.

187

In spite of the wide differences in historical circumstances and forms of legitimation surrounding the birth of social security in the four countries discussed, there is nevertheless a common underlying theme. In each case the introduction of compulsory social income protection was deemed necessary for the protection of the economic, social, and political order. It was primarily the concern with a public good, as perceived by political and administrative leadership, that was the driving force. This concern with survival and stability of existing institutions was a much broader concept, in my opinion, than the idea of "social control" advanced by writers like Piven and Cloward (1971).[9] Nevertheless, both views imply a system of protection inspired by collective interests, as seen by the leadership, rather than notions of individual social rights. It is not that the idea of social rights did not exist before World War II, but that it was only after the war that it became a driving force. This force for universal, comprehensive protection at rising levels of comfort, contrasts with the earlier notion of a basic floor of protection mainly for those most at risk.

III. The Post World War II Reforms

The present difficulties of the social security systems in the western industrial countries have their roots in the postwar reforms and in the forces which propelled those reforms over time. There were two elements in the postwar reforms that eventually proved difficult to combine successfully. The first of these elements was the abandonment of the traditional idea that social insurance was designed primarily for a segment of the population considered particularly at risk, namely the wage workers. Social protection was now increasingly treated as a social right to which all citizens were entitled, not merely the economically weak. Universalism and comprehensiveness became goals of social policy. The second element of the postwar reforms relates to the level of protection. The traditional idea of social protection aiming at a minimum floor to avoid the hardships of poverty was abandoned in favor of a level of protection which aimed at maintaining standards of living. The impetus for the immediate postwar reorganization of the welfare state had two major historical sources: the memory of economic suffering during the interwar period and the hardships of wartime. The experience with economic planning during the war and the expectation of high unemployment following it also predisposed many countries toward a greater governmental role in the management of the national economy. A comprehensive system of welfare programs was to be an integral part of postwar economic reconstruction.

The most influential reform program was contained in the Beveridge Report (1942) prepared for postwar Britain.[10] It quickly became an international reference standard. The insecurity of the war inspired the goal of "security for all," expressing thus the hope for a better postwar world. The Beveridge vision of universal and comprehensive social security became embodied in the 1944 "Philadelphia Declaration" of the International Labor Conference, in the 1948 United Nations Universal Declaration of Human Rights, and in the constitutions of many countries.

Although the Beveridge Plan was an outcome of conditions prevailing in Britain, its objectives of universal and comprehensive protection of all citizens against all major risks had very wide appeal. The war had obliterated many social distinctions and suppressed many political squabbles. The war induced sense of social solidarity, which made a national consensus around the Beveridge Plan possible in Britain, was also a powerful phenomenon in other countries. In France, the political right and left, which had fought each other bitterly before the war, were brought together in the Resistance movement. Their common goals and experiences generated the sense of solidarity that inspired the postwar rebirth of French social security. The Beveridge Report was a strong influence on the *Conseil National de la Résistance*, which in March 1944 drew up the *Charte de la Résistance*. Among other postwar objectives, the Charte called for "a complete plan of social security designed to ensure the means of existence for all citizens."

The underlying concept of the Beveridge Report was the social right to freedom from want. This was, in Beveridge's words, a right to a "guaranteed minimum income needed for subsistence." In Britain, this minimum was to be secured primarily through a flat contributory social insurance benefit. Although flat rates of contribution and benefit were traditional in British social insurance since 1911, they reflected also the Beveridge view that the state ought to provide no more than a minimum of subsistence and that this minimum should be the same for everybody. His argument was that "in insurance all men should stand on equal terms." There should be no differentiation based on income levels or cause of insecurity. This egalitarian "Dunkirk spirit" applied also to family allowances, which were payable regardless of income, and to the provision of social services, which were to be provided equally to all. For those who were not able to earn the minimum benefit through contribution, a means-tested relief through public assistance would be available. Beveridge hoped that means-tested relief, which brought unpleasant memories to mind, would play a minor role and diminish over time. He expected that the compulsory system, supplemented by social services and individual efforts, would be the main element of income security. The whole approach was built on the assumption that the government would pursue an active full employment policy.

The Beveridge Plan illustrates the new emphasis on universalism and comprehensiveness, but with regard to benefit levels and financing it was still very traditional. It remained tied to the subsistence minimum, which Beveridge did not expect to rise much over time in real terms. After a twenty year transition period, Beveridge expected that the system would be self-financing without subsidies from general revenue. This expectation rested on the assumption that benefit levels would remain at the subsistence level and that gradually the vast majority of citizens would have paid for their benefits through years of contribution. There would be little need for a substantial role for public assistance. Although there were some unsettled issues in his plan, he strongly believed that social insurance was ideally suited to provide this floor of protection for all citizens against all the major sources of poverty. In the years immediately following the war, the British Government reformed the welfare system along the general lines of the Beveridge Plan, but economic and social changes quickly undermined the acceptability of minimum benefits tied to previous contributions.

The second new element in postwar reforms—the deliberate abandonment of the idea that the function of social insurance was to provide only a floor of protection—is best illustrated by the German pension reforms of 1957. These reforms were enacted after many years of debate and after alternative proposals advanced by the major political parties. By 1957, economic conditions had changed drastically for the better in Europe and especially in Germany when compared with the immediate postwar years. Economic growth and rising wages inspired the German reformers to take a forward-looking approach. In this rising tide of prosperity, the idea was adopted that social insurance was not simply a contract between the individual and the state, but a social contract between generations, between those in the work force and those who have retired or become disabled. Intergenerational solidarity was interpreted to imply that those at work were committed to maintain the standard of living for those whose working life had ended, and in return they could count on similar support from the succeeding generation. This was a far cry from the traditional alleviation of income interruption. The central idea was explained in 1955 by Adenauer's Minister of Labor as follows: "Originally pensions had the objective of providing merely a supplement toward subsistence, not even an existence minimum, and much less a guarantee for a standard of living. . . . This conception of the old-age pension has undergone substantial change, not only here but in the entire world. Today the task of old-age pensions is to safeguard for those no longer at work, and under their special conditions, the standard of living they had earned through a lifetime of labor."[11]

This objective was built into the pension reform by tying pension levels to the growth of real national income. Not only were pensions to be protected against loss of income due to inflation, they were allowed to move with the rise in real national income. This approach was ideally suited to an expanding economy with a growing population. It severed the rigid link between contribution and benefit levels which had dominated traditional German social insurance and which was still a guiding principle of the Beveridge plan.

Germany was not alone in deviating in this manner from Beveridge. As it turned out, inflation and prosperity during the 1950s and 1960s made the egalitarian subsistence approach impossible to maintain, even in countries like Britain and Sweden, where it was traditional. In both countries inflation eroded the real value of the established nominal minimum, and rising real wages created a widening gap between the incomes of pensioners and active workers. The increasing inadequacy of the egalitarian minimum benefit led to further growth of inequality of protection by stimulating the development of voluntary occupational pensions. In Britain, low flat benefits required more and more supplementation through means-tested public assistance, something Beveridge had hoped to avoid. It was not possible to raise the level of the flat benefits without abandoning the principle of equal contribution for equal benefit or putting an excessive burden on the lowest paid workers, or undermining the importance of financing through contributions. In both Britain and Sweden, the introduction of superannuation, that is, the imposition of differentiated benefits on top of flat pensions, involved complex issues and a lengthy debate among the interested groups. But both countries eventually enacted earnings-related pensions, while the link between individual contributions and pensions became increasingly tenuous.

The unanticipated prosperity of the 1950s and 1960s would seem to be the main force that enlarged the concept of social rights that had emerged from World War II. In a world of sustained economic growth, increased social mobility, and rising wages, the prewar subsistence level concept of social protection was no longer compelling. There were widely differing conceptions with regard to the precise objectives of social policy, but they generally agreed that it should aim at providing a higher quality of life. Social policy had acquired an integrating function. Social rights enhanced the value of citizenship, of membership in the postindustrial society. Social policy was the means to overcome the major defects of capitalist society in a world of rivalry between capitalism and socialism. Universalization of coverage, high employment, and rising wages increased the revenues of the various social programs. At the same time the general acceptance of pay-as-you go financing made rising benefits easy to achieve. Under such circumstances, expansionist policies were nearly irresistible. The immediate cost was often small, the needs for improved benefits were easily demonstrated by an interested program bureaucracy, and the political advantages were readily apparent to interested legislators. Whatever the specific combination of forces, all the major countries experienced significant growth in social expenditures, especially after 1960. Table I presents the growth of the major OECD countries. The data include pensions, health care, education, family allowances, and unemployment compensation. It is striking that in this period of high GDP (Gross Domestic Product) growth (1960–1975) the growth of social expenditures exceeded economic growth in each of the countries. The years of unprecedented sustained economic growth generated an unprecedented and unsustainable growth in social expenditures. In the United States, the United Kingdom, and in a number of other OECD countries, the rate of growth of social expenditures was more than twice the rate of growth of GDP. In addition to

Table I
Social Expenditures Growth for Selected Countries: 1960–1981

	Social Expenditures as % of GDP		Annual Growth % of Real GDP		Annual Growth % of Real Social Exp.	
	1960	1981	1960–75	1975–81	1960–75	1975–81
Australia	10.2	18.6	5.2	2.4	8.6	2.4
Belgium	17.0	38.0	4.5	3.0	9.1	4.6
Canada	12.1	21.7	5.1	3.3	9.5	2.9
France*	13.4	23.8	5.0	2.8	7.4	7.6
Germany	20.5	31.9	3.8	3.0	6.7	1.9
Italy	16.5	29.1	4.6	3.2	7.4	3.1
Japan	8.0	17.5	8.6	5.1	9.7	8.9
Sweden	14.5	33.5	4.0	1.0	8.4	4.0
United Kingdom	13.9	24.9	2.6	1.0	5.6	3.3
United States	10.9	21.0	3.4	3.2	7.7	2.9

*Excludes education.
Source: *OECD Observer* No. 126 (Jan. 1984), p. 5.

the general economic and political factors mentioned earlier, various program related elements contributed to the rise in expenditures, including the addition of new risks, such as health care in the U.S., the aging of the population, the maturing of pension programs, and the advances in medical technology and in health care utilization.

IV. Social Security in Crisis

By the mid 1970s the postwar era of sustained economic expansion had come to an end and with it much of the optimism about the welfare state. Severe recessions in 1974–75 and 1980–82, high unemployment rates, and high inflation rates increased the need for social expenditures but at the same time diminished the available resources under the nearly universal pay-as-you-go financial systems. As Rosa noted: "In recent years a significant change has affected public attitude toward mandatory social security systems. Criticism of their side effects on the economy and their inequities, plus fears for their long-term viability have replaced praise for social insurance as the greatest social triumph of the second half of this century. While contributors are protesting against increases in the payroll tax, the insured wonder whether they will have a sufficient income when they retire."[12] The fiscal crisis of the system stimulated a great deal of critical opposition, more than at any time since the birth of social security.

It was not only the financial difficulties of social security that created a sense of crisis. There was a growing, if belated, realization that the vast expansions of the previous decades had fundamentally altered the role of social security. In most countries, social security turned out to have an impact rather different from what had been anticipated. This observation is especially relevant for the United States where major changes had occurred with practically no public debate, other than the health care debate. The flexibility of the pay-as-you-go approach made many improvements seem almost costless, or at least the cost could be delayed into the future while benefits could be provided immediately. There was no great postwar debate in the United States over any changed role for social security. The expansion was politically attractive and carried out in an incremental fashion, with technical expertise provided by the Social Security Administration.

Until the 1970s, the American scholarly community paid little attention to the postwar development of social security. Milton Friedman wrote in 1962: "The 'social security' program is one of those things on which the tyranny of the status quo is beginning to work its magic. Despite the controversy that surrounded its inception, it has come to be so much taken for granted that its desirability is hardly questioned any longer."[13] Friedman, of course, had serious reservations, but they were reservations of a classic libertarian who had a small following at the time. It was only after the expanded social security structure was in place and in the context of the fiscal crisis that the American debate over social security was reborn. The public debate centered on the high taxes and on the reported anticipation of "bankruptcy" of social security. The payroll deductions, which once were almost negligible, were rising rapidly, while for younger people the confidence that they would ever collect commensurate benefits was decreasing. The scholarly debate focused partly on social security itself, but even more importantly on its economic impact. An extensive debate has taken place over whether social security has a significant impact on capital formation and on the supply of labor. The outcome of the debate, as far as I know, is still in doubt.[14] There seems to be less doubt about the impact of health insurance, including Medicare and Medicaid, on the cost of health care, and of unemployment compensation on the rate of unemployment.

My concern here is less with the outcome of the debate than with the fact that it has been going on. Matters that appeared to be settled have once more become controversial, because our social security system has evolved into something very different from what it was at the time of its inception. Yet, there is a certain irony to this belated debate, because it occurs at a time when the die is cast. Politically, the options for substantial change are very limited, at least for the foreseeable future. The manner in which the social security amendments of 1983 were formulated and enacted offers a good illustration of how even limited changes require an adroit balancing of competing political interests. Competition among political groups for a share in the enlarged transfer income has become one of the fundamental characteristics of the modern welfare state, as Robert Morris has recently emphasized.[15] It is a consequence, in his view, of democratization, the weakening of traditional values of mutual assistance, and the development of modern social rights. I want to emphasize the contrast between this political competition for benefits characterizing the modern welfare state and the social values that legitimized its origins. At that time, protection of the economically weak was the major objective and the political interest was that of collectivity, as we saw earlier. The generalized eligibility of all citizens for social protection today, and the higher benefit levels, have put the political contest over benefits into the foreground. The gainers will be the politically strong. The American welfare state provides rather well for the economically strong, those with strong earning records, but it leaves those with low and irregular earnings in a difficult position.

When we look at other countries, we find many similarities in the underlying problems. In Germany the financial problems have been particularly acute because of the rapid expansion of benefits since the 1950s and a rising aged dependency ratio until the late

1970s. Although in Germany social policy has always been a more important subject of scholarly analysis than in this country, the debate has considerably intensified over the last fifteen years. During the years of rapid economic expansion of the 1950s and 1960s, German public opinion supported massive growth of social expenditures. According to Hans Zacher, "The notion of a social growth dividend became current, and in social policy making it was taken for granted that the economy would automatically generate the resources for any desired redistribution. . . . And this entire approach was justified in the name of democracy."[16] As Table I above shows, Germany already had one of the highest levels of social expenditures in the world in 1960, but the spending level kept on rising. By the mid 1970s, amidst recession, inflation, and a rising dependency ratio, it became obvious that major cost containment efforts had to be made. A long series of cost-cutting and revenue enhancement measures were introduced, but no serious attempt was made to change the fundamental structure of social security rights. In this regard, the experience of the 1970s and 1980s recessions was dramatically different from that of the Great Depression. In the early 1930s, the German government used its emergency powers to reduce social benefits even more than the amount required to maintain financial stability. The recent changes were carried out much more democratically and aimed mainly at slowing increases in expenditures through changes in benefit conditions and curtailed adjustments to higher prices.[17] In the early 1930s the government was clearly determined to cut down the size of the welfare state. The measures taken over the last ten years do not indicate any such intentions. Broadly speaking, the German government has attempted to adapt the welfare system to the country's economic capacity. As in the United States, there has been an important shift in attitude. Zacher describes it as follows:

> The expectations of voters from the political process have changed. During the expansion phase there was a general anticipation of constantly new distributions of benefit increases for as many voters, and as many significant voter blocs as possible. Now there is the dual hope of preserving the social system and its chief functions while shifting the necessary sacrifices to someone else.[18]

If the German government did not take any steps to dismantle its elaborate social security system, neither has it taken any steps to solve its long term deficit. Most measures taken have been directed at short-term deficits. The fundamental problem, as seen by a number of writers, lies in the country's declining birth rate, which is expected to result in a 1.12 worker/pensioner ratio by 2030.[19] It will become necessary in the not too distant future either to cut benefit levels or to raise the already high tax rates even higher. To deal with this problem in an equitable fashion, several writers have suggested that the number of children raised by a family should count as a contribution toward social security.[20] As mentioned earlier, when the pension program was reformed in 1957, one of the guiding ideas was that old-age pensions represent an intergenerational social contract. The contract can be maintained through time only if the working generation supports the aged and at the same time raises a succeeding generation of producers. The contract therefore covers three rather than two generations, but the burden is not shared equitably. While all workers pay taxes to support the aged, those with children bear the main burden to keep the system going. In order to safeguard the concept of intergenerational solidarity, the old-age insurance tax rate should be adjusted to the number of children in the family. Müller and Burkhardt suggest, for instance, that for a family with husband and wife and only one earner, the contributions should be set at 12 percent of taxable wages if there are no children, 9 percent for one child, 6 percent for two children, 3 percent for three children, and zero for four or more children. These rates would be applicable throughout the working life, "in order to make it transparent, that the contribution in kind represented by bringing up children is a solidaristic contribution which assures the survivability of the pension program beyond the child-raising period."[21] The differential rate would of course not apply to employers. This proposal is but one of a number that have been considered in recent years to find new ways to share the burden of social security more equitably.

In Great Britain the demographic outlook is considerably more favorable than in Germany in terms of its impact on projected dependency ratios. Moreover, the total welfare state burden is also much lower, as pointed out earlier. The Thatcher government's preference for private solutions and privatization has not resulted in any overall reductions in welfare spending. While there were some cuts, mainly in the form of delayed inflation adjustments, real expenditures on social security increased by 20 percent during the first four years of the Thatcher government, mainly as a result of high unemployment.[22] Because of the State Earnings Related Pension Scheme (SERPS) which began in 1978, it is recognized that future contribution rates may have to be raised substantially above present levels. Barring a significant increase in dependency ratios, the projected contribution rates "should not be unsustainable."[23]

Nevertheless, there seems to be considerable dissatisfaction with the way in which the Beveridge ideal of a simple universal and egalitarian system has been transformed since the 1960s. In the words of some recent critics: "There are now simply too many benefits, administrative costs are extremely high, and many of those who need benefits are not receiving them despite the enormous resources devoted to their payment. As unemployment and the size of the pensioner population have risen, the strains on the system have multiplied. Today, social security has fallen into severe public disrepute."[24] How widely these sentiments are shared among the population is not clear. It is evident that the Beveridge scheme under which everybody paid the same flat tax, unrelated to income, and received the same subsistence level benefit was not workable. It has been progressively abandoned since the 1960s, culminating with the SERPS, which was enacted in 1975 after a twenty year debate. When the SERPS becomes fully operative, around 1998, it will add ten to fifteen billion pounds to the social security budget,[25] and it will do so in a manner that will benefit primarily higher income receivers. In the meantime, many people at the lower end of the income scale not only receive inadequate benefits but are trapped in poverty by the relief system, because of the manner in which benefits are reduced when income is earned. It is ironic that the Beveridge plan, under which the vast majority of citizens were to pay for their egalitarian benefit, has been displaced by a system which tends to favor the higher paid workers and which maintains only a weak link between contributions and benefits.

Because of the shortcomings of the present system, a number of far-reaching reform proposals have been advanced. The most recent reform plan is probably the one advanced by Dilnot, Kay, and Morris (1984), which involves replacing the entire social security tax and benefit structure with a system based on tax and benefit credits related to individual circumstances and incomes. This is a modified negative income tax approach; all citizens would pay a flat rate social security tax up to an income ceiling, and all benefits would be means-tested. The social security and the income tax systems would be integrated. The proposed reform has obvious virtues of efficiency, but it is doubtful whether such a wholesale dismantling of benefits could be carried out in a democratic country, except in an extreme emergency situation.

I noted earlier that in France the leaders of the Resistance committed themselves to a universal and comprehensive system of social insurance at the end of World War II. Between 1945 and 1975 this objective was realized, but not in the manner the Resistance leaders had anticipated. Their conception was that of a uniform, integrated national system along the lines of the Beveridge Plan. This system of national solidarity did not survive long after the German occupation. The traditional tendencies for diverse groups to go their own way with separate programs became manifest again after the war. A general plan was created for wage workers in industry and commerce, but the self-employed farmers, artisans, and merchants wanted to remain separate, each group with its own plan. Civil servants and employees of nationalized industries also received their own programs. On top of these programs, separate complementary occupational programs were created, which were later regrouped into two national federations, one for workers and one for supervisory and managerial personnel. Finally, there is a state-guaranteed minimum pension for all citizens aged sixty-five or older, regardless of their participation in other pension programs.

In lieu of the integrated national system envisaged in 1945, France thus expended the social rights momentum generated during the war on the creation of a highly complex patchwork of programs. A nationwide system of social protection was created, but one that is confusing and marked by inequities and irrational cross-subsidization. The whole system is financed on a pay-as-you-go basis, partly from general revenue, but mainly from payroll taxes borne two-thirds by the employer. As in other countries, high economic growth, expansion of coverage, and a relatively favorable dependency ratio allowed the pay-as-you-go system to grow rapidly until the mid 1970s. Since then: "A combination of improving benefits, rising health care costs, a worsening demographic ratio and the prolonged economic crisis has . . . generated chronic deficits in particular funds, if not in the social security system as a whole. Forecasts indicate, moreover, that even without further improvements in benefits, the situation is likely to get worse. The general regime as a whole ran an annual surplus until 1974, at which time it went nearly four billion francs into the red. Large deficits were incurred also in 1975, 1976, and 1978."[26] The Giscard government produced a series of measures to deal with the short-term financial imbalances, but did not tackle the long-term problems. When the Socialists came to power in 1981, they quickly proceeded to make good on their electoral promises to raise benefits at the lower end and to eliminate some of the system's inequities. These benefit improvements only increased the deficits, which quickly forced a halt to the improvement programs. The Socialists had belittled the fiscal problems of the social security system while they were out of power, but by 1982 they had to accept the need for austerity and the struggle to find both short-term and long-term financial solutions.

The projected demographic trends for France are more favorable than for Germany, but there is nevertheless a sharply declining ratio of workers to pensioners. By 2030 the present ratio of 2.82 is expected to fall into the 1.64 to 1.87 range, depending on birth and labor participation rates.[27] As the reform minded Mitterand government discovered the hard way, there are no longer any easy solutions. Coverage cannot be extended further to include new contributors and taxes are already among the highest in advanced industrial countries. Reforms can only mean redistribution of benefits or burdens. Freeman considers the outlook for needed reforms rather unpromising: "The combination of fragmented, sector specific programs and overall high levels of spending means that the latitude for a reform-minded government is limited. A large part of the population is organized and willing to fight to maintain its privileges under the status quo. Even among the working class in the general scheme, proposals to direct more effort toward the least well off will meet resistance. There simply is not a majority constituency for structural or redistributionist reforms of the system. Too many people have too much to lose."[28]

V. Summary and Conclusion

Social security was initially established in the industrial countries to provide a subsistence floor of protection against the major risks threatening the continuity of wages or salaries. In most instances, the traditional forms of poor relief were liberalized and to some extent integrated with social insurance. The dominant concept seems to have been that a basic level of economic security for the wage dependent population was a requirement for the stability and productivity of an industrial society.

After World War II, this original concept gave way to the notion that social protection was basic human right of all citizens. This was not a new idea but its full impact was not realized until after the war. The first aspect of the postwar reforms, symbolized by the Beveridge Plan, was to extend social security to more or less the entire population and to cover all social income risks. This aspect responded to the aspirations for greater human solidarity, equality, and security, stimulated by experiences during the war. The second fundamental aspect of the reform was the abandonment of protection based on subsistence and the adoption of maintenance of the standard of living as the aim of social protection. This aspect, which was symbolized by the German reform of 1957, was a response to unanticipated sustained economic growth and the flexibility of pay-as-you-go financing of expanding systems.

By the mid 1970s, a sense of crisis began to overtake the expansionist atmosphere. Expansion was not halted, but growing deficits in spite of high and rising taxes clearly indicated that there were definite limits to social protection. Most countries began to reexamine their welfare system, while they introduced marginal changes to lessen short-term imbalances. In spite of high expenditure levels, no convincing evidence could be found in any of the major industrial countries that social security had significant adverse effects on the rate of saving or on the supply of labor. A return to higher economic growth, however, does not offer expansive possibilities beyond the growth rate, because everywhere existing programs have built-in significant increases of the future economic burden on the working population. At the same time, from almost everywhere demands are made for reforms to increase the fairness of protection, or to redistribute its burden. Unless the future burden on the working population is to be increased further, major reforms to protect the less well off can only come at the expense of those who receive benefits "they don't need." There is no evidence in any of the major countries about an emerging concensus on a new redistributive philosophy. Just as there is no lack of sentiment to vigorously defend social benefits that have already been acquired. The feelings of social solidarity that promoted social rights immediately after World War II now seem to get crowded out by the political conflict over the distribution of rights and the allocation of burdens.

Notes

1. For a sampling of the comparative "crisis" literature see P. Fisher, "The Social Security Crisis: An International Dilemma," *International Social Security Review*, vol 31, No. 4 (1978), pp. 383–96; Jean-Jacques Rosa (ed.) *The World Crisis in Social Security* (San Francisco: Institute for Contemporary Studies, 1982); P. Flora, "Solution or Source of Crisis? The Welfare State in Historical Perspective" and G. J. Room, "The End of the Welfare State" both in W. J. Mommsen, *The Emergence of the Welfare State in Britain and Germany* (London: Croom Helm, 1981); G. V. Rimlinger, "The Economic Limits of the Welfare State," *The Humanist* (March-April, 1977) pp. 17–20; H. Heclo, "Toward a New Welfare State" in P. Flora and A. J. Heidenheimer, *The Development of the Welfare State in Europe and America* (New Brunswick: Transaction Books, 1981). For recent contrasting appraisals of the U.S. welfare system see Charles Murray, *Losing Ground* (New York: Basic Books, 1984) and Richard D. Coe and Greg J. Duncan, *Years of Poverty, Years of Plenty* (Ann Arbor: University of Michigan Press, 1984).

2. K. Polanyi, *The Great Transformation* (New York: Farrar, 1944), p. 150.

3. H. Hatzfeld, *Du Paupérisme à la Sécurité Sociale* (Paris, 1971), p. 69.

4. Ibid., Chap. V; also J. E. S. Hayward, "The Official Social Philosophy of the French Third Republic: Leon Bourgeois and Solidarism," *International Review of Social History*, vol. 6 (1961), pp. 19–48.

5. B. Gilbert, *The Evolution of National Insurance in Great Britain* (London: Michael Joseph, 1966), p. 60.

6. G. V. Rimlinger, "The Emergence of Social Insurance: European Experience before 1914," in P. A. Köhler and H. F. Zacher, *Beiträge zu Geschichte und aktueller Situation der Sozialversicherung, Schriftenreihe für Internationales und Vergleichendes Sozialrecht* (1983), vol. 8, p. 116.

7. J. Douglas Brown, "The American Philosophy of Social Insurance," *Social Security Review*, vol. 30 (March, 1956), p. 3.

8. "Hearings Before the Committee on Ways and Means on H. R. 4120" 74th Congress (1935), p. 241.

9. Frances Fox Piven and Richard Cloward, *Regulating the Poor: The Functions of Public Welfare* (New York, 1971).

10. See Sir William Beveridge, *Social Insurance and Allied Services* (American edition, New York: McMillan, 1942).

11. In Max Richter (ed.), "Grundgedanken zur Gesamtreform," *Die Sozialreform: Dokumente und Stellungnahmen* (Bad Godesberg; Asgard, 1955–1968) Section B/111/1 p. 14.

12. Rosa, *World Crisis in Social Security*, p. 2.

13. Milton Friedman, *Capitalism and Freedom* (Chicago: University of Chicago Press 1962), p. 182.

14. For an excellent summary of the economic debate, see Henry J. Aaron, *Economic Effects of Social Security* (Washington, D.C.: Brookings Institution, 1982).

15. Robert Morris, "The Future Challenge to the Past: The Case of the American Welfare State," *Journal of Social Policy*, vol. 13, No. 4, pp. 383–416.

16. Hans Zacher, "Der gebeutelte Sozialstaat in der wirtschaftlichen Krise," *Sozialer Fortschritt*, vol. 33, No. 1 (Jan. 1984), p. 1.

17. Detlev Zöllner, "Soziale Sicherung in der Rezession," *Sozialer Fortschritt*, vol. 32, No. 3 (March 1983), pp. 49–59.

18. Zacher, "Der gebeutelte Sozialstaat," p. 4.

19. Karl Heinz Juttemeier and Hans-Georg Petersen, "West Germany" in Rosa, *World Crisis in Social Security*, p. 183.

20. Theodor Schmidt-Kaler, "Kinder statt Beiträge," *Die Politische Meinung* vol. 25 (1980), pp. 66–76; J. Heinz Müller and W. Burkhardt, "Die 3-Generationen-Solidaridät in der Rentenversicherung als Systemnotwendigkeit und ihre Konsequenzen," *Sozialer Fortschritt*, vol. 32, No. 4 (April 1983), pp. 73–77.

21. Müller and Burkhardt, "Die 3-Generationen-Solidaridät," p. 77.

22. Michael O'Higgins, "Privatization and Social Security," *Political Quarterly*, vol. 55, No. 2 (April-June, 1984), p. 129.

23. Richard Hemming and John A. Kay, "Great Britain," in Rosa, *World Crisis in Social Security*, p. 46.

24. A. W. Dilnot, J. A. Kay and C. N. Morris, *The Reform of Social Security* (Oxford: Clarendon Press, 1984), p. 42.

25. *Ibid.*, p. 26.

26. Gary Freeman, "Socialism and Social Security," in John S. Ambler (ed.), *The French Socialist Experiment* (Philadelphia: Institute for the Study of Human Issues, 1985), p. 99.

27. Rosa, *World Crisis in Social Security*, p. 18.

28. Freeman, "Socialism and Social Security," p. 112.

8 _____
Comment

I. Richard M. Coughlin

I am pleased to have the opportunity to comment on these three fine papers. Although diverse in the specific topics they address, these papers are connected by a common theme, which, in a broad sense, is the same theme that brings all of us together on this occasion. I am referring to the enduring significance of social security in the changing economic, political, and social conditions of the past half century. Not only has social security endured the test of time, if anything its significance—social, political, and economic—has increased over the past fifty years. The importance of social security today, both as a set of programs in the U.S. and as an attribute of developed nations worldwide, can hardly be overstated. Through the dramatic expansion in terms of budget and coverage, social security has wrought profound changes in the political economy of the nation. It has affected how individual citizens view their government (including present and future expectations of protection against economic insecurity), and, even more pervasively, social security has played a key role in changing the essential nature of individual responsibility in modern society, from patterns of familial support to conceptions of the wider civic obligations perceived and acted upon by the citizenry. Social security has, in short, changed the way we all live.

These changes are still occurring. A host of questions old and new remain unresolved—a fact amply attested to by the richness of the analyses by Achenbaum, Freeman, and Rimlinger. I will confine my remarks today to four general points raised explicitly or suggested by these papers.

First, a matter that seems to be as vexing now as it was fifty years ago is the functional discontinuity between status equality and economic equality in social security. The notion of status equality embodied in the universal coverage of social insurance programs is, of course, a central feature not only of U.S. social security but of the postwar welfare state. What Rimlinger terms the "Dunkirk spirit" of the Beveridge Plan—equality of the rights of all citizens to social protection, benefits not linked to proof of need—signified a rejection of the traditional model of poor relief that stigmatized recipients and relegated them to second-class citizenship.

Yet, the very social insurance programs that conferred this brand of status equality upon the lower strata of society have been of only limited effectiveness in redistributing income to those who need it the most. This is especially the case where social security programs are financed by regressive payroll taxes, as they are in the U.S. Although the net redistributional effects of social security are difficult to sort out, it is probable that the overall impact of Old-Age, Survivors, and Disability Insurance (OASDI) is regressive, despite all the progressive elements built into the benefit formula.

Obviously, this is a sensitive issue to raise in the context of a conference celebrating the durable achievements of those responsible for the Social Security Act of 1935. Merely to mention it is to risk being identified as part of the camp whose opposition to social security borders on passion and whose attacks use the redistributional issue as an opportunity to caricature the present system and to offer simplistic and potentially disastrous solutions. My purpose in raising the question of redistributive impact is simply to highlight what I regard as a central paradox of contemporary social security in the U.S. and elsewhere: namely, that the approach to social security that preserves equality of status among individual citizens may be fundamentally at odds with the effective downward redistribution of income. Conversely, the "most efficient" (as economists use this term) mechanisms of income redistribution to the poor tend to reinforce status differences among individuals, and, as recent experience demonstrates, programs targeted on the poor are far more vulnerable to political attack than programs with universal coverage and hence larger and more diverse constituencies.

A second and related point concerns the changing meaning of the concept of "social rights" of citizenship. Both Achenbaum and Rimlinger note that the concept of the right to a *minimum* standard of living—that is, a mere floor of protection—has been superseded in recent years by a more expansive conception accompanied by higher expectations on the part of the public. These rising expectations, I would argue, have been especially apparent among the relatively secure middle class. The most vocal demands for increased levels of protection come from those who have something to protect. Certainly the prospect of a "risk free" society would be, at best, remote to the experience of segments of the population who have borne the brunt of high unemployment rates in recent years, to those whose livelihood is threatened by the inexorable decline of the industries in which they work, and, perhaps, most of all, to those long-term dependents of public assistance programs who have seen their benefits eroded by inflation over the past decade.

This presents yet another paradox: as we face the prospect of balancing popular expectations for social protection against competing national priorities within constraints imposed by the reluctance of political leaders to propose and the American people to accept the tax burden implied by these myriad commitments of government, those most likely to be asked (or forced) to make sacrifices are those least in the position to do so. On this point, I question whether Freeman is premature in rejecting the demand model as a key to understanding contemporary social security politics. Recall that even during the depression era, pressures for economic relief came not only from the impoverished unemployed and disaffected. In pressing for a monthly old-age pension of $200—an extravagant sum considering wage and price levels during the 1930s—the followers of Dr. Townsend presaged the emergence of contemporary middle-class program constituencies. Perhaps the period covering roughly 1940 to 1977 represented an exception to the rule, and that today we are witnessing a reappearance of the pressure-group politics and some of the political divisions that characterized social security's early years.

Along these same lines, I want to underscore the significance of the point raised by Achenbaum about the divergence of the expansive conception of social rights from rather narrowly circumscribed legal rights to benefits under social security. The promise of full-fledged social rights, which suggests a full range of protection, may inspire popular expectations that the political system will be unable to satisfy, and thus be the source of growing mass discontent about the overall efficacy of government.

This brings me to a third point, which concerns the role of social security as an instrument of social control. The conventional depiction of social security as a response to the threat or fact of social unrest among the masses is in need of revision. While it is true that socialist organization of industrial workers spurred development the first major social security programs in Bismarck's Germany, and that the spectre of spreading social unrest during the 1930s influenced the policies of the New Deal, the social control implied by these events is not a major force shaping social security in the U.S. and other modern societies today. As Rimlinger notes, social security increasingly fulfills a broader set of functions, such as legitimizing government, promoting social integration, and fulfilling long-range goals of economic development. Such functions embody social control in the broad sense of reconciling and rationalizing elements of modern social and economic relations that would otherwise remain irreconciled and unrationalized. Of course, the details that lend substantive meaning to this broad function across nations and over time still need to be filled in. I suggest that explanations drawing on the concept of the state as actor, which Freeman explores in his paper, offer an inviting opportunity to deepen and enrich our understanding of the forces shaping this broad social control function of social security.

Fourth and last, I think that the current debate over the future of social security, which is a concern of all three papers presented here today, needs to be liberated from its preoccupation with the idea of upper limits in the benefits the program can deliver and the revenues it can muster. Undoubtedly these upper limits exist, but it is by no means certain that OASDI has yet come anywhere near this point, or that it will necessarily approach or exceed it in the early part of the twenty-first century, when large numbers of the baby boom generation retire. In any case, the tolerance of the American public to continue supporting social security remains an unknown, and it will likely remain so for as long as the trust funds remain healthy.

I am more interested in the question of lower limits, of how little social security this nation can afford, and how much human misery it is prepared to tolerate. This question is raised less often and with less vigor than I think it should be. At the base of many contemporary critiques of social security is nothing less than a utopian vision of the free market. Social security, because it constrains people from pursuing their narrow economic self-interest, is cast in the role of the villain. This criticism is largely beside the point. It overlooks the fact that market mechanisms sometimes fail—as was the case during the Great Depression—and that the major raison d'être of social insurance is to provide coverage to those who would otherwise be unprotected. Returning old-age pension and disability insurance coverage to the private sector would not work simply because it would leave too many workers and their families without any protection against these risks. There are already enough holes in the safety net of social protection, already enough human deprivation amid affluence, to occupy the attention of scholars and policy makers alike.

II. Charles E. McClelland

Fifty years ago, Congress brought forth the social security system, as we all are here to recognize today. That it did so is perhaps mute testimony that the Sage of Baltimore and scorner of American political wisdom, H. L. Mencken, was not always right when he denounced as "pishposh" the usual products of the deliberations of Congress. Perhaps Mencken was aware of what I think is probably an apochryphal quip by his distant relative, Count Bismarck. (Bismarck's mother was also a member of the legendarily witty Mencken clan.) Bismarck, allegedly, once said "God protects madmen, drunkards, and the United States of America."

Bismarck was sometimes accused by his enemies of being a madman and a drunkard himself. And he certainly professed a belief in God's intervention in human affairs, a view consistent with his conservative beliefs. But he also founded the first social security system of the modern world, testifying that man and the state, even a conservative one, rather than God, must look after the population most at risk in modern society, to use Professor Achenbaum's term. And as Professor Rimlinger has pointed out, he expected these new rights to result in a heightened sense of responsibility to the German state on the part of the workers covered.

I hope you will indulge me today as I speak for a few minutes not so much about the welter of specific points raised by the excellent and thought-provoking papers we have heard, but about the international and comparative context of social security.

One theme present in all papers is the tendency of social security to have grown over time from a national mutual insurance scheme into a vehicle for the welfare state, at least in the expectations of many beneficiaries and even critics. The term *welfare state* need not occupy us here. It is a political catchword, not a useful scientific concept. Hitler, an avowed enemy of socialism, nevertheless retained the German social security system and justified it with the Nazi slogan, *Gemeinnutz geht vor Eigennutz* (common welfare takes precedence over personal welfare). Current West German parlance unites socialists, liberals, and conservatives on the phrase *Generationenvertrag* (a compact among generations). But whatever we call our system, it is clear, if I may amalgamate the titles of our three papers, bureaucrats have created a system that minimizes risk, maximizes rights, and that is consequently in trouble. Since its origins, social security has become much more comprehensive and has taken on welfare dimensions originally lacking.

All three of our papers focus particularly on the old-age insurance side of our national system. It is certainly valid to do so, since by a purely financial reckoning, this is the program involving the most money. Yet when we speak loosely of the social security systems of other industrialized countries, we are in a way comparing apples and oranges. Our system still lacks a comprehensive medical-care component, and its treatment of the disabled and dependent poor (as opposed to the American middle class) does not compare favorably.

These are not unimportant points. An American retired person receiving social security old-age and Medicare benefits may still be spending a large portion of those benefits on medical care, not on maintaining an adequate standard of living.

By comparison, the oldest social security system of the world, Germany's, began not as a retirement plan but as a medical-insurance scheme that was later expanded into a disability and old-age insurance plan. Instead of covering the majority of the working population against poverty in old age, as the American system was designed to do at the outset in the 1930s, it originally covered only the workers most at risk. Widows, orphans, and some salaried employees were added in 1911. But not until 1967 were all salaried employees embraced in the system. The significant point is that the self-employed, professionals, and other "independent" people were long considered capable of providing for their own needs, and even today some ten percent of West Germans are not covered. For the rest, however, no major risk (including illness at any age) is left uncovered, except by the free choice of the person concerned.

The inclusion of medical coverage in most advanced industrial countries other than the United States may be a major reason why those systems appear less open to criticism than ours and why most of them are willing to ask vastly higher contributions from workers and employers and—this almost unthinkable in Washington—even heavy contributions from the national budget. Still, improved medical care, whether insured or not, has caused a number of startling changes in social security systems over the last century. Life expectancy was so much lower a century ago that old-age insurance was really a kind of guarantee against the unlikely event of a covered person reaching the requisite age to collect benefits. Today, demographic swings in cohort size aside, the situation is quite reversed.

Another point that the German experience illuminates is that of Professor Freeman's policymaking models. Clearly the Democratic Politics Model cannot explain the origins of the system in Germany, either. Yet there is another kind of public opinion to which Bismarck and Roosevelt both responded—that of academic specialists and civil servants who urged social insurance even in the face of apparent indifference by the workers at risk. Small but influential academic groups, such as the *Verein für Sozialpolitik* (Social Policy Association), may have had more indirect impact on Bismarck's paternalistic policies toward workers than many newspapers or election slogans. I was also a little puzzled by the distinction Professor Freeman drew between a bureaucratic and statist model, one that depends on the separation of powers and lack of a European-style parliamentary system in the United States. Yet Germany had only a pseudoparliamentary system under Bismarck, and the bureaucracy would not have understood the notion that they did not represent the state in its highest incorporation. Disagreements nevertheless abounded. Why should their similar presence in American social security politics cause complications in model-building?

The German experience would seem to indicate that a statist and paternalistic impulse could lead to a system administered by a decentralized and ad hoc bureaucracy derived from the various interested parties (covered persons, employers, and the state), which in turn to some degree represents at least some of the interests implicit in the democratic model. While social solidarity usually has not been a feature of class-ridden Germany society, the German state has often been viewed by the people, and certainly by its own functionaries, as "standing above the parties," able and duty-bound to compose social fissures.

One thing that struck me about Professor Achenbaum's paper was its emphasis on litigation. Is there another industrial society that litigates rights under social security as much as ours? Does this penchant indicate a weakness of Professor Freeman's preferred bureaucratic model of control and decision? Or does it perhaps arise from the centralized nature of our social security system compared to that of Germany? Suspicion of "big government" is harder to arouse when one of its central sets of services is administered in a highly decentralized way.

For these and other reasons, Germany has not yet witnessed a major political crisis or divisive debate involving the elimination or serious refunctioning of such a central feature of national life— whether under three Kaisers, two republics, Hitler, and even—in East Germany—communism.

I do not wish to minimize the Germans' problems with their own system—in thirty years, theirs may be the hardest to cope with of all industrial countries, with a possible ratio of 1.12 worker to every retired person. Worker and employer contributions may have to rise from a little over the current 18 to 32 percent of gross salary. The U.S., by the same pessimistic estimates, will have "sunk" to the present ratio of workers to retirees in Germany.[1] If the American system can be saved, for example, by raising contributions to the current level (or less) of Germany, then we might do well to study what kind of social and moral consensus has kept their system going through all the traumas of the twentieth century.

In this sense, Germany might be seen to stand somewhere between the self-understanding of Japan and America. As a comparison of the last two societies recently put it, Japan operates on an ancient ethos of solidarity and self-protection derived from the concept of *wa* (harmony), while the motto of American society might be "I've got mine, you get yours."[2] If Germany has been a society less attuned to self-reliance and individualism than America, it has also been a highly competitive one. Certain areas of national life have, however, been ruled out of bounds for competition, for example, adequate health care. Germany's wartime devastations and catastrophic inflations in this century may also explain why Germans are not inclined to denounce "welfare bums," since millions of cripples, bankrupts, and shelterless families arrived at that state through no lack of willingness to work.

One can only hope that America will not have to experience such trauma to achieve again a consensus on the next fifty years of Social Security.

Notes

1. Richard F. Tomasson, "Government Old Age Pensions under Affluence and Austerity: West Germany, Sweden, the Netherlands, and the United States," in Michael Lewis (ed.), *Research in Social Problems and Public Policy*, vol. 3 (Greenwich, CT., 1985), 217–72 (see especially 220–30).

2. Murray Sayle, "Japan Victorious," *New York Review of Books*, 28 March 1985, p. 39.

PART III

Specific Studies

9

Introduction

Perception of a crisis in social security systems of the 1980s—a dominant theme in Part II of this volume—is not new. Throughout the twentieth century, in capitalist as well as noncapitalist societies, the search for economic as well as social security has been a dominant concern. Sometimes that search has been motivated by ideology—as in the Soviet Union or in Nazi Germany. In other nations, such as Great Britain and the United States, the process has been less doctrinaire, and was a pragmatic response to the vicissitudes of their economies. In pluralistic societies the forms of social security that they adopted varied widely and were extensively debated by contemporaries and later critics alike.

Such public discussion also characterized the adoption of the Social Security Act of 1935, and its modification as well as its administration in later years. The enactment of this landmark legislation was no sudden inspiration, but the fruit of more than three decades of deliberation over essential elements of a social security system in the United States. And such deliberation certainly did not cease with the passage of the law. The first fifty years of the Social Security Act thus provided a convenient watershed from which to appraise not only the original act, but subsequent amendments, and its administration, for these elements marked the creation of the American welfare state.

Such an assessment required a detailed as well as a broad analysis. Both approaches were reflected in the discussions at the special conference at the University of New Mexico. Three historians subjected details of the act to special scrutiny. Dr. Blanche Coll focused on the curtailment of the original concept of a comprehensive system of social security in the New Deal legislation. She described how some framers of the law—such as Arthur Altmeyer—hoped for a very broad program of insurance, public assistance, and services to lessen economic insecurity. But the social security system was fractionated from the beginning, with the public assistance program among its most despised components. Dr. Coll argued for the revival of the original concept of a comprehensive program for all citizens, not only for special groups in the population. Only in this way can Americans remove the stigma that has attached to those receiving funds from the Aid to Families With Dependent Children program administered by the states.

Another uncertainty of the Social Security Act of 1935 was financing of the Old-Age pension program. Professor Mark Leff argued that such uncertainty has impeded that particular program from the beginning and created uncertainties about its stability in the 1980s. During the 1935–1950 period Congress refused to increase social security taxes. Inadvertently, such a short-range view was to have long-range consequences in due time. After 1950 Congress gradually increased the social security payroll taxes. Still, the roots of a future crisis lay in that first decade of the act's operation. As long as the economy expanded, some balance between contributors and recipients seemed feasible. But when the pace of economic growth slowed after 1970, the failure to create an ample reserve for the future created difficult problems that Americans would face as the twentieth century drew to a close.

Professor David Berkowitz drew attention to the differences between disability insurance and other provisions of the Social Security Act. Support for government aid to the disabled was widespread in 1935 because the concept had developed from workmen's liability laws in the states which had been in operation for more than three decades. But what its supporters did not anticipate at the outset were numerous administrative problems within the context of the New Deal legislation and its expansion by amendments in

1956. These problems included excessive court litigation and administrative conflicts between medical and vocational experts and social workers as well. The very definition of disability was a continuing source of controversy over the years. Unlike old-age insurance—where age determined eligibility—evaluating a disability involved a wide range of subjective judgments. Professor Berkowitz indicated that if the social security system is to be fully understood, its various component parts need to be analyzed in depth and future legislation cannot ignore past experience.

While the historians dealt with rather detailed and sometimes technical analyses of the social security system as it had evolved in the fifty years since 1935, the commentators chose to deal with the broader context of social welfare legislation in their presentations. Professor Fred Harris, a former United States Senator, candidate for president of the United States, and a political scientist, directed his attention to the larger issue of poverty in America, and its relation to the question of income distribution. He noted that in an advanced technological society like the United States, some members of the general population may be unable to participate in the work process through no fault of their own. People without a job are not necessarily lazy or incompetent, Harris emphasized. This group may include the technologically unemployed, the young, the old, and the disabled. Harris pointed to myths surrounding social security. These include the belief that the needy are mainly unemployables, that most cheat welfare systems, and that all they need is some good advice. Most prevalent, he argued, is the myth that social security is a charity system and that recipients should pay their own way. In reality, he emphasized, social security is in the national interest, for without it a technologically sophisticated, democratic society would have a difficult struggle to survive.

That reality was also stressed by Professor David Hamilton, a professional economist. In the United States it was not ideology but technological necessity that led to the gradual evolution of a social security system. If there was any theoretical influence that affected the growth of the American welfare state, Hamilton maintained, it emanated from the British economist, John M. Keynes. His general theories were applied to social welfare policies in England during the 1940s and were advocated by various groups in the United States during the succeeding decade. Many business leaders and organizations such as the Committee for Economic Development advocated income maintenance to sustain purchasing power and even a guaranteed annual income under government auspices to maintain economic stability. If Congress did not fully accept all such proposals it nevertheless extended the social security coverage during the Eisenhower era. Thereafter, the Vietnam War and increasing fiscal stringencies weakened income maintenance programs. Yet their impact was not wholly ignored, Hamilton noted, with increasing recognition in the years after 1970 that a wealthy society cannot afford to ignore its poor.

Taken together, the scholarly essays and the accompanying commentaries in this part provide a retrospective appraisal of the Social Security Act of 1935—both in its specific provisions as well as in its broad significance.

10

Public Assistance:
Reviving the Original Comprehensive Concept of Social Security

Blanche D. Coll

"Public Assistance: Reviving the Original Comprehensive Concept of Social Security"—this is Arthur Altmeyer speaking twenty years ago. In his book, Altmeyer deplores the fact that social security has come to refer exclusively to old-age, survivors, and disability insurance. There is no question that Altmeyer expressed both in word and in deed a strong preference for social insurance. Yet to Altmeyer social security meant "comprehensive social insurance, public assistance, and services designed to prevent or ameliorate the hazards causing economic insecurity."[1] My own research leads me to conclude that this was not only Altmeyer's conception but that it represented his and the Social Security Board and Administration's policy during "the formative years," the years of his tenure from 1935–1953.

Other scholars have different perspectives. Martha Derthick, writing in 1979, asserted that public assistance was a "despised program" and that the Bureau of Public Assistance occupied an inferior position in relation to the Bureau of Old-Age and Survivors Insurance.[2] Jerry Cates, in a book published in 1984, goes much farther than Derthick, asserting that "a fundamental conflict of interest existed for the ssb/ssa during the period under study: that given the SSB's overwhelming commitment to the primacy of conservative social insurance, it did not do an equitable job of developing America's public assistance system."[3] Derthick has very little to say about public assistance. Cates, to his credit, has a great deal to say. He has correctly recognized the importance of the interrelationship between insurance and assistance. But both of these scholars are in disagreement with Altmeyer. Although I will cover some of the same ground as Cates, the intention is to broaden the area of knowledge and, in doing so, not simply revive public assistance as related to social security but restore in some measure its place in an honorable tradition.

Two choices made at the very beginning—in 1935—were crucial to the course of development of public assistance programs. The first of these involved the nature of the public assistance titles; the second, the profession selected to administer the programs established. The original Social Security Act contained three public assistance titles—Old Age Assistance, Aid to Dependent Children, and Aid to the Blind—and authorized federal matching grants to states for their administration. The choice of these categories was a conscious one. A group of social work leaders called in as an afterthought by Secretary of Labor Frances Perkins had unsuccessfully argued for a comprehensive welfare component. These social workers recommended a federal grant-in-aid, state administered program to cover all needy persons, a general assistance program, with national oversight vested in a federal department of welfare.[4]

In opting for categorical rather than general assistance, the Committee on Economic Security and the Congress selected programs that were already operating in many states. Equally, if not more important, these programs were usually referred to as pensions— old-age pension, mothers' pension, blind pension. Thus the programs under the authority of the Social Security Board exhibited, on the surface at least, an appearance of symmetry. Confusion was certain; the ultimate outcome anyone's guess. Although one may agree with Derthick that Altmeyer and other social insurance advocates "intended" public assistance to "wither away," this outcome was far from predictable in 1935. In fact, old-age pensions did not begin to wither until the 1950's, while mothers' pensions—the Aid to Dependent Children category—are still very much alive.[5]

The profession chosen to administer the public assistance categories was social work. Why? Why not administer public assistance with the same type of staff as would be hired to administer old-age insurance and unemployment compensation? In each one of these programs, applicants would be lining up to receive money conditioned upon specific proofs of eligibility. Yet no one suggested that the Bureaus of Old Age Insurance or Unemployment Compensation and their field offices be staffed by social workers, while everyone assumed that the Bureau of Public Assistance as well as state and local agencies belonged to the dominion of social work.

Doubtless earlier plans for administration influenced this crucial choice most directly. At first Old Age Assistance had been slated for assignment to Harry Hopkins's Federal Emergency Relief Administration. Aid to Dependent Children was to go to the Children's Bureau, then it too was shifted to the emergency relief agency on the organizational chart. Unquestionably the Children's Bureau was dominated by social workers. To a considerable extent also, social casework had penetrated the agencies that administered mothers' pensions, less so those dealing with pensions for the elderly. Of overriding importance in the choice was the evolution of public and private charities, the relationship of one to the other as a source of assistance to the needy, and the development of social work as a profession.[6]

The profession of social work originated in protest against public charities, those charities that were rooted in state and local Poor Laws. The organizers of private charities feared that charity in public hands would be claimed as a right and would result in pauperization of large segments of the citizenry. They also feared political corruption—that votes would be bought with grocery orders—votes from both grocer and pauper. The realities of the Great Depression modified but did not eradicate these attitudes.

The private charities that nurtured the social work profession were not always adverse to accepting public money, but they preferred public money to be dispensed by private charities, or, at the very least, through social case work methods of investigation and supervision used by private charities. Social casework had evolved out of earlier assumptions that the applicant for charity was at fault and therefore must be changed in some way. As casework came under the influence of the mental hygiene movement and psychoanalytic theories in the early twentieth century, relief (as charity was now designated) given by private agencies was often conditioned upon the recipient's willingness to come to grips with his inner conflicts. In this context, relief became a "tool in treatment."[7]

These social work views were challenged by Harry Hopkins as

head of the Federal Emergency Relief Administration when he ruled that public money must be administered by a public agency, and also by Josephine Brown, a social worker who was one of Hopkins's assistants. Brown defined a new role for social workers in the public welfare agency. She declared it inappropriate for a government agency to mingle relief with social casework as was done in private agencies. As Brown saw it, "much of social casework practice is directed towards the treatment of problems inherent in individuals and families—their inadequacies, their failures, their personality difficulties," while "the administration of unemployment relief is directed at a common problem which is outside the individual and beyond his control." Granted the unemployed might have personal problems, "it is not the function of the relief administration *per se* to inquire into these problems or to treat them." The social worker's job in a public assistance agency was exclusively to determine need and the extent of need—in other words, to conduct a means test. The applicant cooperated in this process, supplying facts and references that were then checked out "on a business-like basis, maintaining a self-respecting relationship." Nevertheless, Brown believed that public assistance workers should be trained, not only in the routines of the job, but in core elements of social work—"appreciation of human values" and "handling the human elements in the relationships." She asserted that "in the administration of unemployment relief we are creating a new type of social work and of public welfare. . . , adapting whatever is applicable from the rest of social work and adding the results of our own experience in standards, methods, training, and terminology."[8]

In truth, social workers who dispensed relief, whether from public or private funds, had never been popular. The depression experience made them less so. Resentment and dislike were widespread. Although some of this feeling was encouraged by conservatives who regarded social workers as overgenerous humanitarians and by politicians who wanted patronage restored, at bottom lay a grassroots revolt against the instruments of the means test. To usually independent persons reduced to dependency, even Brown's formulation minimizing social casework would not satisfy their main objection.[9]

There was considerable expectation that categorical assistance under the Social Security Act—pensions as the common understanding had it—would be relatively free of social casework. As Corrington Gill, Hopkins's chief statistician put it early in 1935, the supervision to be extended to the aged and women with dependent children receiving public assistance through the Social Security Act required study. It seemed "plain" to him, however, "that these households should not be constantly subjected to the annoyance and disturbance of casework investigation, as they did not require as constant and intimate supervision as is customarily extended to chronic incapables. They should receive pensions or insurance benefits and be permitted to arrange their lives as they see fit."[10]

The selection of social work to administer the public assistance categories seems all the more amazing after a look at the state of the profession in 1935. Although widely recognized as a group with unique interests and skills, social work differed markedly from other professions. There were social workers and trained social workers. Trained social workers had received a certificate or a masters degree in social work after attending a one- to two-year postgraduate course at an institution usually affiliated with a college or university. But unlike teachers or nurses or pharmacists, let alone doctors and lawyers, most practicing social workers were not "trained"—they got their training on the job. Many, perhaps most, had not finished college or taken a single course in a school of social work. Most telling of all, social work was women's work.[11]

It should be noted, however, that Jane Hoey, the woman selected to head the Bureau of Public Assistance, held a certificate in social work from the New York School of Social Work as well as a master's degree in political science from Columbia University. One of her brothers was a New York politician and friend of Al Smith. She had more than a passing acquaintance with Franklin and Eleanor Roosevelt. Harry Hopkins, for whom she had once worked, favored her for membership on the Social Security Board itself and Perkins sent her name to the White House, noting that the choice of Hoey would carry more political weight than that of Josephine Roche.[12]

Despite Hoey's qualifications, the amorphous character of the social work profession made it all the more uncertain just how a new, and in many ways different, assignment would be handled and how the actions taken in respect to public assistance would affect the comprehensive program. Two case studies will contribute to an understanding of the nature and consequences of the policy and practice followed. The first is centered on the unsettling question of old-age security and the solutions offered in the 1939 amendments; the second focuses on Aid to Dependent Children.

With two programs directed toward the aged—insurance with coverage limited to workers in commerce and industry and not scheduled to begin payments until 1942, and assistance ready to go at state option in January 1936, the Social Security Board found itself in the middle of extraordinary pressures—pressures so strong as to threaten the basic premises of the Social Security Act itself. Old Age Assistance (OAA) dominated the actions of governors and state legislatures taking precedence over plans for Aid to the Blind and to Dependent Children. By June 1937, forty-four states and the District of Columbia had established programs for OAA, at least ten more than had Aid to the Blind and Dependent Children programs. In the states, the number of persons found eligible for OAA rose rapidly and substantially, doubling during the fiscal year 1937 to reach a total of 1.2 million recipients.[13]

The effort to set the aged apart from other needy groups appeared in many guises, not the least in the use of the term *pension.* Whenever the Bureau of Public Assistance heard "pension," it cried "need." In the Bureau's view, the federal government could not match state payments to persons who were not needy. The general counsel was not so sure. Thomas Eliot, a drafter of the original bill, remembered disagreements in congressional committees about defining need and pointed out that the adjective *needy* occurred only in the preamble—the so-called hot air section of the OAA title. He thought the omission in the substantive portions of the title had been deliberate. In December 1935 he let Executive Director Frank Bane know of his uncertainty "that we have any right to read 'needy' into the definition of old age assistance." But when confronted with several state plans that offered pensions at age sixty-five with no income or property limitations, the board, relying on the preamble, sided with the bureau.

The pension-at-sixty-five plans presented a very clear-cut proposition, one that ignored need completely. Far more difficult to deal with were state proposals that sought to accomplish much the same thing in more circuitous ways. Everyone agreed that the states alone had the power to define and establish standards for old-age assistance. Nothing in the act specified one particular method or several alternative methods for defining need or setting standards. The Bureau of Public Assistance could only make suggestions which the states were free to accept or reject.[14]

The method favored by the bureau was family budgeting, an

individualized casework process that measured an applicant's income and resources against a community standard for maintaining health and decency. Public officials with a strong pension philosophy favored a flat-grant-minus-income method over family budgeting. Under the flat-grant system, the state old-age assistance statute specified a minimum dollar amount and named various exemptions before looking at income and resources.[15]

Those favoring a flat-grant-minus-income system argued that most of the elderly would fare better under this system than under family budgeting. This was not the only reason they were for it. It was simpler to administer, and while not completely automatic, it minimized discretion on the part of the decision-maker. Administration of the program would be conducted along the lines of a well-run business. Honesty and common sense were the qualifications to be sought in the program's directors and staff. No social workers need apply. Their lengthy, detailed investigations would be unnecessary.[16]

In opposing the flat-grant-minus-income process, Hoey and her staff in the Bureau of Public Assistance pointed to the inequities created by it. The system seemed to be even-handed because most individuals received about the same amount of assistance payment. In reality those entirely without means had to get by with only the minimum standard; those who had something to start with got the minimum on top of exempted income or assets. Such inequities were compounded, they pointed out, when states faced financial crisis—a crisis that could be induced by unsound planning for generous assistance to the aged. When such a crisis was met by applying across-the-board percentage cuts to grants, the indigent received less than the minimum standard while those better off to start with continued with at least the minimum, some with more.[17]

In the five or six states—California and Colorado among them—that adopted a flat-grant system, OAA payments were relatively high, at or above the federal matching level of thirty dollars in a large percentage of cases. Yet comparably wealthy states that used the family budgeting system proved only slightly less eager to grant exemptions that would ensure higher grants. Exemptions on income and resources were common to both systems. Most states exempted a home, though some placed a limitation on the value of such property. A great many states exempted the value of personal property and savings or investments of modest amounts. States with a flat-grant system often exempted small amounts of earnings. Exemption of earnings was not usually specified in states on the family budgeting system, but allowance was made for extra food and work expenses.[18]

Hoey had seen what was coming as early as October 1936. Old-age assistance and old-age insurance were on a collision course, she told Executive Director Frank Bane. Barring some drastic change, contributory old-age insurance would suffer total demolition. She pointed to the statistics. Forty-two states already had old-age assistance programs. The 1937 legislative sessions were sure to bring in several more. Look at the average grant level—more than $18 a month. Consider the pressures to abolish the means test. Flat grants to the aged were far from untried. In fact, most European countries adhered to a flat-grant system, though many also required contributions from employer and employee. Hoey noted also that European governments had found it necessary to supplement employer-employee contributions to ensure solvency to their old-age pension funds.

Replying to Bane's request for suggestions on possible amendments to the Social Security Act, Hoey warned:

> If there is a lapse of five years before the contributory scheme goes into effect and the average grant after five years of contribution is less than that which can be secured under the non-contributory scheme, it would seem to me to be practically impossible to put into effect the contributory plan. . . . We have made a great point of the fact that persons could receive the pension as a right on the contributory basis. If, however, in a five-year period, the means test is lessened and the right of the individual is established for the non-contributory scheme, then the distinction between the two systems is eliminated.

Hoey concluded that payments under old-age insurance must begin "much sooner than 1942," even if initial contributions had to be raised and a federal supplement made.[19]

Altmeyer was equally if not more concerned. Noting in December 1938 that forty, fifty, even sixty dollar a month old-age pensions at age sixty were being seriously discussed, he warned of a huge fiscal burden. But he and George Bigge, a Board member, saw the folly of slamming the door on all strategies backed by the old-age pension movement. Too rigid a stance might drive the moderates to support more extreme measures. Equity was one thing; fairness another. Altmeyer thought the states sought fairness in exempting modest accumulations:

> It may be wise public policy to exclude certain things in determining need. There is no hard and fast rule that can be laid down. You have to say that within reason certain things may be exempted. And why should they be exempted? Perhaps to encourage that old fashioned virtue of individual initiative and thrift, because if a person can benefit to some extent, then you have encouraged him to make some provision. That is true whether he is able to take advantage of it or not; at least, you have extended the encouragement to him.

Altmeyer had a simple explanation for social worker opposition to automatic exemptions: social workers feared that state legislatures would rob them of their professional skill. Altmeyer agreed that this skill was a very fine thing—"an idealistic thing. Individual case work, recognizing the family as a unit, taking into consideration its whole past history and making grants accordingly is the best way," he conceded to an audience composed of Bureau of Public Assistance staff. But there simply were not enough social workers to handle each case on such a refined basis. As a practical matter, Altmeyer lectured, the board had to allow state legislatures some leeway. "If we don't, they will go the whole way and we will get flat grants," perhaps even flat grants paid from federal funds, at which point, "we will sink."[20]

During a board discussion of the California flat-grant plan, Hoey drew a fine line of distinction between a state's right to determine need and a state's right to determine the method of measuring need. When Altmeyer expressed interest, Hoey went on to advocate a new policy. The board should insist that all resources available to an individual be considered in investigating the need of each applicant with no exclusion of regular income.[21]

It was in this exchange that the first step was taken toward the amendment adopted in 1939 which provided that the states, in determining need, must consider any other income and resources of individuals claiming assistance. The income and resources clause was one of a number of significant amendments that helped to remove old-age insurance from the threat posed by OAA. The 1939 amendments made clear, once and for all, that public assistance, including OAA, was for needy individuals. This was done by inserting the word *needy* in the definition of OAA and the other assistance titles. More important than these brakes upon public assistance were the amendments that liberalized old-age insurance. As signed into law by the president on August 10, 1939, the date for beginning monthly old-age insurance payments was advanced from 1942 to 1940. A supplementary allowance for elderly wives of insurance beneficiaries was provided. Survivor benefits, to be paid monthly rather than in one lump sum, were authorized for widows age sixty-five and over, and for all widows with dependent children. The level of benefits was increased by changing the method of calculation to use an average of past earnings rather than a total of accumulated wages as the base. All of these changes followed the administration's recommendations. However, on its own initiative, Congress raised the maximum amount for federal matching in OAA from thirty dollars to forty dollars but turned down the administration request to extend old-age insurance coverage to agricultural workers, domestic servants, and employees of nonprofit organizations.[22]

Little noticed during the framing of the Social Security Act, more or less slipped in to round things out, then funded on a less comprehensive basis than OAA or Aid to the Blind, the program for Aid to Dependent Children (ADC) continued in obscurity during the shakedown years when support for the elderly emerged as the dominant issue. The Bureau of Public Assistance was backed by the Social Security Board in its assertion that excessive attention to the needs of the aged led to disregard of the needs of children.

ADC was designed to cover unusual cases of need. The vast majority of American children had one or two adults responsible for their support, adults who, if unemployed, were eligible for public work or unemployment compensation. Under Title IV of the Social Security Act, the unusual cases consisted of children "deprived of parental support or care by reason of death, continued absence from the home, or physical or mental incapacity of a parent."[23]

The Children's Bureau, whose chiefs had drafted Title IV in full expectation that they would be its administrators, thought in terms of a small, select program. "Not all fatherless families can possibly qualify for mothers' pensions—probably not more than half of them," the bureau informed the Committee on Economic Security. Edith Abbott, dean of the University of Chicago's school of social work and sister of a former head of the Children's Bureau, had assured the Ways and Means Committee that "the children are really nice children and the families are nice families." By taking half of the 358,000 female-headed families currently on relief rolls, the Children's Bureau arrived at 179,000 "qualifying" families. When this figure was added to the 109,000 families currently receiving state mothers' pensions, roughly 300,000 families with about 700,000 children would seem to be eligible for ADC. The Committee on Economic Security went along with these estimates in its report to the president.[24]

The number of children receiving ADC quickly matched estimates. In June 1938, 243,000 families with over 600,000 children were on the rolls. By the following year families numbered 298,000; children, 718,000. Nevertheless, the board's Office of Research and Statistics thought the program was failing to reach a large number of needy children, estimating that no fewer than one million were potentially eligible for ADC, with a likelihood that almost two million needy children were in the pool of eligibles.

In an article written for the 1939 *Social Work Year Book*, Hoey suggested several reasons for the estimated gap between assistance required and assistance received. Most obvious was incomplete coverage. Eight states—Connecticut, Illinois, Iowa, Kentucky, Mississippi, Nevada, South Dakota, Texas and the territory of Alaska—had no ADC program, although these states continued to grant some assistance under their mothers' pension laws. Moreover, reports from the states with ADC programs raised puzzling questions. On the whole, state plans followed the liberal lines of the Social Security Act. Why, then, were more than 50 percent of the families headed by widows?

The number of women aged fourteen to thirty-four years who were widowed was somewhat fewer than those divorced. Yet only 28 percent of ADC families were headed by a woman whose spouse was absent from the home due to divorce, separation, or desertion. Parental disability accounted for 22 percent of ADC cases. Was disability being defined too narrowly? Were illegitimate children— ninety births per one thousand—getting more than token consideration? Only 2 percent of children living with unmarried mothers were represented in the caseload. In five states no illegitimate children were accepted; eleven other states carried fewer than fifty of these cases.

The great variance among states in the proportion of children aided could be explained only in part by state fiscal capability. The number of children receiving assistance, compared to the total population under sixteen years, averaged twenty-four per one thousand, ranging from more than forty per one thousand in seven states to sixteen or less per one thousand in eight others.

Drawing on reports from her field representatives, Hoey attributed the puzzling characteristics of the program to "opinion and attitude." Restrictive qualifications regarding the mother's character were no longer obtrusive in state ADC law and regulation. But the viewpoint that pervaded the administration of mothers' pensions remained potent, subtly but surely affecting the administration of the new program. Often the welfare agency recognized need but chose to place a family judged "unqualified" for ADC on the state or local general assistance rolls at a lower grant and less sense of permanence.

Hoey spoke for the board in announcing her stand to her peers in social work, putting miles between the Bureau of Public Assistance and the Children's Bureau:

> Denying children this form of aid because their parent's behavior does not conform to a certain pattern is coming to be recognized as no solution of such problems. Yet transfer from general relief to aid to dependent children is still frequently made on a basis of "promoting" the "nice" families.

Hoey knew that many of these needy families fell below accepted middle-class standards, but she insisted that "in many borderline cases the family—which may have genuine values for the child in spite of its inadequacies—can be kept together if the parent can be offered practical and constructive guidance." State and local practice should be derived from objective criteria laid down in federal and state law, so that equitable provision be made for all families with eligible dependent children. This meant more than determination of eligibility and a cash grant, basic as these were. Equally important were services to help the family deal with problems of housing and health, and if necessary, to provide guidance in planning for the well-being of the children in the family setting. The overall goal was "adequate and appropriate assistance and service for each child and each family in accordance with its particular needs."[25]

After considerable study of alternatives, the board decided to try the usual inducement offered in a federal-state program: more money. As the law then stood, the federal share in ADC was one-third, with a maximum of eighteen dollars for the first child and twelve dollars for each additional child, no specific allowance for the mother. For the participating states, the monthly payment per family averaged $31.29. Except in the higher payment states, most families could not get along without supplementation from another source—work outside the home or assistance from general relief. ADC looked particularly inequitable when compared with OAA. The average ADC family of 3.5 persons received less than half the amount of money granted to a sole recipient of OAA. With such facts on the line, there was good reason to expect favorable action to increase the amount of federal financial participation, and to raise the maximum.[26]

In their final form the administration's recommendations for the 1939 amendments included three proposals directed exclusively at Title IV: (1) grants to states to be authorized on a 50 percent matching basis as in OAA and AB; (2) the federal maximum for payments to individual children to be increased, although no definite amounts were suggested; and (3) the age limit to be raised from sixteen to eighteen years for children regularly attending school. However, several other proposed amendments would, if adopted, bear significantly on ADC. On the public assistance side was the radical scheme for variable grants to states, the restriction of assistance to needy individuals and the requirement that all income and resources be considered in establishing need. On the insurance side was the very important addition of survivors' (widows and dependents) insurance to Title II. The proposal viewed as most important was the scheme to change the federal match from the uniform 50 percent to a formula related to a state's fiscal capacity. The board was deeply concerned about the extremely low public assistance payments—to the aged as well as dependent children and the blind—that were common in the poorer southern and southwestern states. Many of these states also had long waiting lists of applicants. By allowing for some degree of equalization between wealthy and poor states, "variable" grants would help the poor states bring their assistance payments to a health and decency standard and extend coverage and, at the same time, quiet demands for a federal takeover of OAA.

As enacted into law, the 1939 amendments extended social insurance coverage to widows caring for minor children of insured workers, authorized 50 percent matching for ADC, and increased

the age limit from sixteen to eighteen years with the school atten-
dance proviso. Eligibility under each of the public assistance programs had to be based on establishment of need after consideration
of income and resources available to the applicant. The variable
grants scheme and the increase in the ADC maximum were rejected.[27]

During the clearance process on the 1939 amendments proposal,
the Bureau of the Budget, citing the president's desire to extend
greater protection to children, expressed a desire to force the states
to apply any increase in federal funding for ADC directly to that
program. Assistance payments to current recipients should be
raised, additional families assisted, or a combination of both instituted. States should be prevented from diverting savings in ADC
to other programs. The board, not least the Bureau of Public Assistance, while alert to this danger, saw a greater one on the horizon.
Surely special conditions placed upon the states could not be con-
fined to ADC. Although the administration had not recommended an
increase in federal funding for OAA, it was expected that such an
attempt—probably successful—would be made once the bill
reached Congress. Under these circumstances it seemed preferable
to make all additional federal funds freely available to the states.
Similar thinking influenced the decision not to place a dollar
amount on the recommendation for an increase in the ADC maximum.

In a letter drafted by the general counsel's office and approved by
the Office of Research and Statistics and the Bureau of Public
Assistance, Altmeyer gave the Bureau of the Budget the board's
reasons for opposing special conditions to the ADC increase. After
considering the possible results of imposing such conditions in
relation to OAA and AB as well as ADC, the board had concluded that
"the disadvantages outweigh the advantages since in some states it
might prevent desirable readjustment of the expenditures made for
various social services financed in part through federal grants." As to
ADC specifically, Altmeyer judged it "practically certain that almost
every state will spend at least as much and probably more . . . than
it has been spending in the past since that is a field that has been
relatively neglected." As to OAA, some states might be able to lower
their expenditures for this category and apply the money to more
adequate financing of ADC and other social service programs.

As Cates emphasizes, the board's desire to protect the old age insurance program probably weighed heavily in its decision in this matter as in many others. It does not follow that ADC was abandoned. On the contrary, Altmeyer knew as well as Hoey that more liberal funding of ADC was possible only in the presence of restraint in OAA. The ADC program did grow, both in numbers of recipients and in expenditures. So did OAA but not by nearly as much. ADC recipients—families and children—increased 14.3 percent from June 1940 through June 1941; expenditures rose 22 percent during this period. The increase in OAA recipients was 10.1 percent; expenditures rose 11.3 percent.

In reporting these increases the board stopped short of assigning a direct cause and effect relationship to liberalized federal financial participation, pointing out that other factors were also involved. However, the evidence seemed sufficient to indicate that "a considerable rise in total payments to recipients has resulted from the higher matching ratio or maximum monthly amounts" under the 1939 amendments. At the same time, the board expressed regret at the failure to offer support to the poorer states through variable grants and renewed its recommendation for reconsideration of this approach to improvements in public assistance.[28]

Altmeyer predicted that about 20 percent of potential ADC children would collect insurance beginning in the next decade, and that the numbers would increase as coverage was extended. If this turned out to be correct, many of the "nice families" would never appear at the door of the welfare office. Although the Bureau of Public Assistance renewed its attempt to get the states to break away from the mothers' pension–Children's Bureau philosophy, it was in no position to take its message directly to local communities where decisions on eligibility were made. By law, the bureau was restricted to working at the state level. By custom, the bureau could offer advice to states only when asked to do so. During the 1939 hearings on the amendments, Altmeyer received a number of sharp questions from congressmen about supposed interference from regional representatives.[29]

By the early 1940s, Hoey and her staff could cite some progress toward a more liberal interpretation of ADC, but the program continued to fall far short of the bureau's ideal. During World War II years, ADC rolls dropped. But those families that stayed on were forced to subsist on very low assistance payments.[30]

Not content with its own studies and analyses and far from content with the seeming failure of the ADC program to fulfill its promise, the Bureau of Public Assistance employed Grace Marcus, a social work leader in the private sector, as a full-time consultant during 1943–1944. Although Marcus agreed with the bureau that the mothers' pension tradition constituted a drag, that maximums on federal financial participation led to undesirable restrictions and inadequate assistance payments, and that state and local general assistance funds were insufficient to meet need not covered by ADC, she found no way to reach the mutually desired goal—assistance to all needy children—through the instrument of ADC. On the contrary, she was convinced that ADC "as a category" was "fundamentally defective." To work well, an assistance category must be easily defined in objective terms, as was the case with old-age assistance and aid to the blind. Categories such as these called attention to characteristics of the group that were easily accepted by the public as "innocent and justifiable reasons for dependency." Not so with ADC:

> Children eligible for aid to dependent children must be sorted out of the mass of dependent needy children according to combinations of parental circumstances, and of these circumstances only death is easily determined and accepted as an objective cause of need. In actuality, the characteristics of parental absence and incapacity undermine the appeal that a category for children might otherwise carry, and they divert, rather than strengthen, the concern with need.

The more Marcus commented, the more she sounded like the welfare agencies out in the field. No wonder the public assistance worker tended to play it safe, she remarked. In actual practice it was very hard to draw the line between absence, unemployment, and nonsupport. Even more difficult to determine was incapacity:

> To escape from the present narrow constructions of incapacity that recognize only the extreme and incurable conditions is to risk irresponsible and slipshod acceptance of all sorts of complaints and behavior as evidence of mental incapacity. This risk would be so grave that it is socially wiser to accept the present exclusion of real mental incapacities as an injustice to be met only as adequate public health facilities can be established.

Good social worker that she was, Marcus also expressed concern about the program's underlying tendency to encourage family breakup. It was not so much that fathers left home to put the family on ADC as it was that being on the rolls stood in the way of reconciliation.

Since ADC was not meeting and, Marcus thought, could not meet the physical, psychological and social needs of children, the program should be replaced:

> As middle ground between some such measure as children's allowances and a comprehensive general assistance program covering the need of all families with children, whatever the cause of need, aid to dependent children has had some justification, but this justification exists only as long as it is impossible to obtain a better provision.

As published in the February 1945 *Social Security Bulletin*, the Marcus article encouraged action for legislative change. This, then, was one way the bureau might go—seek a general assistance category or a system of children's allowances. The bureau decided to promote an amendment to authorize federal financial participation in general assistance when a favorable opportunity developed.[31]

Meanwhile, a careful reading of Marcus's report opened up another possibility. Though no specific recommendation had been made, the report contained several pointed references to requisite qualifications and abilities of welfare agency staff. With this approach very much in mind already, the bureau determined to emphasize the need for experienced social workers. The 1939 Amendments had stipulated that state plans must provide for "establishment and maintenance of personnel standards on a merit basis." Not necessarily social workers, to be sure, but that is another story. And in 1949, the Social Security Administration recommended the addition of a general assistance category. Congress refused to go this far but did agree to pick up a large part of this group for federal matching under a new title—Aid to the Permanently and Totally Disabled.[32]

The public assistance programs established under the Social Security Act were, and, in many respects continue to be, integral to the comprehensive concept—the safety net—signed into law by President Franklin Roosevelt fifty years ago. That public assistance has been overtaken by social insurance is a fact of history, and like all significant historical developments, it did not just happen. From the president on down, the leaders of the administration greatly preferred insurance. But for nearly one-half of social security's existence, Old Age Assistance was the larger program, not only making payments to the needy aged who were not covered by old-age insurance, but also supplementing insurance payments that were insufficient to support persons according to a standard of health and decency. During these years the two programs very much needed each other.

The eventual triumph of old-age insurance was greatly assisted—perhaps unknowingly—by the social workers. Had Hoey and her bureau relaxed in the face of the flat-grant movement, sided with the general counsel, allowed the old-age pension philosophy to go unquestioned, who knows what the outcome would have been? But then, of course, they would not have been social workers.

In retrospect, it seems plausible also that once the social workers set the Aid to Dependent Children program on a liberalizing course they—again with the best of intentions—stripped it of its viability as a category. Today we have social security, Supplemental Security Income (ssi), and "welfare." ssi includes three public assistance programs that parallel insurance titles of the act—the aged, the blind, and the disabled. This program has been federalized, financed from general revenues and administered by employees of the Social Security Administration in its district offices. Surviving widows have for a long time now presented their claim for themselves and their children at social security offices. Only the Aid to Families with Dependent Children remains a state administered welfare program, a despised program.

In the development of policy and administration, differences of interpretation and approach among members of the Social Security Board and administration led to lively debate but seldom if ever to acrimonious conflict. At the top and through the ranks, the persons in charge were bureaucrats in the best sense—young, bright, creative, hardworking, dedicated. It never occurred to them to undermine one program in order to advance another, much less to go about trying to redistribute wealth on any grand scale. Rather they hewed to the law that had been approved by duly elected representatives in a capitalist democracy.

Notes

Abbreviations: bpa, Bureau of Public Assistance; fdr Library, Franklin D. Roosevelt Library; fsa, Federal Security Agency; na, National Archives;

NFRC, National Federal Records Center; RG, Record Group; SSA, Social Security Administration; SSB, Social Security Board.

1. Arthur J. Altmeyer, *The Formative Years of Social Security* (Madison: University of Wisconsin Press, 1966) pp. 167–68; 272–73.
2. Martha Derthick, *Policymaking for Social Security* (Washington, DC: Brookings Institution, 1979) pp. 159–60.
3. Jerry R. Cates, *Insuring Inequality: Administrative Leadership in Social Security, 1935–54* (Ann Arbor: University of Michigan Press, 1983) p. 104.
4. Josephine Chapin Brown, *Public Relief, 1929–1939* (New York: Holt, Rinehart and Winston, 1940; reprinted by Octagon Books, 1971) pp. 304–06; Letters, Perkins to Dorothy Kahn, Nov. 16, 1934 and Kahn to Perkins, Nov. 19, 1934, NA RG 47, Committee on Economic Security, Public Employment and Public Assistance; Informal Report of a Special Committee Advisory to the President's Committee on Economic Security, Nov. 24, 1934, signed by Dorothy Kahn and Walter West, NA RG 47, Committee on Economic Security, Public Employment and Public Assistance, Minutes of Meetings.
5. Derthick, *Policymaking for Social Security*, p. 160; *Social Security Bulletin, Annual Statistical Supplement*, 1983, Tables 158, 183. Aid to the Blind continues under Supplemental Security Income.
6. Charles McKinley and Robert W. Frase, *Launching Social Security, 1935–1937* (Madison: University of Wisconsin Press, 1970) pp. 180–81; Edwin E. Witte, *Development of the Social Security Act* (Madison: University of Wisconsin Press, 1962) pp. 71, 162–63; Altmeyer, *Formative Years of Social Security*, pp. 36–37. Old Age Insurance was referred to as Old Age Benefits until after the Supreme Court decision in 1937.
7. Blanche D. Coll, *Perspectives in Public Welfare* (Washington, DC: Department of Health, Education, and Welfare, 1969) pp. 35–62; Brown, *Public Relief*, Chap. 2; Roy Lubove, *The Professional Altruist* (Cambridge: Harvard University Press, 1965) Chaps. 1–4; John H. Ehrenreich, *The Altruistic Imagination* (Ithaca: Cornell University Press, 1985) Chaps. 2,4.
8. Brown, *Public Relief*, pp. 184–86, 229–30; Harry L. Hopkins, "The Developing National Program of Relief," *Proceedings, National Conference of Social Work*, 1933, pp. 66–67; Josephine Brown as quoted in *The Survey*, July 1935, pp. 217–18. *See also* Bonnie Fox Schwartz, *The Civil Works Administration, 1933–1934* (Princeton: Princeton University Press, 1984) for an extensive discussion of the social worker-social engineer conflict in one Hopkins public works agency.
9. Joanna C. Colcord and Russell H. Kurtz, "Unemployment and Community Action," *The Survey*, Jan. 1935, pp. 23–24; Apr. 1935, p. 111; Jun. 1935, pp. 183–84; Brown, *Public Relief*, pp. 252–53, 275–77, 308, 395–97; BPA, Transcript, Staff Meeting, Sep. 29, 1938, NFRC, BPA files, RG 47, 321.2.2.

10. Corrington Gill, "How Many Are Unemployable?" *The Survey*, Jan. 1935, pp. 4–5.

11. Lubove, *Professional Altruist*, pp. 127, 131–37; Ehrenreich, *Altruistic Imagination*, pp. 108–10.

12. Blanche D. Coll, "Hoey, Jane Margueretta," *Notable American Women: The Modern Period* (Cambridge: Harvard University Press, 1980) pp. 341–43; Interview, Jane M. Hoey, Oral History Collection, Columbia University; Memorandum, Perkins for the President with attachments, Aug. 15, 1935, FDR Library, OF8, OF1710a.

13. SSB, *Annual Reports*, 1936, pp. 29, 35, 37; and 1937, pp. 27–28, 32, 36.

14. Memo, Eliot to Bane, Dec. 6, 1935, NA RG 47, SSA, Executive File Unit 600; SSB, *Annual Report*, 1936, p. 31; Altmeyer, "If," *Proceedings of Social Security Conference*, Nov. 16–17, 1960, pp. 13–14; Memo, Eliot to Executive Director, sub: Need of Applicant as Condition of Approval of Plans for Public Assistance, May 3, 1937, NA RG 47, SSA Central Files 621.1.

15. Robert T. Lansdale, *et al, The Administration of Old Age Assistance* (Chicago: Public Administration Service, Social Science Research Council, 1939) pp. 83–84, 86–87; SSB, *Annual Report*, 1938, pp. 102–03; Memo, Hoey to John J. Corson, sub: Monthly Report, BPA (November), Dec. 7, 1937, NFRC, BPA 317.2/21.2, Oct. 1937; Eveline M. Burns, *Social Security and Public Policy* (New York: McGraw-Hill, 1956) pp. 22–23.

16. Lansdale, *Administration of Old Age Assistance*, pp. 86–88; Burns, *Social Security and Public Policy*, pp. 21–25.

17. Memo, Hoey to Corson, sub: Monthly Report, BPA (November), Dec. 7, 1937.

18. "Analysis of Grants to 586,000 Recipients of Old Age Assistance," *Social Security Bulletin*, Nov. 1938, pp. 13, 15–17; Property and Income Provisions in Approved State Plans for Old Age Assistance, Nov. 20, 1937, NA RG 47, SSA Chairman's Files, 632.13, Payments; Memo, Gertrude Gates, BPA for Chief, Division of Public Assistance Research, Nov. 23, 1940, sub: Reports on Consideration of All Resources, NFRC, BPA file 621, Jul. 1940; Transcript, Luncheon Meeting, Dec. 14, 1938, NFRC, BPA file 321.2.2, Dec. 14, 1938, Conference.

19. Memo, Hoey to Bane, Oct. 15, 1936, sub: Amendments to Social Security Act, NA RG 47, SSA Chairman's Files, 011.1 Public Assistance.

20. Transcript, Luncheon Meeting, Dec. 14, 1938.

21. Notes of Proceedings of the Social Security Board, Informal Notes, May 4, 1937, NA RG 47.

22. Public Law 379, 76th Cong. approved Aug. 10, 1939 (53 Stat. 1360) The Social Security Act Amendments of 1939; Altmeyer, *Formative Years of Social Security*, pp. 101–03, 106, 111, 113.

23. SSB, *Annual Reports*, 1938, pp. 99–101; 1939, pp. 116–18.

24. SSB, *Social Security in America* (Washington, DC: Social Security Board, 1937) pp. 248–49; Security for Children, Summary of the Recommendations of the U.S. Children's Bureau. . . , Dec. 1, 1934, NA RG 47, Committee on Economic Security, Advisory Council, Misc.; *Report of the Committee on Economic Security*, p. 36; House Ways and Means Committee, Hearings on HR 4120, Economic Security Act, p. 496.

25. SSB, *Annual Reports*, 1936, p. 30; 1938, p. 76; Jane M. Hoey and Zilpha C. Franklin, "Aid to Dependent Children," *Social Work Year Book 1939* (New York: Russell Sage Foundation, 1939) pp. 30–31; U.S. Department of Commerce, Bureau of the Census, *Historical Statistics of the United States*, Bicentennial Edition, Series A 160–171; B 28–35; B 216–220, 1940 figures.

26. Hoey and Franklin, *Social Work Year Book 1939*, p. 34.

27. Altmeyer, *Formative Years of Social Security*, pp. 90–93, 96–98, 104–07, 111–13; Public Law 379, 76th Cong., approved Aug. 10, 1939 (53 Stat. 1360) The Social Security Amendments of 1939.

28. Ltrs, D. W. Bell, Bureau of the Budget, to Altmeyer, Mar. 18, 1939 and Altmeyer to Bell, Mar. 23, 1939, NA RG 47, SSB Central Files, 011.1; Cates, *Insuring Inequality*, pp. 133–34; Transcript, BPA Joint Field Staff Meeting with Bureau of Employment Security, 1939 Amendments to the Social Security Act, Oct. 2, 1939, p. 5, NFRC, RG 47, BPA files, 011.1; SSB, *Annual Reports*, 1940, pp. 101, 110; 1941, pp. 111, 115–16, 119, 194–95.

29. Bureau of Public Assistance–Bureau of Employment Security, Joint Staff Meeting, 1939 Amendments to the Social Security Act, Oct. 2, 1939, NFRC, BPA files, 011.1; House Committee on Ways and Means, *Social Security Act Amendments of 1939*, Hearings, pp. 2382, 2393–94.

30. Division of Administrative Surveys, BPA, SSB, FSA, *Aid to Dependent Children: A Study in Six States*, PA Report No. 2, Nov. 1941; Statistics and Analysis Division, BPA, SSA, FSA, *Families Receiving Aid to Dependent Children*, Oct. 1942; *Social Security Bulletin, Annual Statistical Supplement*, 1983, p. 248.

31. Grace M. Marcus, "Reappraising Aid to Dependent Children as a Category," *Social Security Bulletin*, Feb. 1945, pp. 3–5.

32. Public Law 379, 76th Cong. approved Aug. 10, 1939 (53 Stat. 1360); P.L. 734, 81st Cong. (64 Stat. 477), approved Aug. 28, 1950.

11

Speculating in Social Security Futures

The Perils of Payroll Tax Financing, 1939–1950

Mark H. Leff

With the possible exception of his stamp collection, perhaps nothing gave Franklin Roosevelt more satisfaction than his social security system. And for good reason. No legacy of the New Deal has been as prominent or enduring; it is the linchpin of the American welfare state. But this result did not obtain as smoothly and automatically as one might assume. I will be arguing here, in fact, that the early years of financing the old-age insurance program demonstrate considerable uncertainty about the program's direction, and that the system revealed vulnerabilities that would reemerge in the recent social security crisis.

In pursuing the checkered history of social security finance after the initial formulation of old-age insurance, I found myself, in short order, in a rather anomalous period. Analysts who chart and interpret the system's evolution tend to use as their primary reference points the inauguration of the program in 1935, and the steady, though not entirely regular, expansion of benefits and costs that occurred after 1950. The experience of the fifteen years between 1935 and 1950 fits rather oddly into this general pattern. The maximum employee and employer tax for old-age insurance has indeed risen from thirty dollars each at its inception to well over two thousand dollars by 1985. The first decade and a half of the program was scheduled to be part of that growth pattern, with tax increases programmed at three-year intervals until reaching a ceiling in 1949. Instead, in 1949, a quarter of the way home to 1985's sixty-nine-fold increase in the top employee tax payment, the maximum tax still held at thirty dollars. Again and again, in 1939 and then seven more times between 1942 and 1947, Congress turned back scheduled tax increases. It has become a cliché to talk about the extraordinary power and influence of the Social Security Board/Social Security Administration (hereafter ssb/ssa); yet the ssb/ssa almost unceasingly opposed the freeze of the payroll tax and lost every time.[1]

This essay, then, examines a slice of social security financial politics from an unfamiliar, fluid period. Although we tend today to see the old-age insurance system through the prism of its expansion and of ssa influence, the 1940s represent a fundamentally different context: before the modern pattern of expansion culminating in fiscal crisis was established, and before the scope of debate over the program's future direction had been critically narrowed. By freeing the early years of social security finance from the effects of the distortive lens of modern social security politics, the early dynamics of the system may more truly emerge, and, paradoxically, the choices inherent in today's system may be clarified.

Even at a very basic level, one can offer a ready resolution for this paradoxical contrast between the modern pattern of rising social security taxes and the 1940s pattern of inertia. A little knowledge, plus a nodding acquaintance with certain common assumptions about political behavior, might turn the trick. Congressmen, one can fairly assume, never seek to increase taxes if they can avoid it. In the late 1930s and 1940s, they *could* avoid it, because:

1. They saw no need to build up a reserve fund. Their short-term outlooks immunized them to FDR's insistence on stowing away payroll taxes from the system's early years in a reserve fund whose interest yield would help finance future pensions. In fact, the amassed trust fund, like the payroll tax, was seen only as a potential source for current pensions.

2. A tax freeze would never become a damaging political issue. Public understanding of social security finances was very limited. In a 1941 poll, a high percentage of Americans did not even realize that paying social security taxes would qualify them for an automatic retirement pension; if voters did not understand this, their comprehension of the very complex financial role of a reserve fund must

have been scant indeed. Accordingly, public pressures for higher taxes to expand the reserve fund (and thus secure their payroll tax investment in a future annuity) were negligible.[2]

3. Pension costs were low. The high ratio of contributors to beneficiaries in the early years of the program made it possible to cover current disbursements with a minimal tax rate. Moreover, social security taxes are obviously related to the level of benefits that they need to support. Thus, until recent years, it has been the norm to pair tax hikes with benefit increases. Though there was an important revision of social security benefits in 1939, there were no further benefit increases in the 1940s, a period in which the ratio of pensions to preretirement wages dropped to the lowest level in the history of the system. This may be a significant step to resolving the paradox: one could simply find out why the benefits failed to increase, and an explanation of the strange stasis of the tax rates would follow (the two sides in the tax freeze debate said as much themselves, each accusing the other of using recondite financial rationales either to block or to facilitate future hikes in benefits).

These explanations, which contain a powerful core of truth and common sense, nevertheless beg several questions and oversimplify others. The rather cavalier treatment of the reserve fund in the 1940s is less an explanation than a clue to more vexed questions about the rationale and eventual character of the system. The inchoate state of public opinion on old-age insurance also cuts more than one way. The congressmen of the 1940s, after all, bore no electoral guilt for the tax increases mandated in the 1935 law. Simple inactivity, no stranger to the congressional job description, could have allowed the 1935 provisions to go into effect. While imprecise public conceptions about the program were unlikely to produce a groundswell of pressure for a fortified reserve fund, neither is there convincing evidence that voters were sufficiently informed and committed to penalize congressional acquiescence in the automatic tax increases. In short, public pressures in the 1940s on a financial issue that was neither highly salient nor well understood do not seem a solid centerpiece to any explanation of the repeated, often eleventh-hour decisions to forestall the mandated increases. A focus on the third explanatory factor, the temporary stabilization of benefits, would have its advantages. The temptation is great to flee the technical world of financial considerations (even Senator Arthur Vandenberg, the main sponsor of tax freezes in the late 1930s and 1940s, introduced the subject with an apology that "this subject is technically dull,"[3] scarcely a heartening sign to a historian intending to devote months of his life to it) to explore the more human world of politics and the changing status of the elderly. And political explanations, at least on a surface level, seem readily available: the subordination of domestic programs (especially for nonworker soldiers) once the U.S. entered World War II, the suspicion that the wartime economic growth that would have allowed higher pensions would only be temporary, and Republican congressional ascendancy in the war's immediate aftermath. But, alas, it will become clear that benefit payments were only part of a more complex calculus of decision-making that prompted the tax freezes. So to follow the rabbit down that hole by making a detailed examination of the benefits freeze would only divert me from the central issue of financing. Finally, the impact of the benefits calculus should not be oversimplified. The ease with which the small pool of initial annuitants could be covered carried with it the corollary knowledge that this was perforce a temporary situation; even popular periodicals showed awareness of an inevitable day of reckoning.

While none of these qualifications to the basic line of common sense reasoning is determinant, taken collectively they prevent the analyst from dismissing too quickly the aberrant state of suspended animation into which the financing of old-age insurance fell after the program's inception. It is still necessary to explore more carefully the political and economic context in which Congress actively thwarted both the dictates of the Social Security Act of 1935 and the counsel of social security administrators. For what the stagnation of the 1940s represented was in some respects a deliberate suspension of construction of a partially completed edifice of old-age insurance. To see a fledgling program in a protracted state of arrested development should alert the observer to the probability that considerable disagreement about the character of the program lurks beneath the path of least resistance charted by Congress in 1939 and the 1940s. Of most concern, of course, is what this postponement portended for clear thinking on the future financial basis of the program.

Skewered on a Technicality?: The "Rule of Three"

On the surface, the tax freeze has an enticingly simple explanation. Congressional sponsors in World War II commonly observed that Congress had adopted a formula for determining the reserve level and that the reserve fund vastly exceeded that guideline so as to make further taxes superfluous.

Interestingly, the source of that guideline was Secretary of the Treasury Henry Morgenthau, who with FDR in 1935 had successfully pressed for a very different sort of old-age insurance, one structured to build up a large reserve in its first several decades in order to assure that the system would always be self-supporting. In 1939, however, Morgenthau, in throwing his support behind the effort to repeal the payroll tax hike scheduled for 1940, seemed to endorse a pay-as-you-go system in which each year's benefit obligations would be paid out of that year's payroll tax receipts (supplemented perhaps in the remote future by other government revenues). He no longer depicted the reserve fund as a financial pillar of the program; instead it would be a financial pillow, protecting it against any unforeseen drop in tax collections or jump in benefit outlays. In congressional testimony, the treasury secretary thus put forward the following confusing but simple formula: Estimate the maximum annual benefits that would need to be paid out over the next five years, and then set the reserve at no more than three times the expected benefits for that year.[4] Congress duly mandated that the Board of Trustees of the social security system should report if the reserve rose above the level prescribed by this "rule of three."[5]

Morgenthau, responding to SSB concerns, allowed for "a somewhat larger contingency reserve" during the first "few years" of unrepresentatively low benefits, citing difficulties of early forecasts and the need to cement public understanding of the need for payroll taxes.[6] In opposing later tax freezes, SSB leaders made the most of this codicil. But they were, often intentionally, missing the point.[7] In fact, treasury economic advisers had initially suggested a reserve of only "two years benefit payments when the system is mature"; they designed the multiple of three precisely to accommodate higher reserve ratios in the system's earliest years.[8] More importantly, the very principle behind Morgenthau's rule of three—the minimal reserve—was indeed inconsistent with the bloated reserve fund levels of World War II.

Before rushing to invest the rule of three with too much explanatory power in accounting for subsequent tax freezes, however, it is essential to recognize that the depth of commitment to this formula, even on the part of Morgenthau himself, is decidedly questionable.

The Morgenthau guideline is a case study—an instructive one for the early years of the Social Security Act—in how to make a fundamental decision without really trying. The primary impetus behind Morgenthau's testimony in 1939 was his desire to meet business demands for tax reduction. The widely-supported "contingency reserve" conception may be seen without undue exaggeration as the tail that ultimately wagged the dog, legitimizing the reduced reserve produced by the combined tax freeze and benefit rise.

In putting forward his "rule of three," Morgenthau—not the most systematic or technically astute thinker at his best—never had to confront its implications. Treasury actuarial estimates suggested no year—the near future included—in which it would be exceeded.[9] This allowed Morgenthau to more casually pass along the recommendation of his economic advisers, less as an endorsement of their intent to block any deflationary reserve accumulation than as a numerical dramatization of the sort of protective role that his proposed contingency reserve would play. The prospective operational irrelevance of the Morgenthau rule made it all the easier to focus on an immediate set of priorities—lower taxes for business, accelerated payments to aggrieved retirees, heightened economic growth—that subordinated the financial future of old-age insurance. A similar logic applied to Congress. It too accepted the Morgenthau rule with little regard for its possible consequences.

World War II brought an embarrassment of riches to complicate the Morgenthau guideline: prosperity, inflation, and new job opportunities for young and old alike doubled the predicted yield of payroll taxes and cut total benefit outlays to 50–55 percent of what had been expected.[10] They suddenly confronted an unanticipated future. By 1943, although payroll tax freezes had blocked scheduled increases, the reserve fund was even larger than had been projected on the basis of the higher scheduled tax rates: twenty times annual outlays, and more than eight times as high as maximum annual benefit payments over the next five years. SSB representatives could protest that the changed economic situation outmoded the "rule of three"—that wartime prosperity had greatly increased the future benefit claims of a more fully and profitably employed society—so that the current reserve fund/benefit ratio was terribly deceptive. Unfortunately, however, the Morgenthau rule had not been offered with any qualifiers to alter its application to changed economic circumstances. No one had dreamt that this guideline could be so vastly exceeded even while there was such a great gap between the actual tax rate and the premium needed to maintain the system over time. To invoke the expectations generated by the Morgenthau rule as decisive, however, would ultimately be unsatisfying, even had the treasury secretary himself or the Congress more carefully considered the rule's possible consequences. Only rarely do policy questions have the same dynamics as legal cases that can be won on clever technicalities. Succeeding invocations of this rule depicted it as a financial straitjacket. But it might better be seen as a ready rationale that helped ventilate more fundamental issues: the rejection of reserve financing and the absence of a clearly defined and widely assimilated vision of the future of the old-age insurance system.

The Case Against the Reserve Fund

The shifting economic conditions generated by World War II would have triggered debate over the size of the reserve even without the Morgenthau guideline. Accordingly, the question of payroll tax increases was bound to receive intensified scrutiny. That boded well for payroll tax freeze advocates, for the accumulation of a sizeable social security reserve fund had already shown signs of political untenability. The adjustments codified in the 1939 Social Security Amendments had made that eminently clear. The original conception of a huge prospective reserve fund had basically been a two-man show, introduced at the instance of Morgenthau and FDR over the objections of even hand-picked social security drafters. As I have argued elsewhere, the fiscal conservatism that motivated them backfired, at least over the next fifteen years, releasing forces that ironically undermined the fiscal soundness of old-age insurance. For the FDR/Morgenthau plan, with its scheduled tax hikes and snowballing reserve fund, proved shatteringly vulnerable—leaving the system in a state of financial drift in its early years. My earlier work has pointed to the emergence of a sprawling consensus in the late 1930s, running the ideological gamut from right to left, to challenge both this form of reserve financing and the tax increases that would further it.[11] A broad spectrum of labor and reformist interests condemned the original financial arrangements of old-age insurance as socially and economically pernicious. Seeking to use the social security system to redistribute income, many on the political left criticized a large reserve fund for placing the entire social security burden on regressive payroll taxes instead of on supplementary government revenues drawn more heavily from the rich. They went beyond attacks on the adverse social impact of the payroll tax to denounce the macroeconomic effects of the reserve fund that it sustained. Generally sympathetic to Keynesian or other deficit-spending theories that stressed inadequate demand in the economy, these critics feared that the reserve fund drained away needed purchasing power and was thus dangerously deflationary—a theory that seemed validated when (as some had predicted) the introduction of social security taxes was closely followed by the punishing recession of 1937.[12]

Business leaders and other more conservative forces reinforced this pressure from the left. They agreed that the social security reserve put a severe crimp in the economy. They carried their antipathy to the reserve even further, fearing that it might be invested in such socialist schemes as public housing or take-overs of private corporations. Most prominently, they lobbied for lower taxes. And even Republican commitments to increase old-age insurance pensions in the near future (often made in pursuit of political support from the Townsend Movement) militated for drawing down the reserve. With Treasury Secretary Morgenthau pulled into the tax reduction effort to "appease" business into recovery, and with many social security "experts" hostile to a large reserve in the first place, the pressure to cut back was irresistible. Social security founder Edwin Witte and SSB Chairman Altmeyer were highly skeptical, but despite their congressional testimony opposing the tax freeze, they could neither block it nor prevent the substitution of a lax schedule for a "contingency reserve." Witte's response to Morgenthau's "unsound" concessions in social security finance was "a sinking feeling about the future of old-age insurance" and a prediction that the new financing principles could culminate in future congressional payroll tax freezes.[13] Not surprisingly, the SSB and its entourage remained particularly leery of laxity in social security finance, even when the treasury switched to support of a payroll tax freeze in 1939. It was essential, the board explained, "that any method of financing that is proposed should take into account all probable future disbursements so that the interests of both the prospective beneficiaries and the general taxpayers may be properly safeguarded."[14] This concern with the future of the program—understandably intense in the organization administering the system and among the generation that founded it—offered a very hostile environment indeed for the operation of the Morgenthau rule. In their projections, a tax freeze and the Morgenthau rule jeopardized the system's future. The system might either explode—with benefits rocketing once the fiscal discipline of a tight connection between benefits and the payroll tax was severed—or it might implode, as continued refusals to raise payroll taxes might starve the program out of needed funds.[15]

The mere fact that these SSB concerns were overcome in the late 1930s did not definitively assure continued refusals to raise the payroll tax. Macroeconomic arguments on the deflationary impact of the reserve fund and the dangers of piling a tax increase on an already crippled business sector had been important in blocking the scheduled tax increase for 1940. These concerns were, of course, fated to lose force in the midst of the World War II boom. In fact, economic arguments cut the other way in World War II. A strong case—though a tricky one given the effort of the SSB to promote social security as a self-contained insurance program whose finances should be totally determined by its future obligations—could be made (and was insistently made by the Treasury Department and FDR) that the deflationary effect of the payroll tax was just what the doctor ordered to curb wartime inflationary pressures. At minimum, opponents of the freeze pointed out, the transition from depression to prosperity removed the excuse that the economy could not bear the tax. On the contrary, "with the federal treasury badly in need of revenue and with the people and the corporations literally drunk with excess cash," the economy was in a better position to absorb a tax increase than might be true in later, less favorable, economic conditions.[16] The economic picture was more mixed in the war's aftermath, but persisting inflationary concerns undermined any macroeconomic rationale for lower payroll taxes.

A similar fate befell another pillar of the case for the tax freeze in the late 1930s. The very size of the original projected reserve was daunting—"eight times the amount of money then in circulation in the United States; nearly five times the amount of money in savings banks; enough money to buy all the farms in the United States, with $14 billion to spare."[17] Concern with this behemoth, along with the allied fear of social security funds financing socialist inroads into the private sector, tailed off in the 1940s. A much expanded economy and a much more visible government sector lowered the relative prominence of the social security reserve; the over two hundred billion dollar war debt could absorb it before it could move into more "dangerous" channels. Finally, the argument that payroll taxes burdened the poor and favored the rich lost some of its force. This reflected the evaporation of pressures from left of the New Deal, especially the tendency to mobilize in defense of social security and the New Deal rather than snapping at those programs for not going far enough. As had always been true, some conservative critics were willing to adopt the regressivity argument as their own. They asserted the unjustifiability of "levying an income tax on the lowest income group in our country and giving them no exemptions whatever,"[18] especially since these taxes were used to fund benefits that exceeded the actuarial value of contributions even for the wealthy. But such arguments could no longer make the impact that they had in the New Deal years.

Yet with all these factors having shifted against it, the movement for a payroll tax freeze met with repeated successes. Roosevelt administration support for the scheduled taxes—extending to presidential letters, veto threats, a critical paragraph on the freeze in the overridden veto of the Revenue Act of 1943, and ssb and Treasury Department testimony and lobbying—all proved unavailing. The Truman administration's Treasury Department abandoned the fight altogether,[19] putting forward its own tax freeze in 1945 and acquiescing in the 1946 and 1947 freezes under the rationale that taxes could later be raised in conjunction with the administration's expansion of old-age insurance.[20]

Shifts within Congress partially account for the strength of the tax freeze forces. In the 1940s, the congressional conservative coalition grew substantially—a crucial factor, since urban liberal supporters of expanded New Deal reform comprised the core of support for higher payroll taxes. In World War II, the payroll tax suffered the fate of other New Deal domestic measures that could not forge convincing links to the war effort; as the one tax specifically earmarked for a social, nonwar expenditure, it proved especially vulnerable to resentments over rising tax bills. And Republican gains in the war's wake provided a still less hospitable atmosphere.

Yet the financial and political vulnerabilities of old-age insurance transcended these congressional shifts. The 1939 amendments had already sent storm signals by unceremoniously—and permanently—jettisoning the original 1935 provision for a large reserve that would carry a significant share of the future old-age insurance load. Support for minimizing the reserve remained quite strong in the 1940s, partly because it could be formulated as a question of whether, or how much, the government's domestic functions and commitments should be expanded. The endlessly repeated argument was that social security finance socked the taxpayer coming and going. First, the payroll tax itself, through the subterfuge of a trust fund that was immediately invested in government bonds, would be squandered through increased spending "for whatever fantastic scheme may be incubated within the inner circle of the boondoggling fraternity of the New Deal."[21] Payroll taxes paid in for old-age insurance would thus be paid out for God-knows-what; in the cryptic words of Senator Robert Taft, "we don't want to build a house that someone else is going to occupy."[22] Then, with the taxes already spent, the public would have to pay again when the pension obligations came due, partly in the form of interest on this paper reserve. In vain, social security defenders itemized a somewhat difficult counterargument to what they saw as this specious if intuitively persuasive scenario: a. *Someone* had to purchase the government debt; b. By purchasing government securities, the Trust Fund simply transferred the destination of future interest on the debt (to social security benefits instead of to those who otherwise would have held the bonds); c. Accumulation of a reserve thus significantly reduced burdens on future generations, since it allowed them to provide for the elderly through interest payments (on the government bonds) that they would have owed anyway.

Freeze proponents still were not convinced, arguing that Trust Fund purchases would not replace those of private holders but would instead somehow generate new government spending. Just as dangerously, the very existence of this phantom reserve, some feared, would encourage still greater promises to current workers for future pensions.[23] Because of these fears, it was often the case, confusingly from today's vantage point, that freeze advocates supported liberalized old-age pension payments for most current retirees precisely in order to draw down the reserve and thus avert both the long-term expansion of the old-age insurance system and the short-term expansion of other government programs.

To fully understand how such a perspective could gain a foothold, one must appreciate the political imperatives of a pay-as-you-go system of social insurance. In the first years of any such system, while workers are building up their pension rights through their payroll taxes, relatively few elderly qualify for these pensions, and the ratio of taxpayers to pension recipients is naturally quite high; contributions of a few tenths of a percent could suffice to cover the benefits for the earliest annuitants. In the 1940s, it was still possible to take advantage of this politically pleasant situation. In fact, the high contributor/beneficiary ratio, combined with the unexpectedly large revenues, seemed to assure continued old-age insurance surpluses for a decade or more.[24] Down the road, as the pool of annuitants grew relative to contributors, future pensioners might pay much more and get relatively much less. Because the short and intermediate-term picture was so bright, and because the reserve fund was itself suspect as an instrument of current and future liberal policy, it was all too easy to defer consideration of such possible inequities.

Visions of the Future for Old-Age Insurance

To argue that the social security financing debates were often guided by short-term considerations is not to imply that certain long-term interests were not being served as well—albeit sometimes very passively. Nor should it obscure the concerns of those who *did* have a definite vision for the future of old-age insurance. This section will examine the alternative visions considered in the debates of the 1940s. As I argued at the outset, these prove to be more diverse than contemporary social orthodoxy might lead one to expect.

The starting point is almost axiomatic—a social security program, more than most government programs, must make provision for the distant future. More is involved here than selfless consideration for future generations, of course; a worker's security and thus perhaps eagerness to shell out payroll tax payments is dependent on expectations of future pension rights. To this imperative, participants in the financing debate over old-age insurance responded in different ways. For tax freeze advocates, the long view presented special problems. They often responded by finessing the issue of the future altogether. On the one hand, they rejected the need to spell out a longterm view. They denied that a tax freeze fundamentally altered the prospects of the system and they scorned any capacity to foretell the future anyway. The most popular argument of all was to pooh-pooh the actuarial projections suggesting that a frozen tax rate would culminate in a whopping fiscal crisis in twenty years or so. Discrediting such forecasts was not a politically challenging task. Politicians are famed for time horizons that only extend to the next election and for their willingness to favor the present at the expense of the future; the longer-term perspective necessary to building a secure old-age insurance system could thus become a joke. "Why worry about something twenty years hence?" one freeze advocate chided Altmeyer.[25] It is true social security projections were hardly a shot in the dark, rooted as they were in established actuarial methods. Nevertheless, not until the general explosion of interest and methodological refinement in general forecasting techniques two decades hence would such long-term planning begin to seem more commonplace, if still unreliable and faintly disreputable.[26] To the precybernetic generation of the 1940s, large-scale social projections were akin to science fiction. Indicative of Washington's outlook on—even suspicion of—coherent long-term planning was the demise of the National Resources Planning Board in 1943. In such a climate, J. Douglas Brown could respond to predictions of rising social security deficits in the distant future with flippancy: "We'll all be dead."[27] "Après nous le deluge."[28]

This dismissive attitude was all the more natural because World War II had so drastically compromised the actuarial projections of only a few years before. As the Chairman of the Ways and Means Committee put it, the Social Security Board had provided "the wildest guessers with whom I have ever attempted to work."[29] Worse yet, freeze proponents could not fail to notice that there appeared to be method to their wildness; SSB representatives, in crying wolf, had underestimated future tax collections and overestimated prospective benefit outlays. Over the 1940s social security defenders suffered from too much good news: high employment rates and burgeoning incomes bettered the system's financial position over both the short- and long-term, largely because of the weighted benefit formula that prescribed a higher relative return to lower-income than higher-income contributors. The disinclination to come to terms with the future was thus intensified both by the

255

uncertainty of that future and by the recent improved status of the fund.

Advocates of a tax freeze had a further reason for failing to act on threats predicted for the remote future. While moving beyond the individualist notion that each wage earner helped pay his or her own way with taxes that built up a personal right to a pension, they argued a limited notion of social responsibility between young and old that discounted obligations to the future. Instead, under a pay-as-you-go system "each generation [would] provide for its own aged in terms of its own ability."[30] Under this formulation, future considerations were not entirely irrelevant. "The younger workers," it was explained, "get a quid pro quo for their current sacrifices in the Federal assurance that when they too are sixty-five they would similarly receive benefit payments provided by the output of goods and services by workers then on the job."[31] But advocates of a tax freeze were often content to leave the precise nature of that commitment to future generations.

This ambiguity on future benefits clashed with the definite moral and political commitments incorporated in the benefits schedule set down in the social security law. The difference was not coincidental. Some critics of higher social security taxes and a larger reserve denounced "the binding commitments it makes on future generations," accusing the government of "overpromising."[32] Thus, if a tax freeze lessened public assuredness of future pension rights, that might be all to the good.[33]

But other advocates of a tax freeze were both less conspiratorial and less rigorous in their analysis. Their view of the future of social security encompassed basic revisions of how the system would be financed, and/or how benefits would be calculated. They dismissed doubts about future financing with the assumption that government's general revenues would come to the rescue, or that the whole system might need to be changed by replacing the current benefits schedule with a uniform minimum pension.

Planning for a Government Contribution

We tend to forget today that one of the so-called fundamental principles of social security—that the system should be self-supporting, with no supplementary government contributions—was very far from etched in granite in the system's early years. From the earliest stages, drafters of old-age insurance had assumed some government contribution. Though President Roosevelt and Secretary Morgenthau overruled this government role, their rigorous self-supporting plan was in turn rejected by the 1937–38 Advisory Council, by the Social Security Board, by the Congress, and even, ultimately, by Morgenthau himself at the end of the 1930s. Most importantly, the Social Security Act Amendments of 1939 had incorporated what Edward Berkowitz has called "a vague promise that government revenues would enter the system sometime in the future."[34] Divining legislative intent, always a hazardous enterprise, is made particularly difficult by Congress's failure to make explicit provision for future general revenue contributions or to spell out legislative guidelines for dealing with the future deficit that it built into the program. But when the 1939 law expanded benefits over the near term while temporarily reducing taxes, even the failure of congressional committees to provide deficit forecasts beyond 1955 could not hide the fact that something would ultimately have to give. And since there was not yet enough faith in the economy to raise expectations that economic growth could bail out the system, supplements from the government's general revenue collections were the leading candidate. Thus, Senator Vandenberg stated categorically during the 1939 debate that "There must be a general public contribution to offset what would have been the contribution obtained through the interest on the reserve fund," and the Finance and Ways and Means Committee reports noted that either "other general taxes" or higher payroll taxes would be needed to fund any future revenue deficiencies once the system got past the ten to fifteen years in which the small reserve and taxes already authorized would suffice.[35]

To many, the message sent by Congress was not that obscure. Soon after the passage of the 1939 Amendments, J. Douglas Brown, who had chaired the 1937–38 Advisory Council, explained that in Congress's provision for a mere contingency reserve "the United States has adopted, in effect, the principle that the government should participate in the financing of the system by means of appropriating supplemental contributions."[36] By 1940 and 1941, federal officials were almost offhanded in their assessment that "it is now rather generally admitted" that an eventual government subsidy was "necessary" and "inevitable."[37]

To some extent, such comments were wishful thinking (the alternatives of lower benefits or frightfully high payroll taxes were both dreaded in the SSB). But this assumption, though not universally shared (members of the House Ways and Means Committee in the 1940s were particularly likely to assert their commitment to the system's future self-support), extended well beyond the SSB. The Senate Finance Committee went so far as to declare in 1943 that a government commitment to subsidize old-age insurance if needed to maintain its solvency "is inherent in the decision made by Congress in 1939" to "change to the basis of contingent reserves" and pay-as-you-go financing.[38] A 1944 Senate floor amendment, which was retained in conference and thus entered the law, went one step beyond this. Introduced at the initiative of the SSB and with the support of the leader of the profreeze forces Arthur Vandenberg, this amendment authorized a government subsidy to the Trust Fund whenever necessary to cover benefit payments.[39]

There is probably less to this proviso than meets the eye. It was more a consoling symbol than a firm provision for general revenue financing. To Senator Vandenberg, it represented a declaration of good intentions, to show that he was not using the tax freeze to slash future benefits; for the SSB and the sponsor Senator Murray, it was a way to hold Senator Vandenberg to his promises of future solvency while underlining their concern that some provision be made for the future deficits generated by the freeze.[40] Still, this so-called Murray Amendment survived a vote by the House to repeal it in 1946 and stayed on the books until the 1950 Amendments.[41] And it did seem, as *Newsweek* pointed out, to clearly establish "the intent of Congress to use general tax funds" when necessary to meet old-age insurance commitments.[42] This was not merely a defensive gesture. Senator Vandenberg himself termed it a "general social obligation" to which Congress was "now committed."[43] Many now took such a future government contribution for granted; for example, a briefing book for the secretary of the treasury in 1949 stated categorically that "Present law has already recognized that [government contributions] will be necessary ultimately."[44]

One should be cautious in drawing conclusions from this congressional commitment. It would be silly, for example, to assume that any large number of congressmen acted in pursuance of the more refined rationales (such as asserting a general public responsibility for old-age security or counteracting the regressive effect of payroll taxes) for a general revenue role. The allowance for supplementary government financing was too casual for that. But that is precisely the point. The prospect of general revenue contributions served the convenient purpose of justifying an often short-sighted effort to shift current tax burdens to the future, but the general revenue authorization would not have prevailed if the notion of a self-contained, self-supporting old-age insurance system had been sacrosanct. The lack of devotion to this sort of self-sustaining system smoothed the way for a payroll tax freeze.

The Flat Pension Alternative

Also contributing to the freeze was a more frontal assault on the received principles of old-age insurance: the proposal to provide a uniform pension to all the elderly, regardless of past contributions. This is another chapter of the social security story that has received too little attention. Analysts have understandably been riveted by the neat fit between contributory social insurance, with its ties between benefit levels and the previous earnings of recipients, and American work ethic/free market values. Concern with the flat universal alternative is thus sometimes subordinated. Interestingly, though, it is certainly not a chapter that social security officials of the time were likely to dismiss. Arthur Altmeyer, for example, concluded that pressures in Congress were so great that "we were fortunate that the committees with which we had to deal were money-minded committees. Otherwise we would have had a flat general pension. There's no question about that."[45]

The flat-plan threat points to vulnerabilities of the old-age insurance system; as a persisting challenge to its basic operating assumptions, the existence of the flat-pension alternative helps to account for the decisions to freeze taxes and to raise early benefits and thus deplete the reserve fund. Despite the notorious infeasibility of its generous two hundred dollar monthly flat pension, the Townsend movement's strength is legion and needs no elaboration here; its influence extended from the 1930s (in the 1939 election, for example, the Townsend movement focused considerable attention on the inadequacy of old-age insurance in meeting current needs and gained at least nominal commitments to the Townsend plan from most Republicans elected to the House) through the 1940s (when well over a third of elected Congressmen carried Townsend endorsements) and into the 1950s (in 1953 a discharge petition for a Townsend-sponsored bill gained 161 congressional signatures). But this strength was only a symptom of a broader questioning of the adequacy of, and the assumptions behind, old-age insurance and old-age assistance.[46] Arthur Altmeyer in fact concludes that if old-age insurance had not gotten "off the ground in a hurry" through the 1939 provisions for markedly increased benefits in the near future, flat pensions would instead have prevailed.[47] Opinion poll data on this question is ambiguous, but it is clear that the public rejected the early pension levels for both old-age assistance and old-age insurance as too low, and considered it a federal responsibility to increase them. Even immediately after the passage of the liberalized 1939 amendments, pressure for raising minimum pensions to a much higher—and perhaps flat—rate was intense, and the administration registered the effects.[48] Between 1939 and 1941, the Congress of Industrial Organizations (CIO), for example, repeatedly endorsed the replacement of old-age insurance and assistance by a uniform pension financed by income and wealth taxes.[49] One of the more revealing incidents came in March 1940, when Paul McNutt, the head of the Federal Security Agency (within which the SSB was then housed), tried to boost his presidential prospects by proposing a renovation of the social security system. The current system, he charged, was economically dangerous, failed to redistribute income, and still relied heavily on an old-age assistance program with a humiliating means test. His proposal, which set forth a position already taken by certain leading administration economists, was to scrap social security in favor of a flat federal universal pension financed from income tax revenues.[50] This speech was never given, because Altmeyer prevailed on the president to quash what he rightly considered to be a fundamental if "casual" assault on "the basic principles of contributory social insurance, which automatically relates benefits to wage loss."[51] McNutt's proposal, Altmeyer warned, would only lead FDR's opponents to offer even more generous pensions.

Though McNutt was silenced, the public concerns to which his original speech appealed could not so easily be suppressed. By May of 1940, the Social Security Board had felt compelled, despite profound distaste for the whole idea, to draft for FDR's possible use a double-decker social security system which would institute a flat universal pension to be supplemented by contributory graduated benefits.[52] The 1940 Democratic platform went so far as to call for "the early realization of a minimum pension for all who have reached the age of retirement and are not gainfully employed."[53] FDR then kicked off his presidential campaign with what seemed to be a call for a double-decker system: a "bare minimum" old-age pension, coupled with a provision for building up "additional security."[54] FDR was characteristically ambiguous—he actually had said that no "needy person" would lack such a minimum pension, thus suggesting a mere extension of old-age assistance—but his speech was clearly a response to public doubts as to the adequacy of social security. These doubts were voiced most compellingly in a 1941 investigation by Townsendite Sheridan Downey's Senate Subcommittee to Investigate the Old-Age Pension System. Downey zeroed in on philosophical vulnerabilities of the old-age insurance plan—vulnerabilities that would in turn make it easier for congressmen to depart from the payroll tax rises that the SSB deemed essential to its view of responsible contributory social insurance. Downey denounced the unfairness of a system that could give affluent retirees astronomical returns—basically a subsidy—on their previous payroll tax payments while other, more needy, elderly could qualify for nothing beyond a paltry means-tested old age assistance grant. As the senator had explained it earlier, social security was "hardly at all a contributory plan but almost wholly a fake scheme of social dividends in which payments of public money will be disbursed in the inverse order of need; that is, substantial payments to the prosperous and meager pittances to the miserable."[55]

In a similar way, even in the late 1940s, after war priorities and other factors had largely neutralized a flat-plan threat from the left, conservative attacks on old-age insurance revealed continued questioning of certain fundamental social security principles. Carl Curtis, a leader of Republican social security critics in the House, also put forward a plan for uniform pensions, taking the existing system to task for "paying a privileged few," those with greater resources for retirement in any case, "many, many times more than what they have paid in," while the poorer elderly were failing to qualify for insurance benefits.[56]

Such proposals may be a throwback to what Gaston Rimlinger identifies as a more traditional emphasis on only meeting minimum needs instead of establishing a broader "social right" to maintain one's standard of living. And the proposals were often quite conservative in their objective of reducing long-term—and sometimes even current—social security costs.[57] But the fact remains that they represented a continued challenge to old-age insurance principles. In such an atmosphere, it was difficult for supporters of old-age insurance to make a convincing case for a payroll tax increase. By the end of the decade, a presidential staff memorandum reported that "most careful observers" agreed that "it is nip and tuck as to whether the Townsendites and other advocates of a general pension system may win out in the race between insurance and pensions."[58]

Nightmares at the SSA

SSB/SSA leaders did not, of course, simply capitulate to these challenges. For they too had a vision of the future, one that reflected their ideological and organizational commitment to the long-term viability of old-age insurance. And that vision was a nightmare. Both the flat-pension movement and the periodic tax freezes, they thought, would attenuate the relationship between contributions and benefits. This would weaken carefully drawn distinctions between insurance and welfare—thereby, they feared, undermining the philosophical foundation that safeguarded the program's long-term support. They thus responded to the tax freeze movement in the most apocalyptic terms: "Whether we realize it or not, we are deciding the whole future course of social security in this country—whether we shall have a genuine contributory social insurance system where benefits are paid as a matter of right or whether we shall have a system of government handout or dole, requiring the taking of a pauper's oath."[59] And a double-decker system with a flat-pension base seemed just as menacing, for "political pressures might inevitably result in a continued increase throughout the years in the basic uniform amount. . . , thus weakening and eventually destroying the rationale of a contributory social insurance system under which benefits, contributions, and wage loss were interrelated."[60]

A tax freeze, SSB leaders initially thought, posed parallel dangers through its assumption that old-age insurance represented an intergenerational transfer rather than an assurance that a worker's contributions would accrue toward future benefits. This could overinflate current pension levels by producing a political bidding war to take advantage of the existing reserve. Stationary benefit levels throughout the 1940s eventually alleviated this fear, only to have it give way to the opposite concern: refusal to raise taxes would tend, argued the AFL point-man on social security, "to freeze not only the present contributions rate but the present inadequate benefit provisions."[61] This argument became a major SSB theme as the board orchestrated the attack on freeze opponents.[62] As a Ways and Means Committee minority report, actually drafted by the SSB, asserted: "The real reason why many people advocate keeping the contribution rate at a level below the true cost of the benefits provided is that they fear the accumulation of a reserve fund will create a demand for an increase in the size of the benefits."[63] Altmeyer had good reason to be sensitive on this score. In a memorandum to an assistant to President Roosevelt, he revealed the very expansionary motives for the scheduled tax increases that some conservative freeze supporters darkly suspected. "It seems increasingly possible," he observed with evident satisfaction, "to provide cradle-to-the-grave insurance against unemployment, sickness, permanent disability, old age and death, without any increase in the employers' payroll taxes beyond the automatic step-up schedule now contained in the Social Security Act, if there were equal three-way contributions by employers, employees, and the government."[64] Payroll tax freezes could torpedo this vision, a threat which hit home when the freeze enacted by the Republican Congress in 1947 reduced all future slated payroll tax rates, dropping even the maximum scheduled tax on employers and workers from 3 percent each to 2 percent each.

But even the pension obligations already on the books, SSB leaders feared, faced a potentially crippling challenge from any movement toward a more strictly pay-as-you-go system. Though they themselves had endorsed a marked reduction in planned reserves from those scheduled in the original 1935 law, they had always opposed the pay-as-you-go principle and refused to credit the mushy congressional endorsement of that principle that most others recognized in the 1939 Amendments. Their concern was as much actuarial as political: the "mathematical certainty that the longer the present payroll tax remains in effect the higher the future payroll tax must be."[65] Without the accrued interest provided by a trust fund, the ever-diminishing contributor/beneficiary ratios would ultimately necessitate heavy payroll taxes or large government subsidies—either one of which, they worried, could sink the program. The trouble with high payroll taxes was that future generations might not want to pay "many times as much for the same insurance protection" as early annuitants, especially if their eventual annuity would be smaller than their payroll taxes could have "obtained . . . from a private insurance company."[66] (This prospect of actuarially excessive "contributions" was a particularly sensitive one, for the regressive impact of those taxes on current workers would be more embarrassing and less excusable if they could no longer be justified as a good personal insurance investment). The track record on social security finance, after all, was highly discouraging. As an SSA-drafted speech put it, "If we reduce contributions below scheduled rates when we fear unemployment [1939] and if we also reduce contributions when employment and wages are at peak levels [World War II], a breakdown of the old-age insurance program must follow."[67]

What was the alternative? Government subsidies had appeal as a way of avoiding excessive future tax rates and of compensating for the "unearned" payments in the early years of the system and repeatedly received qualified support from the SSB. Yet this alternative was met with some ambivalence, partly because of the argument that government subsidies were inappropriate while the system excluded so many taxpayers, but mainly because the board had serious doubts as to whether Congress would come through with the money. It was not unimaginable that a future Congress would bridle at making a substantial general revenue commitment to cover pensions vastly in excess of the actuarial value of earlier contributions; SSB supporters pointed to the inconsistency between freeze advocates' blind confidence that future Congresses would raise the requisite taxes and their cynical belief that current Congresses would "raid" the Trust Fund for extravagant projects. Such political uncertainty—the removal of "security" from social security—was precisely what the SSB feared. For in a system that justified payroll taxes as a way of "earning" future pensions, public support might wither at the possibility that the promised retirement checks would never arrive.

The SSB's arguments had a compelling logic that even some opponents could not deny. Senator Vandenberg, for example, had to concede that the pay-as-you-go rule might need some revision, since the "reserve fund won't be sufficient when the real load of social security payments falls due, as it soon will."[68] Newspapers and magazines increasingly echoed this theme; the *U.S. News*, for example, predicted a "future financial headache" in the latter part of the century as deficits built up, while *Newsweek*, in an article entitled "Social Insecurity," warned that "from a long-range standpoint . . . the system is insolvent."[69] Even some prestigious business journals departed from their customary opposition to taxation, fearing that the freeze would ultimately lead to a shrinking reserve and a federal subsidy that would probably "be borne chiefly by business."[70]

Yet as we have seen, such "realities" could not prevent the repeated enactment of payroll tax freezes. It was not in the cards. The trust fund, even by the end of the 1940s, exceeded outlays by a multiple of sixteen. Continued disagreement over some of the program's most basic principles attenuated the perceived need to build up a trust fund. Despite hectoring from the SSB/SSA, Congress had drifted through the 1940s without any of the scheduled tax increases; its only real provision for the future of the program lay in an uncertain commitment to general revenue financing. The SSA's nightmare showed distressing signs of prophecy.

Reconstructing Social Security Finance: The Social Security Act Amendments of 1950

In 1949 and 1950, however, Congress abruptly reversed direction. For the first time, it allowed a slated payroll tax rise (to 1½ percent for 1950) to go into effect. The ensuing Social Security Act Amendments of 1950 highlighted the theme of "self-support," scheduling future payroll tax increases to allow the old-age insurance reserve fund to continue to grow over the next several decades.

This talk of self-support was less impressive than it appeared. In the politically sensitive short-term, payroll taxes would be no higher than those already programmed, and only in the 1960s would rates surpass the 2 percent employee payroll tax ceiling scheduled in the 1947 law. The preponderant burden of meeting future expanded pension obligations still rested on subsequent generations, who were slated ultimately to bear rates more than twice as great as current ones. And even this formula for building up a substantial reserve eroded in practice. By the end of the 1950s, program expansion—even when ritually accompanied by minor tax increases—led Congress to ease back into its approximation of a pay-as-you-go system, in which annual tax receipts—supplemented by the small interest yield on the previously accumulated reserve—roughly equaled annual outlays. Still, though the Eisenhower administration briefly flirted with another payroll tax freeze for 1954, a revised political dynamic—one that allowed repeated payroll tax hikes over succeeding decades while banishing the alternative of general revenue supplements—had taken root.

What is most striking here is the starkness of the congressional shift. Wilbur Mills, of the Ways and Means Committee and the dominant figure in the shift, even engaged in the closest thing to self-criticism that one can expect from a congressman, confessing himself and most of his colleagues "guilty . . . of doing what now appears to be a very ill-advised thing over the years" in repeatedly deferring the tax.[71]

This reversal represents something of an enigma, one that has thus far yielded no definitive solution. My own research on this is still at a preliminary stage. But a number of hypotheses do seem to have at least some explanatory power in accounting for the program's shift in direction. Perhaps the most convincing and direct source of this shift may be found in Martha Derthick's focus on the House Ways and Means Committee.[72] With the notable exception of the tax freeze issue, in which Senator Vandenberg most commonly took the initiative, that committee has been the key congressional actor over the broad history of social security. When this powerful committee acts on such a complex and technical issue, the rest of Congress tends to go along. That pattern certainly applied to the committee's 1949 decision to return the program to its 1935 emphasis on self-support.

The Ways and Means Committee thus put its unique stamp on the financial structure of old-age insurance. In so doing, it rejected not only a decade of tax freezes but also a series of recommendations (by its own expert technical study in 1945–46, by the Advisory Council on Social Security in 1947–48, and by the Truman administration in 1949) for partial government financing.

The committee's mission seems crucial to understanding this glaring rejection of advice and precedent. The Ways and Means Committee has been the foremost money committee, with more reason than any other to be sensitive to programs that involve substantial future outlays from the government's general fund; a program that "paid for itself" had inherent appeal. Committee leaders also had a proprietary interest in this popular program and more particularly in the principle of earning one's right to a pension through past contributions which they had originally placed at its center. Though committee members had gone along with, and even on occasion initiated, the continued tax freezes they had always shown more commitment to the contributory principle and much less openness to future general revenue contributions (even voting unsuccessfully in 1946 to repeal the Murray amendment's government subsidy pledge).

Admittedly, this characterization of the Ways and Means Committee's mission might seem more convincing if the committee had given more scrupulous attention to the impact of its actions on the program's future. Instead, through the late 1930s and 1940s, its members seemed to share the short time horizons of other congressmen. One is tempted simply to brand the committee as fickle, a temptation heightened by the comment of one observer of the committee's deliberations in 1949: "In that whole process, the shift of individual members from the beginning to the end was almost amazing, as they became informed on particular points. What they'd be against, maybe three weeks later they'd be for."[73] But from the perspective of the SSA this had less derogatory implications; the committee had simply been coached—by what was increasingly seen as one of Washington's most influential and respected bureaucracies—to see the light. The 1950 amendments required the committee to undertake a full-scale analysis of this difficult program. This provided an opening for SSA experts and their focus on higher payroll taxes to secure the financial future of old-age insurance. (SSA chief actuary—and, incidentally, general revenue opponent—Robert Myers, for example, temporarily served as actuary to the committee, where he assisted Wilbur Mills in his new crusade for a "self-supporting" system.)

One can perhaps best make sense of the Ways and Means Committee's actions by placing its inclinations toward "fiscal responsibility" and contributory social insurance in the context of broader

trends that shaped the social security system. These trends acti-
vated the committee's fiscal conservatism not so much by direct
reinforcement as by more circuitous routes: a. by threatening val-
ued committee approaches; and b. by creating a more permissive
atmosphere for change in the system, allowing the committee scope
to act on its inclinations.

The threat had become unmistakable by the late 1940s, pressing
old-age insurance into great political prominence. As war inflation
ate away at the purchasing power of benefit levels, they appeared
more and more inadequate. The contrast with old-age assistance
became particularly discomfiting. Despite a tendency today to assume that American "anti-statist" "free-market" values of "self-
help" severely restricted old-age policy options—an assumption
that public opinion data and the whole social security debate of the
late 1930s and 1940s call into question, the non-contributory old-
age assistance program (OAA) had proved far more vigorous than
old-age insurance in the 1940s. Many in fact thought it *too* vigorous,
complaining of its "political attraction" and of "the irresponsible
expansion by several states of their 'give-away' old-age assistance
program."[74] By the end of the 1940s, just over a fifth of the elderly
received OAA payments, and in a few states it was over half.[75] More
of the elderly received OAA than old-age insurance benefits, and the
average benefit was 70 percent higher (OAA benefits having more
than doubled from 1939 to 1950).[76] With old-age insurance payments literally having become a joke, with thousands of letters to
Congress complaining that their paltry insurance benefits were not
enough to live on, and with even these old-age insurance benefits
vastly exceeding the actuarial value of past contributions, old-age
assistance—to quote Gaston Rimlinger—had reached a "turning
point . . . where the contributory system would have to become
substantially more effective or would have to yield to the attacks of
the advocates of universal flat pensions."[77] The social security bat-
tleground of 1949–50 was littered with such observations. A White
House staff report asserted "the extreme importance of a *very
substantial* increase in insurance benefits . . . to head off any general pension movement.[78] This link did not elude the Ways and
Means Committee:[79]

> There are indications that if the insurance program is not strengthened
> and expanded, the old-age assistance program may develop into a very

costly and ill-advised system of noncontributory pensions, payable not only to the needy but to all individuals at or above retirement age who are no longer employed. . . . The financing of such plans may become chaotic, their economic effects dangerous. There is a pressing need to strengthen the basic system at once before it is undermined by such forces."

A major expansion of old-age insurance thus became irresistible. Both the Republican and Democratic 1948 platforms had endorsed an increase, and the Democratic victory after a campaign that highlighted the need for strengthening the social security system assured this issue a leading place on the agenda of the next Congress. Also, the prosperity of the past decade, along with the growing faith in further economic growth, had the effect that Professor Rimlinger discusses in his paper of fostering more ambitious social security systems. The Social Security Act Amendments of 1950 jacked up benefits by 77 percent, enough to compensate for the inflation of the 1940s.

Yet however compelling the need for liberalizing benefits, the benefit rise alone cannot explain the Ways and Means Committee's decision to jump-start the stalled financial engine of the program. The frozen tax rate could have covered the new benefits for at least a couple of years—and well beyond that had the committee been willing to dip into the system's reserve, which was well above "contingency" levels. But in an expanding system, such a financing approach would have too deeply undercut the social insurance principles espoused by committee members. As it was, the committee had stretched the notion of contributory earned annuities to the breaking point. To meet the demands for an instant jump in pensions and for their extension to new groups, it had not only boosted benefit levels but it had further subordinated the role of past accrued contributions by sharply kicking up the minimum benefit, by easing qualification requirements for pensions, and by updating the "average monthly wage" to reflect higher current incomes on which benefits were calculated. The committee would have been hard pressed to retain any credibility for the contributory principle if it had enacted all of these instant benefits while allowing contributions to coast along at the same minimal rate. Just as importantly, the powerful pressure for higher pensions brought home the menacing prospect of escalating charges on the federal treasury. By spelling out a schedule of future taxes that would provide for the program's self-support, and by establishing a framework in which benefit increases would be paired with tax hikes, the committee slammed shut what it saw as the 1944 Murray amendment's open invitation to future profligacy (as one member put it, "the sky is the limit," since the availability of general revenues would only heighten the political proclivity to call for higher pensions).[80]

The confusing and double-edged politics of social security were at work here again; higher payroll taxes could legitimize expanded provisions for old age even as they blocked future *over*-expansion into undesired channels. Yet the unfreezing of the payroll tax cannot alone be explained by the irresistible political demand for more generous pensions. Even a reduced sense of crisis in the 1950s and the fading specter of rampaging pension increases could not refreeze the payroll tax. Other factors instead sustained a more permissive atmosphere for payroll tax increases. Perhaps most importantly, economic growth allowed any tax increase to be paired with more sizeable benefit increases (this particularly applied to the first departure from the freeze in 1950, when the tax rose from 1 percent to 1½ percent in anticipation of the 1950 act's show-stealing 77 percent pension increase). Fiscal conservatism had never before come so cheaply. Social security tax increases—until the crisis of the later 1970s—were an almost painless political choice. In fact, worker support for old-age security made the payroll tax a relatively popular one.[81] And finally, pressures for a looser financing scheme drawing on general revenues proved weak at key points. Organized labor, formerly an opponent of the regressive payroll tax, had joined the SSA in viewing the payroll tax as a way to secure the system's future expansion. Thus, when Wilbur Cohen of the SSA rather casually acquiesced in Congressman Mills's proposal to repeal the Murray amendment's general revenue authorization for old-age insurance, both the AFL and the SSA viewed this as a small price to pay for the more secure financial footing provided by the Ways and Means Committee's more rigorous commitment to payroll tax financing.[82]

The Legacy of the Payroll Tax Freeze

In the last analysis, the pattern of stasis in the 1940s—the great nondecision to defer repeatedly higher payroll taxes—has disturbing implications. SSA leaders had survived another crisis, but even in its resolution one can glimpse the seeds of future crisis. The economic vitality of the 1940s would have permitted a very different path for payroll tax rates from the flat trajectory that obtained. But two major factors intervened. First, Congress proved exquisitely responsive to politically painless solutions and to economic fluctuations that allowed, but hardly mandated, procrastination. Second, time had not yet sanctified the "fundamental principles" of the program, easing departures from its financial schedule.

The revamping of old-age insurance in 1950, combined with the Eisenhower administration's subsequent endorsement of this expanding system, stilled debate over the alternative visions of how the program might develop. But the narrowing of debate over the future of old-age insurance could not secure that future. The dynamic that gave impetus to many of these alternatives—the vaguely defined and ever-changing relationship between what contributors paid in and what they got back, with all that implied about divisions of responsibility between and within generations, would return to haunt social security deliberations. True, in the 1950 amendments, Congress scrupulously drafted an ephemeral reserve and tax schedule that diverged from previous failures to make explicit provision for the program's future viability. Yet the political calculus that underlay the tax freeze—one that focused on short-term needs— remained essentially unchanged, as the social security crisis of the late 1970s and early 1980s may have indicated.

This political calculus should give us pause in the celebration of the Social Security Act Amendments of 1983. These amendments provide for a huge trust fund to be built up in the 1990s and the early twenty-first century to cover commitments for the later part of the century. The reserve levels that facilitated the tax freeze discussed in this paper are scheduled to be surpassed many times over (from under 5 percent of the Gross National Product through the 1940s to perhaps 25 percent or more in 2015–2020. So much has changed since the 1940s, of course, that comparisons are hazardous. The firmer current consensus on certain basic principles of social security, especially the rejection of substantial general revenue financing and flat pensions, would seem to require a more careful financial basis for the program. Economic prosperity in the 1940s (with consequent trust fund levels that so greatly exceeded predictions) provided more fertile soil than we have any reason to expect today for lowering payroll tax schedules. The congressional endorsement of a "contingency reserve" formula in 1939 and the 1940s provided a context that eased the rejection of payroll taxes to boost the reserve balance. The salability of the current call to use social security reserves to raise the national savings rate might also better allow for fuller reserve financing in succeeding decades than in the 1940s, though the failure of macroeconomic logic to push through a larger anti-inflationary reserve in World War II may call into question the potential persuasiveness of this argument. And perhaps the most telling difference is the social security crisis itself. With recent talk of bankruptcy and the erosion of faith in receiving future pensions, a secure foundation for the system has become a more exigent issue—a notable contrast to the 1940s, when SSA warnings of a future day of reckoning were cries in the wilderness. We have seen the future, and we know that it doesn't have to work. The slipshod framework for the future in the 1940s, one can argue, can thus never again pass muster.[83]

It is no revelation to observe, however, that one *can* go broke overestimating the historical memory of the American people. There is no better reminder than the 1940s that if social security payments are secure over the short haul, and especially if a payroll tax increase cannot be paired with a benefit rise, scheduled jumps in payroll taxes are far from a sure thing. And more recent expectations of rising old-age insurance benefits may make it even harder to build up the mandated huge reserve. Social Security tax rises thus may well become an issue even before the end of this decade. As in the 1950s period closing this paper, the guardians of social security may be breathing a sigh of relief, for their direst speculations have not materialized. But now as then, the problem of the future remains.

Notes

1. This is not to depreciate two of the sources that have most contributed to this image: Carolyn L. Weaver, *The Crisis in Social Security* (Durham, N.C.: Duke University Press, 1982); and Martha Derthick's particularly insightful and historically sensitive book, *Policymaking for Social Security* (Washington, D.C.: Brookings Institution, 1979). Derthick and Weaver, in fact, offer the best available treatments of the freeze, though neither examines it in any depth.

Even in addition to the surprising triumph of the tax freeze over the powerful SSA, there is irony in the fact that the trajectory of payroll tax rates has largely gone in an opposite direction from other tax rates. During the dozen years in which payroll tax rates were frozen, the personal and corporate income tax both rocketed; someone earning a $3000 income might well have paid no income taxes in 1937 but hundreds of dollars in 1949. By way of contrast, while payroll tax rates have been rising between 1950 and the present, income tax rates have dropped in that period.

2. U.S., Department of Health, Education, and Welfare, Social Security Administration, Office of Research and Statistics, *Public Attitudes Toward Social Security, 1935–1965*, by Michael E. Schiltz, Research Report no. 33 (Washington, D.C.: Government Printing Office, 1970), pp. 82–86. See, for example, *Congressional Record*, 78 Cong., 2 sess., 1944, 90, pt. 7: 8839, 8853, and 8856.

3. *Congressional Record*, 78 Cong., 2 sess, 1944, 90, pt. 1: 41.

4. U.S. Congress, House, Committee on Ways and Means, *Social Security: Hearings relative to the Social Security Act Amendments of 1939*, 76 Cong., 1 sess., 1939, vol. 3, p. 2113. Simultaneously with Morgenthau's testimony, President Roosevelt loosely endorsed this formula. Franklin D. Roosevelt, *Complete Presidential Press Conferences* (New York: Da Capo Press, 1972), March 24, 1939, 13:218.

5. SSB representatives later grasped at the fact that there was no explicit requirement that anyone act on the Trustees' finding. However, the Finance and Ways and Means committee reports not surprisingly make clear that the Board of Trustees was not reporting for its health; the committees in fact made a point of noting that their own projections for the reserve closely conformed to the Morgenthau rule.

6. Committee on Ways and Means, *Social Security: Hearings*, 76 Cong., 1 sess., vol. 3, p. 2114.

7. Witness the contrast between the concern in 1940 to keep the Trustee reserve estimate within the rule of three and the studied campaign in 1942 (once compliance with the rule became totally impossible) to deny the rule's applicability. L. L. Schmitter and B. C. Goldwasser to I. S. Falk, August 24, 1940, "705.1" folder, Office of the Commissioner, Executive Files Unit, Record Group 47, Records of the Social Security Administration (National Archives, Washington, D.C.); Wilbur J. Cohen to O. C. Pogge, August 20, 1942, "710 Jan-July 1942" folder, box 111, Executive Director Files 1948–1941 (accession no. 56–A533), Record Group 47, Records of the Social Security Administration (National Records Center, Suitland, Md.).

8. Henry A. Morgenthau, Jr., Diary, vol. 185, p. 23, Henry A. Morgenthau, Jr., Papers (Franklin D. Roosevelt Library, Hyde Park, N.Y.).

9. Committee on Ways and Means, *Social Security: Hearings*, 76 Cong., 1 sess., vol. 3, p. 2116.

10. Committee on Ways and Means, *Analysis of the Social Security*

System: Hearings on Public Assistance before a subcommittee, 83 Cong., 1 sess., 1953, pt. 5, p. 790.

11. Mark H. Leff, "Taxing the 'Forgotten Man': The Politics of Social Security Finance in the New Deal," Journal of American History 70 (September 1983): 371. I am certainly not the only one to note this. See, for example, Edward Berkowitz's clear, perceptive study of the 1939 Amendments, "The First Social Security Crisis," Prologue 15 (Fall 1983): 133–49.

12. Mark H. Leff, The Limits of Symbolic Reform (New York, New York: Cambridge University Press, 1984), p. 285.

13. Theron F. Schlabach, Edwin E. Witte (Madison: State Historical Society of Wisconsin, 1969), p. 177. FDR, who had gone along with the tax freeze with the greatest reluctance, interestingly had earlier reached a similar conclusion, warning that "if we don't go ahead" and allow the scheduled payroll tax increase, "we'll never get it." Morgenthau Diary, January 20, 1939, vol. 184, p. 335.

14. Social Security Board, "Proposed Change in the Social Security Act," in Committee on Ways and Means, Social Security: Hearings, 76 Cong., 1 sess., vol. 1, p. 8.

15. Such apocalyptic scenarios were not entirely irrational. Many conservative advocates of a tax freeze and a minimal reserve, such as the U.S. Chamber of Commerce and M. Albert Linton, had precisely the long-term objective that defenders of Social Security feared: preventing the government from overcommitting resources for pensions in the distant future. Leff, Limits, pp. 283–84.

16. Chicago Herald-American, December 20, 1943, in Congressional Record, 78 Cong., 2 sess., 1944, 90, pt. 1: 39.

17. Berkowitz, "The First Social Security Crisis," p. 138.

18. Committee on Ways and Means, Social Security Act Amendments of 1949: Hearings on H. R. 2892, 81 Cong., 1 sess., 1949, pt. 2, p. 1250.

19. Challenging tax freezes had proved a losing proposition, especially since veto threats were empty. Most freezes (including the one remotely close—50–35—Senate vote in 1942 to block the first step-up provided in the 1939 Amendments) had been attached to needed tax bills, and the others carried by veto-proof majorities. Altmeyer himself supported the Treasury Department's freeze proposal in late 1945, noting that "the result would be the same whether or not the administration takes the initiative." Arthur Altmeyer to Fred Vinson, September 28, 1945, "OASI Tax Freeze-1946" folder, box 2, Office of the Commissioner, "A. J. Altmeyer's Speeches, Testimony, and Articles" (accession no. 62A–82), Record Group 47, Records of the Social Security Administration (National Records Center, Suitland, Md.).

20. Acting Secretary of Treasury to James E. Webb, August 1, 1947,

"Bill File: August 6, 1947 (H. R. 3818–H. R. 4079)," White House Bill File, Harry S Truman Papers (Truman Library, Independence, Mo.). Truman, however, did speak out against the freeze. *Public Papers of the Presidents of the United States: Harry S Truman* (Washington, D.C.: Government Printing Office, 1963), 1947 volume, p. 53.

21. *Congressional Record*, 78 Cong., 2 sess., 1944, 90, pt. 7: 8845.

22. Transcript of hearing, July 19, 1946, p. 50, Bill File on H.R. 7037, 79 Cong., Records of Senate Committee on Finance, Record Group 46 (National Archives, Washington, D.C.).

23. Robert M. Ball, "What Contribution Rate for Old-Age and Survivors Insurance?" *Social Security Bulletin* 12 (July 1949): 6. See, for example, *Congressional Record*, 78 Cong., 2 sess., 1944, 90, pt. 7, pp. 8843, 8844, 8847, 8858.

24. *Congressional Record*, 78 Cong., 2 sess., 1944, 90, pt. 7: 8838; Committee on Ways and Means, *Amendments to Social Security Act: Hearings*, 79 Cong., 2 sess., pt. 1, p. 85.

25. Committee on Ways and Means, *Freezing the Social Security Tax Rate at 1 Percent for 1944*, 78 Cong., 2 sess., 1944, p. 11.

26. Thomas E. Jones, *Options for the Future* (New York: Praeger, 1980), pp. 5–8.

27. Morgenthau Diary, January 20, 1939, vol. 184, p. 330.

28. Derthick, *Policymaking*, p. 235.

29. *Congressional Record*, 78 Cong., 2 sess., 1944, 90, pt. 7: 8838.

30. "Current Social Security Notes," *American Economic Security* 7 (April-May 1950): 3.

31. Merryle Rukeyser, 1939, in U.S. Library of Congress, Legislative Reference Service, *Public Affairs Bulletin* No. 46 (Raymond E. Manning, "Financing Social Security") (Washington, D.C.: Government Printing Office, 1946), p. 59.

32. Carl Curtis, "Additional Minority Views," Committee on Ways and Means, *Social Security Act Amendments of 1949, H. Rept. 1300 to Accompany H.R. 6000*, 81 Cong., 1 sess., 1949, p. 182; Hugh Butler, in Senate, Committee on Finance, *Social Security Act Amendments of 1950, S. Rept. 1669 to Accompany H.R. 6000*, 81 Cong., 2 sess., 1950, p. 318.

33. "More Social Security," *New Republic* 122 (July 3, 1950): 7.

34. Berkowitz, "The First Social Security Crisis," p. 149.

35. *Congressional Record*, 76 Cong., 1 sess., 1939, 84, pt. 8: 8827; Committee on Ways and Means, *Social Security Act Amendments of 1939, H. Rept. 728 to Accompany H.R. 6635*, 76 Cong., 1 sess., 1939, p. 17.

36. J. Douglas Brown, "Economic Aspects of Social Security Against Life Hazards," *American Labor Legislation Review* 30 (March 1940): 36.

37. Paul McNutt, "Major Problems of Social Security," March 28, 1940, "McNutt, Paul V. 1940" folder, File 062.2, box 158, Office of the Commis-

sioner, Executive File Unit 1935–1940, Record Group 47, Records of the Social Security Administration (National Archives); Daniel Bell to Henry P. Morgenthau, May 8, 1940, "1940" folder, Official File 1710, Franklin D. Roosevelt Papers (FDR Library). McNutt's speech was drafted by the SSB.

38. Committee on Finance, *The Revenue Bill of 1943*, S. Rept. 627 to *Accompany H.R. 3687*, 78 Cong., 1 sess., 1943, p. 19.

39. See the SSB draft in Daniel S. Gerig to I. S. Falk, January 6, 1944, box 2, "A. J. Altmeyer's Speeches, Testimony, and Articles" (accession no. 62A–82), Record Group 47 (National Records Center); and Wilbur Cohen to Arthur Altmeyer, December 16, 1943, "710 November 1943" folder, box 111, Executive Director Files 1941–1948, General Correspondence, Record Group 47 (National Records Center). Also see Vandenberg's discussion of his support for the amendment in one of his many letters to Altmeyer: Arthur Vandenberg to Arthur Altmeyer, October 3, 1944, "Tax Freeze—1945—Miscellaneous Date" folder, box 1, "A. J. Altmeyer's Speeches, Testimony, and Articles," Record Group 47 (National Records Center).

40. *Congressional Record*, 78 Cong., 2 sess., 1944, 90, pt. 1:374; Committee on Finance, *Social Security Revision: Hearings on H.R. 6000*, 81 Cong., 2 sess., pt. 1, p. 54.

41. James S. Parker, "Financial Policy in Old-Age and Survivors Insurance, 1935–1950," *Social Security Bulletin* 14 (June 1951): 7.

42. "Broadening of Social Security Looms as Issue for Congress," *Newsweek*, October 16, 1944, p. 64.

43. Transcript of hearing, July 19, 1946, p. 50, Bill File on H. R. 7037, 79 Cong., Records of Senate Committee on Finance, Record Group 46 (National Archives).

44. Office of Secretary of the Treasury, Technical Staff, "Questions and Answers on Social Security," March 11, 1949, box 85, John W. Snyder Papers (Harry S Truman Library, Independence, Mo.).

45. Arthur Altmeyer interview by Peter Corning, 1966, pp. 122–23, Columbia Oral History Collection (Columbia University, New York).

46. See, for example, Department of Health, Education, and Welfare, *Public Attitudes*, pp. 39–43.

47. Derthick, *Policymaking*, p. 221.

48. For a fuller discussion of this challenge, see Jerry R. Cates's provocative book, *Insuring Inequality* (Ann Arbor: University of Michigan Press, 1983), chap. 3.

49. Derthick, *Policymaking*, p. 113; Congress of Industrial Organizations, *Proceedings of Fourth Constitutional Convention, 1941*, pp. 270–71.

50. "Federal Security Administrator McNutt Advocates Universal Pension Plan," March 28, 1940, "McNutt, Paul V. 1940" folder, File 062.2, box

158, Office of the Commissioner, Executive File Unit 1935–1940, Record Group 47, Records of the Social Security Administration (National Archives).

51. Arthur Altmeyer to Stephen Early, March 28, 1940, in ibid.

52. Arthur Altmeyer to Edwin Watson, May 7, 1940, "1940" folder, Official File 1710, Franklin D. Roosevelt Papers (FDR Library).

53. John J. Corson and John W. McConnell, *Economic Needs of Older People* (New York: Twentieth Century Fund, 1956), p. 134.

54. *New York Times*, September 12, 1940, p. 14. FDR continued to talk privately of the need for a "general old age pension" in 1941. Roy Blough, "Memorandum for the Secretary," September 30, 1941, "Social Security Amendments-Taxes" folder, box 188, Records of Assistant Secretary John L. Sullivan, Record Group 56 (National Archives).

55. *Congressional Record*, 76 Cong., 3 sess., 1940, 86, pt. 14: A1423.

56. Carl Curtis, "Additional Minority Views," Committee on Ways and Means, *Social Security Act Amendments of 1949, H. R. 1300*, p. 75.

57. Gaston V. Rimlinger, *Welfare Policy and Industrialization in Europe, America, and Russia* (New York: John Wiley, 1971), p. 236.

58. Staff comments, "Expansion and Extension of Social Security System," February 14, 1949, Social Security Folder 2, Charles Murphy Papers (Truman Library).

59. "Undermining the Federal Old-Age and Survivors Insurance System," December 2, 1944, "Tax Freeze-1945-Miscellaneous Data" folder, box 1, "A. J. Altmeyer's Speeches, Testimony, and Articles," Record Group 47 (National Records Center). This quotation is actually taken from Rep. Dingell's speech, drafted at the SSB.

60. Arthur J. Altmeyer, *The Formative Years of Social Security* (Madison: University of Wisconsin Press, 1966), p. 126.

61. Nelson Cruikshank to Arthur Altmeyer, December 11, 1944, "Letters from CIO and AFL on 1945 Tax Freeze" folder, box 1, Office of the Commissioner (accession no. 62A–82), Record Group 47 (National Records Center).

62. See, for example, a radio question planted along this line: "Questions Prepared for Robert Watt" for December 9, 1944, "Tax Freeze-1945-Miscellaneous Data" folder, "A. J. Altmeyer's Speeches, Testimony, and Articles," Record Group 47 (National Records Center).

63. "Dissenting Views," November 30, 1944, "Tax Freeze-1945-Miscellaneous Data" folder, "A. J. Altmeyer's Speeches, Testimony, and Articles," Record Group 47 (National Records Center).

64. Arthur Altmeyer to Stephen Early, March 28, 1940, "McNutt, Paul V. 1940" folder, File 062.2, box 158, Office of the Commissioner, Executive File Unit 1935–1940, Record Group 47 (National Archives).

65. *Congressional Record*, 78 Cong., 2 sess., 1944, 90, pt. 1: 49. Alt-

meyer of course noted that a government subsidy could allow an exception to this rule.

66. Parker, "Financial Policy," p. 6; *Congressional Record*, 78 Cong., 2 sess., 1944, 90, pt. 1:49.

67. "The Background and Justification for the Elimination of the Vandenberg Amendment to the Tax Bill," October 3, 1942, "710 Oct.-Dec. 1942" folder, box 111, Executive Director Files 1941–1948, General Correspondence (accession no. 56–A533), Record Group 47 (National Records Center, Suitland, Md.).

68. *Washington Post*, March 13, 1944, p. 5.

69. "What Tax Freeze Means to System for Old-Age Aid," *U.S. News* 17 (December 29, 1944), p. 60; "Pensions: Social Insecurity," *Newsweek*, January 27, 1947, p. 71.

70. "The Pay Roll Tax Rate," *Journal of Commerce*, November 16, 1944, p. 4. Also see Edson Blair, "Payroll Taxes and the Day of Reckoning," *Barron's*, June 19, 1939, p. 4.

71. *Congressional Record*, 81 Cong., 1 sess., 1949, pt. 11: 13905.

72. See Derthick, *Policymaking*, pp. 239–44.

73. Fedele Fauri interview by Peter Corning, 1966, p. 8, Columbia Oral History Collection (Columbia University, New York).

74. M. Albert Linton, "Facing Facts in Old-Age Security," *American Economic Security* 9 (Jan.-Feb. 1952): 23; John J. Corson, "Social Security Needs Modernizing," *New Republic* 122 (May 8, 1950): 10.

75. *New York Times*, October 16, 1949, sec. 6, p. 68.

76. Committee on Ways and Means, *Social Security Act Amendments of 1949, H. R. 1300*, p. 2; Derthick, *Policymaking*, p. 273.

77. Senate, Committee on Finance, *Social Security Revision: Hearings on H.R. 6000*, 81 Cong., 2 sess., 1950, pt. 2, p. 694; Rimlinger, *Welfare Policy*, p. 237.

78. Staff comments, "Expansion and Extension of Social Security System," February 14, 1949, Social Security Folder 2, Charles Murphy Papers (Truman Library).

79. Committee on Ways and Means, *Social Security Act Amendments of 1949, H. R. 1300*, p. 2.

80. Committee on Ways and Means, *Social Security Act Amendments of 1949, Hearings on H. R. 2892*, 81 Cong., 1 sess., pt. 2: 1220.

81. Linton, "Facing Facts," p. 27.

82. Committee on Ways and Means, Subcommittee on Social Security, *Financing the Social Security System: Hearings*, 94 Cong., 1 sess., 1975, p. 625; Derthick, *Policymaking*, p. 243.

83. Alice Munnell and Lynn E. Blais, "Do We Want Large Social Security Surpluses?" *New England Economic Review*, September/October 1984, p. 7.

12

Disability Insurance and the Social Security Tradition

Edward D. Berkowitz[1]

Since the passage of the Social Security Act, its various contents have tended to settle into three discrete piles: welfare, unemployment compensation, and what the general public refers to simply as social security. In the more technical discourse of policy analysts, this last pile has the formidable title of old-age, survivors, disability, and hospital insurance. Sometimes people separate health insurance from this giant amalgam; nearly everyone lumps old-age, survivors, and disability insurance together. In so doing, people miss the differences between disability and the other components of the social security system. These differences merit attention, as does the general relationship between disability and other components of social security.

Precursors

In the deliberations surrounding the passage of the Social Security Act in 1935, disability received little mention. The problems of unemployment and old age crowded other concerns from the policy agenda. As a result, the act cited existing disability programs without creating new ones. Aid to the blind became one of the original welfare categories, preserving and strengthening the blind pensions run by the states. The act also contained a provision related to vocational rehabilitation, a modest grant-in-aid program that provided vocational counselling to the handicapped. Social insurance for sickness or for permanent disability was conspicuously absent from the law that included so much else.

Arthur Altmeyer, the bureaucrat in charge of the daily operations of the Social Security Board, considered disability insurance an important priority. Almost from the first day of the board's operations, he and I. S. Falk, who headed the research and statistics operations of the board, performed research on the question of disability and drafted constantly changing disability insurance bills. As they toyed with ways of uniting disability and old-age insurance, they were mindful of much more than the immediate considerations related to the social security program. Both gentlemen had considerable experience with a disability program that, although not mentioned in the Social Security Act, was, in fact, the most ubiquitous form of social insurance in America before 1935: workers' compensation.

To the extent that historians consider workers' compensation at all, they regard it, and properly so, as an artifact of the progressive era. What historians fail to realize, however, is that workers' compensation, like many social welfare entities, enjoyed a life that extended well beyond the era of its creation. Indeed, it remains a vital program today, drawing over twenty-two billion dollars in insurance premiums from employers.[2]

For Arthur Altmeyer, workers' compensation held a special significance. Even in 1936, experts in social insurance tended also to be experts in workers' compensation, and Altmeyer was no exception. As an administrator of the Wisconsin Industrial Commission, he had worked closely with the program. It was the program on which he had grown up.

Workers' compensation assisted workers injured in the course of employment by providing them with a portion of their lost income and with medical care to treat their injuries. The program arrived in Wisconsin and elsewhere in 1911 and soon spread to nearly every state in the country, although it took Mississippi until 1948 to pass a workers' compensation law. The state workers' compensation laws, therefore, formed extremely important precedents for federal planners who hoped to create a disability insurance program.

One reason for the importance of workers' compensation in the plans of the Social Security Board was that it provided a less than cheerful precedent for the expansion of social security to include disability. By the thirties, the state programs had developed severe and widely recognized problems. A generation after the euphoria of the progressive era, workers' compensation was characterized by legal bickering that added delay and cost to the compensation process and by extraordinarily wide disparities in benefits from state to state that left some states with benefit levels that were, by any sort of measure, inadequate to cover the costs of injured workers.

At the same time that the Committee on Economic Security and its staff sat down to write the Social Security Act, Walter Dodd investigated the administration of workers' compensation for the Commonwealth Fund. His findings confirmed the low opinion that many social welfare experts had of workers' compensation.

Dodd painted a sordid picture of workers' compensation. Illinois and New York offended him the most. In Illinois four of the arbitrators who heard disputed compensation cases had less than three month's experience, and Dodd reported that they spent most of their time "keeping their political fences intact." All owed their appointments to political connections, and some were illiterate. Few expressed any interest in the compensation law itself.

New York, the home of Secretary of Labor Frances Perkins and the political base of the Democratic candidate for president from 1928 to 1944, maintained one of the nation's most liberal workers' compensation laws, and its industrial commission included some of the nations' most dedicated administrators. Still, abuses occurred. Dodd described one hearing in which the representatives of the insurance company began to quarrel with the referee hearing the case. The referee, the representative, and the witnesses all spoke at once, and the stenographer threw down her pencil in despair. Workers' compensation, as practiced in New York was frenzied, with as many as fifty-five to sixty cases being scheduled on a single day, and it was not free of corruption.

Immigrants crowded the hearing rooms, many speaking broken English, unable completely to understand the questions being put to them by lawyers. As in most states, insurance companies nearly always retained counsel for a hearing. Employees fended for themselves unless their union intervened. The practice of sending "runners" to solicit business for attorneys endured in New York. The foreign born constituted between 50 and 75 percent of the New York City caseload, and the runners concentrated most of their attention on this group. As the lawyers hustled for business, the insurance companies cultivated the referees. The commission made an effort to rotate the referees' calendars so that a particular referee did not continue to hear the cases from a particular insurance company year after year. Still, the insurance companies maintained cordial relations with the referees and made it a regular practice to send them what Dodd discretely calls "Christmas remembrances."[3]

Dodd's report posed an implicit question for the social security administrators. How many of the problems in workers' compensation were administrative in nature, and how many were related to the inherent problems of disability? Administrative problems, after all, were remediable in ways that inherent problems related to disability were not. I. S. Falk, true to his background as a public health technician, took pains to differentiate the proposed disability insurance program from the established workers' compensation programs. He noted that workers' compensation forced administrators to make an untenable distinction between disabilities that originated on the job and those that derived from conditions outside of work. From a social rather than a legal or actuarial point of view, the distinction made little sense, and it would be eliminated in social security's disability insurance program. By the very nature of social security, a federal program, differences in benefit levels among states would also disappear under disability insurance.

If I. S. Falk regarded correcting the problems of workers' compensation as a scientific exercise, Arthur Altmeyer saw the problem in more personal and political terms. He realized in ways that Falk did not that workers' compensation already existed and that it could not simply be shunted aside. Too many of Arthur Altmeyer's former colleagues in state government owed an allegiance to workers' compensation; too many insurance companies and labor unions had invested too much in this program to abandon it. The legacy of the progressive era could not be cast aside as yesterday's news. Instead, there needed to be a continuity between the programs of the progressive era and the programs of the late New Deal. For Altmeyer, as well, workers' compensation presented a more cautionary tale than it did for Falk. If so many problems had arisen in workers' compensation, similar problems might arise in disability insurance. Where Falk advocated quick and correct action, therefore, Altmeyer proposed moving with caution and political prudence.

Altmeyer's caution appeared to be well-founded. Even Falk's researchers realized that the problems of disability insurance extended well beyond the administrative concerns of workers' compensation. At base disability remained an elusive concept that was difficult to define and administer. Falk admitted, for example, that disability was an "elastic concept." "Too strict a system invites pressure to swing in the opposite direction," he said. Altmeyer, mindful of the problems in workers' compensation, called disability a matter of "conjecture," because the state of disability rested not on a set of facts but on the conclusions that were drawn from the facts. Social workers, who were just beginning to administer the public assistance program, agreed with Altmeyer. One said that efforts in the welfare program to distinguish between employable and nonemployable applicants and between temporary unemployables and permanent unemployables had proved "impossible." Altmeyer's actuaries also told him bluntly that "precision" was "impossible."[4]

Ever the careful administrator, Altmeyer hoped to tame the problems of disability through a process of tough yet sympathetic administration—no referees who lacked knowledge of the law—superimposed on clear, modern rules. In workers' compensation, true to its origins as the payment of legal damages for an industrial accident, the mere existence of an impairment often led to benefits; in the proposed social security disability program, a "loss of strength, disfigurement, or diseased condition" would not be enough. Instead, an impairment would need to sever someone from the labor market and cause a "loss of earning power for work in general." Each case would be carefully scrutinized by medical and vocational experts to verify this loss of earning power; that is where competent administration entered the picture. In addition, the rules for permanent and total disability insurance would reflect improvements over those for workers' compensation and, it was hoped, reduce legal disputes. In the workers' compensation program, people who were back on the job after an accident could still receive benefits. In the proposed disability insurance program, such an eventuality was impossible and by making it impossible for a person to collect benefits and work, Altmeyer and his colleagues hoped to lessen legal disputes over the severity and extent of a particular disability. Unlike workers' compensation, disability insurance, as proposed by Altmeyer and Falk, made no allowance for partial benefits. By restricting benefits only to the totally and permanently disabled (not the partially disabled who constituted the bulk of disputed cases in workers' compensation), Altmeyer expected social security to have far fewer legal disputes than workers' compensation.[5]

As this discussion makes clear, the history of disability insurance and of old-age insurance differed from one another, even in the planning stage. Not only did disability insurance come later, it also involved the resolution of extraordinarily difficult bureaucratic, administrative, and political problems. Nor were these problems all reflected in the comparison between disability insurance and workers' compensation. In the creation of disability insurance, social security planners also needed to accommodate other traditions in the treatment of disability, such as the ones that favored one sort of disability over others.

To use a particularly graphic illustration, one might consider the sympathetic treatment of the blind, long thought to be among the deserving poor, and compare and contrast it with the treatment of the mentally ill, long suspected of being less than worthy of state aid. Even a cursory look at the archival records reveals preferential treatment of the blind. In a 1946 memorandum, for example, disability was defined as the "total inability to work by reason of illness or injury." The definition stated that a person would be considered unable to work when he "(1) is blind or (2) is afflicted with any impairment which continually renders it impossible to engage in substantial gainful work." A blind person, in other words, could stop working whenever he or she wished and begin to receive permanent and total disability insurance.[6]

The mentally ill received far less cordial treatment. The earliest drafts of the proposed disability program specified that a person suffering from mental illness would not qualify for disability benefits. Although Falk and his co-workers recognized that mental illness was a leading cause of disability, they cited two reasons for not including it in the social security system. In the first place, many of the mentally ill had their needs taken care of in public hospitals and institutions. The notion of deinstitutionalization had not yet taken hold of social policy. In the second place, certain types of mental illness were too hard to diagnose and, by implication, to police in a system of disability insurance. Falk cited evidence from Sweden where benefits for people suffering from "neurosis" were difficult to control. In the case of the blind, the Social Security Administration believed that automatic entitlement "would not result in malingering." In the case of the mentally ill, the threat of their malingering precluded their even being considered for disability benefits, even under the relatively strict terms envisioned by the Social Security Administration. In plain and simple English, the blind deserved benefits and the mentally ill did not.[7]

It is worth pausing at this point and comparing disability and old-age insurance. Old-age insurance makes distinctions based on marital status and age at retirement, yet it treats the elderly as a homogenous group of wage earners who have reached a certain age and been granted the right of retirement. Disability insurance grants younger individuals the very special right of early retirement, if they can prove they are unable to continue working. Unlike old-age insurance, the disabled are not regarded as a homogeneous group. The blind come at the front of the line of people seeking early retirement.

To be sure, by the time disability insurance reached passage in 1956, the Social Security Administration had dropped its reservations about excluding the mentally ill. They received coverage and provided administrators with some of their most challenging cases. When, however, the Reagan administration began aggressively to examine people on the disability rolls in 1982, it singled out the mentally ill, not the blind, for special attention. The mentally retarded and mentally ill topped the list of those removed from the rolls. As for the blind, they obtained special favors in the 1954 disability legislation that preceded passage of disability insurance. Although no exceptions were made for the blind in the 1956 law, the Senate, responding to the leadership of Senator Vance Hartke, added a more lenient definition of disability for the blind in 1965.

The differences among types of disabilities, it should be clear, underscored fundamental differences between old-age and disability insurance. Old age represented a convenient and relatively easily identified attribute. Proof of age posed no insurmountable problems. Disability, by way of contrast, proved to be a much more difficult concept to measure and, therefore, to administer. The condition of being a certain age applied to everyone; the state of disability was difficult to translate from one person to the next. From the very beginning of the planning process, administrators were tempted to use convenient shortcuts such as equating disability with blindness.

Ironies in the Passage of Disability Insurance

The differences between old-age insurance and disability insurance extended to the method of their respective enactments. Old-age insurance came into existence in two fell swoops: 1935 and 1939. The passage of disability insurance was also the product of two major social security laws, but these laws came nearly twenty years later: 1954 and 1956. The disability insurance program was not as complete as the 1939 old-age insurance law until 1960, when workers of all ages became eligible for disability benefits.

The lag in the passage of disability insurance, and Medicare as well, has not been properly interpreted by historians, who commonly make two mistakes. They attribute passage of disability insurance to an "incremental" legislative style, and they fail to see differences in the laws passed in the nineteen fifties and those passed earlier.

These mistakes require correction, for they conceal important and distinctive features of disability insurance. Although disability insurance was not passed until 1956, Arthur Altmeyer had advocated it at least since 1941. The incremental strategy was not in place until 1950. Before that time, the Social Security Board envisioned a very different disability insurance law from the one that was eventually passed. This law, as expressed in such vehicles as the Wagner-Murray-Dingell bill of 1943, would have been part of a comprehensive federal system of social insurance. It would have been linked closely with a federal temporary disability law (that never was passed and never will be), and it would have applied to workers of all ages. The act, as passed, came nowhere close to these attributes.

The famous incremental strategy took years to develop. When the second social security advisory council met in 1947 and 1948, for example, social security administrators refused to sanction a proposal that would have restricted disability payments to people over fifty-five. The Bureau of Old-Age and Survivors Insurance sent Arthur Altmeyer a memo that noted that more than half of disability cases occurred among workers younger than fifty-five "when the worker has heavy family responsibilities and has not had the opportunity to build up adequate protection through savings or insurance." O. C. Pogge, one of the bureau's employees, made a different argument against compromising on a program of disability insurance for people over fifty-five. He said that a general disability program should emphasize the three "R's: recovery, rehabilitation, and return to work." A program for those above fifty-five, on the other hand, would be dominated by "old-age retirement considerations and would be regarded as permanent." Viewed from any angle, he concluded, "a half-way program would inevitably lead to disappointing results."[8]

In the fifties, despite these and similar warnings, the Social Security Administration moved toward a half-way program. As passed in 1956, the program marked an uneasy adaptation of the plans drafted by Falk in the late thirties to the political conditions of the nineteen fifties. The Social Security Administration continued to insist on the importance of expert administration by medical and vocational experts in a successful disability program. In this sense, the 1956 act took its contents from the social security planning memos that had been drafted over the years. Instead of putting the Social Security Administration in total charge of the program, however, the act gave states, acting under contract to the Social Security Administration, the right to make the initial declarations of disability. Just as in the workers' compensation program, each state would make disability declarations. And the act limited benefits to workers, and not their families, who were fifty or older. Yes, there was an incremental strategy in the passage of disability insurance, but it came into existence much later than is commonly supposed. No, the disability insurance program did not mark a simple expansion of social security or the clearing of one of the items on the New Deal agenda for social security's expansion.

In a sense, the employees of the Social Security Administration, eager to gain passage of disability insurance and mindful of the conservative nature of the era, disregarded their own warnings about the volatility of disability insurance. Aware of the need for careful administration, the board acquiesed in the creation of a complex administrative system in which the individual states made decisions about eligibility for disability. Did Congress have any qualms about taking this action? Like the Social Security Administration, the proponents of disability insurance in Congress recognized its controversial nature and searched for any possible grounds of compromise on this highly polarized issue. The passage of time made congressmen and bureaucrats alike receptive to almost any compromise, provided it broke the political deadlock and led to disability insurance.

The conservatives extracted a high price for their reluctant, half-

287

hearted, and less than total support for disability insurance. Instead of expanding social insurance, disability insurance would, according to the congressional documents surrounding its passage, serve the cause of rehabilitating the disabled. A person could apply for disability benefits and rehabilitation at the same state office (of that same vocational rehabilitation program mentioned in the Social Security Act). The entire exercise would take place in an atmosphere characterized by the positive attitude of the rehabilitation agencies.

The differences between old-age insurance and disability insurance were now manifold. Disability insurance involved far more subjective judgments about the condition necessary to initiate benefits. Disability insurance, with its age restriction, covered a far smaller percentage of the population at risk. Disability insurance relied on a state-federal partnership for its administration and on a vaguely defined relationship between a massive social insurance program, paid for and run by the federal government, and a highly selective and quite small social service program, run by the state governments and only partially funded by the federal government. Disability insurance in many ways involved an extension of the employer-employee contributory system of social insurance, yet it amounted almost to a redefinition of the American style of social insurance.

Disability Insurance in Operation: The Rehabilitation Link

What happened to this law once enacted? In the first place, it failed to redefine the American style of social insurance quite as decisively as conservatives hoped it would. The creative link between rehabilitation and disability benefits failed to take hold, a victim of the cynical politics of the passage of disability insurance and, beyond that, of the realities of the American social welfare system.

Congress put political appearances above demographic and bureaucratic realities. The Social Security Administration can be excused from responsibility because few of its employees believed that the rehabilitation scheme would work. It was doomed before it began. Congress wanted the states to rehabilitate people who were, by all practical measures, well beyond rehabilitation. Everyone agreed that of all the barriers to rehabilitation, age and severity of an impairment were the most severe. Congress sent the states nothing but older people with severe impairments and told the states to go out and rehabilitate them.

The states looked for help from the Social Security Administration to transform their limited and highly selective vocational rehabilitation programs into agencies capable of dealing with the problems of the totally and permanently disabled. Here they found another double message. The Social Security Administration wanted to help, but its employees doubted the ability of the states to administer the program and entertained thoughts of running the program by themselves. As Arthur Hess, the social security administrator in charge, expressed the idea in his Columbia Oral History Memoir:

> We had a Social Security program which up to that time was a hundred percent, straight-line federal operation. There were few if any people . . . who were philosophically conditioned to working with a state program. . . . All through the first years in the disability program we had repeated reactions from our field and regional people and from many of the central office people that we ought to get the state agencies out of the picture just as quickly as possible.[9]

From the very beginning, the state rehabilitation directors realized that their new responsibility for running the so-called disability determination services increased their vulnerability to criticism and offered few compensating advantages. Congressmen were bound to wonder why the state agencies were not returning more of the people who applied for permanent and total disability benefits to productive employment. The director of the Florida rehabilitation program complained to Arthur Hess that social security simply dumped cases on his agency, without doing any screening. Social security referred everyone who applied for disability insurance to the state rehabilitation program and expected the state rehabilitation program to respond. That meant more work for the rehabilitation agency, and it caused the number of people rejected for rehabilitation to balloon.[10]

Social security administrators, for their part, could not understand why the rehabilitation agencies reacted so negatively to the privilege of making disability determinations. In a typical late fifties memorandum, one Social Security bureaucrat complained of the "negative attitude" on the part of the Office for Vocational Rehabilitation. Social Security staff felt as though they had given the states one of their most prized possessions. Not only did the states not take proper care of this possession, they regarded it as a burden.[11]

Social security bureaucrats watched with dismay as the states failed to process disability cases as promptly as they would have liked. Unlike social security, state rehabilitation agencies had never regarded the quick and accurate processing of cases as a responsibility of overriding importance. Quickness meant little in a rehabilitation process that often took years; accuracy made little sense to an agency that realized how subjective disability was. Backlogs mounted. By November 1957, the states found themselves with 400,000 disability applications to process.[12]

Shortly after the beginning of the program, the Social Security Administration realized it would have to reach an accommodation with the states. It developed means to refer only motivated applicants for disability benefits to the state vocational rehabilitation program. The states continued to process application for disability insurance. The Social Security Administration allowed the states not to refer people over fifty-five, people who were bedridden, people who were institutionalized, people who were mentally ill and had a negative prognosis, and people who had a worsening impairment to their rehabilitation programs. SSA took this action in 1959.[13]

That meant that by 1959 disability determination had stopped being a recruiting station for rehabilitation as Congress had imagined it would be. In that same year, Robert Ball of the Social Security Administration testified that only a small number of people had been rehabilitated. He said that one reason for the federal-state set-up was a realization that "state determinations would be more acceptable to the groups that had opposed the program." "Now of course you have put your finger on the whole thing," replied Congressman Burr Harrison of Virginia. The congressional dialogue suggested that the federal-state system of disability determination made better politics than social policy. By 1975 more than half of the state agencies responded to a congressional inquiry by saying that the original decision to link disability determination and vocational rehabilitation was no longer valid.[14]

The problems, in other words, were more than transitional ones that attended the start of the program. The relationship between rehabilitation and disability insurance never materialized, even when Congress removed the age restriction from the disability insurance program in 1960. Disability insurance failed to establish a new style of American social insurance, one in which working became an alternative to receiving benefits for not working.

Although the system never worked as intended, it has proved nearly impossible to change. That, in turn, suggests some additional limitations in the incremental approach to social security. Disability insurance has become the nearly classic example of this approach: beginning cautiously with a disability "freeze" in 1954, moving to a limited disability insurance program in 1956, and gradually filling in this program until by 1972, disability and old age benefits resembled each other completely. At the same time, however, disability insurance remains different from old-age and survivors insurance. Once in the picture, the states have remained there. Not all incremental moves are, in effect, remediable. Some, like the decision to share administrative responsibility with the states, have permanent consequences.

Disability Insurance in Operation: Legal Disputes

If one considers the Social Security Administration's desire to escape from the negative precedent of workers' compensation, the persistence of the states in the administration of disability insurance carries with it a sense of irony. Nor do the ironies end there, for like workers' compensation, the disability insurance program has also engendered a great deal of legal controversy and created disputed cases that end in court. All of the disadvantages attributed to workers' compensation apply: disputed cases raise questions about fairness and consistency from one case to another, since some people have access to better lawyers and more sympathetic judges; disputed cases lead to delays as lawyers struggle to carve out time to try the case and judges face crowded dockets; disputed cases encourage people to maintain their "disabled behavior" so as to prove their permanent disability; and consequently disputed cases mitigate against recovery and rehabilitation.

Indeed, the disability insurance system, far more than the other components of social security, has a complexity that might be described as Madisonian. Unlike the rest of Social Security, disability insurance relies on a series of checks and balances. If a person does not like the decision rendered by the executive branch, he can always try the judicial. People who have their claim rejected by the states have the right to ask the states to reconsider. If still rejected, a claimant has the right to appear before an administrative law judge and argue his claim in person. From there a person may take his case to an appeals council and to the federal courts, with full right of appeal in the federal courts.

The administrative law judges, the bureaucratic descendants of the hearings referees described by Walter Dodd, bring elements of a legal culture to a system that is dominated by other concerns. An administrative law judge once described his job as "semi-judicial and hard to understand." Another administrative law judge says with some emphasis that he is "not an accountant." These descriptions underscore the fact that the administrative law judges do not keep the system in front of them when they go to work. Instead, they look at the facts of the individual case that they are to decide. They do not draft their decisions surrounded by thousands of pages of Social Security rules; they write their decisions with an individual's plight, often a troubled individual's plight, in mind. They give an applicant his day in court. [15]

The decision to put a hearings and appeals system in Social Security goes back to Arthur Altmeyer. Wilbur Cohen, the man who knew Altmeyer best, has said that this system represented one of Altmeyer's priorities. In the case of old-age and survivors insurance, the system protects well-defined rights and guards against administrative error. In the case of disability, the system creates another unintended resemblance to the workers' compensation program. Because of the system, disability has become a litigious program that perpetuates the nineteenth century idea of fault and causes people to take legal action against the government. Litigation, apparently, is one of the problems inherent in disability which the Social Security Administration has not been able to overcome.

The administrative law judges bear the brunt of this litigation. The passage of disability insurance led to an epidemic of it. Before 1956 the Social Security system permitted a disgruntled applicant to appeal a case and appear before what were then called referees. Some people took up the system's offer. Most realized the futility of such a move. Facts were facts. Whether or not a person was sixty-five or married to another person allowed little leeway for argument. In the disability program, in contrast, facts were not quite facts. They were pieces of information that led to a conclusion over which reasonable men might differ. Disability produced more grounds for disagreement than did old age. When the disparity among the states in interpreting facts became part of the system, the grounds for disagreement grew.

Between 1955 and 1958, requests for hearings in the social security system rose by more than five hundred percent. The Social Security Administration scrambled to hire more administrative law judges. The number was 30 in 1956, and 110 in 1960. By 1959 requests for hearings reached 1300 per month. Today 800 administrative law judges handle more than 300,000 requests for hearings a year; at least 80 percent of those requests concern disability.[16]

Arthur Altmeyer and his peers intended the hearings to be informal. The presence of the administrative law judge with wide latitude to question witnesses and search out the facts made it unnecessary for a claimant to bring a lawyer. The government never had a lawyer to argue its side of the case.

Even in the early years of the disability insurance program, however, certain pockets of the country, such as the depressed coal mining areas of West Virginia and Kentucky, produced many disputed cases and many appearances by lawyers. In 1960 one administrative law judge wrote candidly of the problem in a letter to his supervisor:

> Inasmuch as the southern half of West Virginia and the eastern half of Kentucky are very depressed areas, with thousands of able-bodied coal miners out of work, I feel that the caseload will be heavy for several years to come. . . . On my last trip to Pikesville, Kentucky there were lawyers representing eight of the fourteen cases which I heard.

As this letter revealed, the appeals process received more of the social pressure on the disability process than did state disability examiners. When a court or an administrative law judge yielded to those pressures, the action was amplified by the legal profession and by others who now saw a real possibility for getting benefits. It was, therefore, the administrative law judge far more than the disability examiners who were forced to hold the line against the forces of expansion that opponents of disability insurance so vividly described and so strongly feared.[17]

The administrative law judges, for their part, did not regard holding the line as part of their jobs. They did not think in terms of lines; they thought in terms of people. In an unguarded moment, an administrative law judge once recorded his impressions of a case. The case was extraordinarily tangled, involving veterans benefits, workers' compensation benefits, conflicting dates of employment, and many of the other complexities that appeared in disability cases. The administrative law judge plunged into these legal questions. He confided to his superior, however, that before the hearing he looked out the window and saw the claimant arriving. The claimant's attorney drove the car, and the claimant's wife helped the claimant out. He climbed the steps to the hearing in obvious pain. He wobbled as he entered the room and approached the hearing table. "He appeared to be frail and sickly," observed the judge, and he "had considerable difficulty in understanding some of the questions directed to him and some moderate difficulty in answering." When the state disability examiner went through the prescribed routine of processing the case, he was not able to give notice to these things. The administrative law judge reacted differently, and he brushed aside the legalisms and declared the person disabled. [18]

Another administrative law judge put the matter this way. "I am not able to give much weight to self-serving declarations, conclusions of law and opinion evidenced by laymen, particularly when there is no opportunity to observe the demeanor of the witness." That expressed the matter nicely: the administrative law judge had a chance to observe the demeanor of the witness, and this observation made a difference. [19]

Few of the applicants, after all, were cheating. The people who came before the administrative law judges included Ed Pullam. He was married and had six children. He had worked in the coal mines until his closed on December 15, 1959. When his mine reopened, his employer refused to hire him. The employer said his physical impairments caused him to work too slowly; he was also too old to rehire, and the employer feared an increase in his insurance premium if he hired Pullam. Pullam drew unemployment compensation, then filed for disability. At the time of his application he was fifty-three years old, a bit old to take his sixth grade education and seek other work. In theory, Pullam could work, however, and the state agency rejected his disability claim. For the administrative law judge, the case represented a close call. Pullam was unemployed.

He was impaired. Perhaps he deserved benefits. The administrative law judge, not the disability examiner, had to stare Pullam in the face and say, no, he was not disabled.[20]

A more recent case heard in Chicago updates the example. A woman enters the hearing room. She is black, very obese, an unmarried mother of five children, four of whom are under sixteen. "My back and legs hurt me so bad. I hurts all over," she says in an indistinct voice. "It be like something pulling me down. I vomits." The administrative law judge asks her to describe the medications she is taking, and she pulls out a haphazardly assembled collection of medicines from her oversized handbag. She appears to be carrying all of her possessions with her. She puts a bottle of medicine "for nerves" down on the table; next she pulls out a different bottle and appears at a loss to explain its purpose. For her high blood pressure, she thinks. The judge breaks the silence and asks, "the administration (actually, the state disability determination office) says that you could operate a feather cutting machine. Could you do that?" "What's a feathercutting machine," she answers.[21]

As these examples reveal, disability poses considerable problems that often require personal hearings to resolve. In this sense, disability insurance differs from the rest of Social Security. Furthermore, hearings invite the participation of lawyers, and the presence of lawyers escalates the level of formality. As late as 1970, claimants appeared with attorneys about twenty percent of the time. Today a resident of Baltimore flips through the Sunday paper and reads the following advertisement:

> Social Security Denied? Call Disability Specialists Jenkins and Block . . . Former Social Security Staff Attorney; Free Consultation; No Money Up Front; No Recovery/No Fee.

This sort of advertising does a lot to increase what social security planners used to call "claims consciousness," and it increases legal representation at social security hearings.[22]

Conclusion

In this manner, disability insurance resembles other disability programs as much as it does the rest of social security. The program makes special concessions to people with certain disabilities, such as blindness, in a way that has no analogue in old-age and survivors insurance (although the kidney dialysis entitlement in medicare comes close). The program depends on the state governments whereas old-age and survivors insurance is a purely federal operation. Finally, disability insurance involves a great deal of disagreement and litigation as does workers' compensation. The rest of social security gets conducted in a much less discretionary way.

The story of disability insurance does not have to be told this way. In many ways its development parallels that of the rest of Social Security. Its benefit structure comes directly from the old-age and survivors insurance program. It pays benefits to a workers' dependents and carries an entitlement to Medicare, just as old-age insurance does. The growth of the program has attracted a great deal of recent attention, just as the growth of old-age and survivors insurance has. Efforts to cut benefits have met with a similar resistance in both programs.

At the same time, it is clear that fundamental differences exist between disability and old-age insurance. The risk of disability has not been institutionalized by the social security program. Instead, it continues to reveal its distinctive features. At the very least, we should appreciate the fact that the giant program known as old-age, survivors, and disability, and hospital insurance contains many disparate parts each of which deserves its own form of special attention. Such attention pays scholarly dividends and helps to clarify thinking about questions related to the broad, generic entity known as social security.

Notes

1. I wish to thank the Twentieth Century Fund for the financial support of the research which contributed to this chapter. Many of these themes are developed at greater length in my forthcoming Twentieth Century Fund study of disability policy. This study also contains a full listing of citations. In developing this article, I also benefited from reading Andrew Achenbaum's *Social Security: Visions and Revisions* (1986) and from reading the chapters in this book by Mark Leff and Gary Freeman. Conversations with Wilbur Cohen and Arthur Hess were also invaluable. None of the people mentioned bears responsibility for the accuracy of this account or for its conclusions.

2. See John D. Worrall and David Appel, "Some Benefit Issues in Workers' Compensation," in Worrall and Appel eds., *Workers' Compensation Benefits: Adequacy, Equity, Efficiency* (Ithaca: New York, ILR Press, 1985), pp. 1–18. The same volume contains Edward D. Berkowitz and Monroe Berkowitz, "Challenges to Workers' Compensation: An Historical Analysis," pp. 158–80 which expands on the themes developed here.

3. Walter Dodd, *Administration of Workmen's Compensation* (New York: The Commonwealth Fund, 1936), pp. 222–86.

4. Falk to Wilbur Cohen, December 3, 1938, File 056.11, Chairman's File, Records of the Social Security Board, National Archives; "Extended Disability Benefits: Administrative and Medical Considerations," February 15, 1949 in Arthur Altmeyer Papers, Box 7, Wisconsin State Historical Society, Madison, Wisconsin; Lucille Smith, consultant on medical social work, to Jane Hoey, February 5, 1942, File 056.11, January-December 1941, Box 20, Accession 56–533, Record Group 47, Washington National Records Center, Suitland, Maryland.

5. "Extended Disability Insurance," no date, no file, prepared for 1947–48 Advisory Council, Box 6, Accession 56–533, Record Group 47, Washington National Records Center.

6. Oscar Pogge to Arthur Altmeyer, February 21, 1946, File 056.11, 1944–47, Accession 56–533, Record Group 47, Washington National Records Center.

7. Falk to Cohen, December 3, 1938, File 056.11, Chairman's Files, Record Group 47, National Archives.

8. For these quotations and more on the passage of disability insurance in 1956 see my forthcoming book as well as such standard social security sources as Martha Derthick, *Policymaking for Social Security* (Washington, D.C.: The Brookings Institution, 1979).

9. Interview with Arthur Hess, Columbia Oral History Collection, pp. 1, 45.

10. Claude Andrews to Arthur Hess, January 20, 1960, File 055.4, 1968, Box 7, Accession 68–888, Record Group 47, Washington National Records Center.

11. George Wyman to Victor Christgau, September 28, 1959, File 055.4, 1957–59, Box 7, Accession 68–888, Record Group 47, Washington National Records Center.

12. "Processing Time for Disability Claims," November 27, 1957, File 752.1, Box 92, Accession 64–751, Record Group 47, Washington National Records Center.

13. Arthur Hess to Robert Ball, November 25, 1959, Box 055.4, 1957–59, Box 7, Accession 68–888. Record Group 47, Washington National Records Center.

14. Subcommittee on the Administration of Social Security Laws, Com-

mittee on Ways and Means, *Administration of Social Security Disability Insurance Program* (Washington, D.C.: Government Printing Office, 1960), p. 26.

15. Thomas C. Fischer Memorandum, September 6, 1960, File Louisville Correspondence, Box 22, Accession 67–278, Record Group 47, Washington National Records Center; Subcommittee on Oversight, Committee on Governmental Affairs, *Social Security Disability Reviews: The Role of the Administrative Law Judge* (Washington, Government Printing Office, 1983).

16. On the rise of litigation see *Administration of Social Security Disability Insurance*, p. 71; George Wyman to Robert Forsythe, May 25, 1959, File 752.1, Box 92, Accession 64–751, Record Group 47, Washington National Records Center, and Marvin Schwartz, *The Trial of A Social Security Disability Case*, privately distributed by the Social Security Foundation.

17. L. Steel Trotter to Robert Hennings, March 20, 1960, Charleston Correspondence File, Box 22, Accession 67–270, Record Group 47, Washington National Records Center.

18. Memorandum of James La Bianca, July 26, 1961, Siegel Correspondence, Box 1, Accession 67A–278, Record Group 47, Washington National Records Center.

19. Ben Worcester to Claire Hardy, July 6, 1960, Siegel Correspondence, Box 1, Accession 67A–278, Record Group 47, Washington National Records Center.

20. Thomas C. Fisher Memorandum (see note 15).

21. Interview with Thomas Ploss, March 21, 1984, Chicago, Illinois.

22. See, for example, the *Baltimore Sun TV Week* for August 5, 1984, p. 21.

Afterword

This essay was written in 1985. Since that time, the Twentieth Century Fund has published my *Disability Policy: America's Programs for the Handicapped—A Twentieth Century Fund Report* (New York: Cambridge University Press, 1987). My thoughts on the fiftieth anniversary of social security have also been expressed in Edward Berkowitz, ed., *Social Security After Fifty: Successes and Failures* (Westport, CT: Greenwood Press, 1987). This volume also contains relevant essays by Mark Leff, Wilbur J. Cohen, Robert Myers, and W. Andrew Achenbaum.

13

Comment

I. Fred R. Harris

Social security is fifty years old this year—venerated like a sacred icon. Alf Landon, in 1936, was the last serious presidential candidate to call it "a fraud and a hoax." Yet, in official circles, welfare components of the Social Security program—like Medicaid and Aid to Families with Dependent Children (AFDC)—are as despised as a thistle. Even the old-age and medical insurance aspects of Social Security, while praised in principle, are continually attacked at the edges. With seasonal regularity, the budget freezers seek to cap the COLAS—cost of living adjustments—and increase the amounts old people have to contribute toward the costs of their own medical care.

Myths and misconceptions about poverty and social security are the software for this programmed opposition. There is the myth that the conditions that make people poor are temporary, short-term aberrations in our system. In fact, while life today is better for most people than when I was growing up in a small Oklahoma town, a side effect of our becoming an advanced industrial society is that we are always going to have people who are unable to work because they are disabled, blind, too old, or too young and others who, from time to time, cannot find work—and whom families or private charity cannot take care of. It is a permanent cost of doing business in our kind of society.

There is the myth that poor people are mostly deadbeats who deserve their lot. This comes from thinking of recipients as statistics. We should particularize and think of the actual people involved—the elderly woman in Truchas, New Mexico, who tries to live on her social security check of $323 a month, for example, or the young Albuquerque mother of two whose husband has just left them and who needs financial assistance—and daycare—while she tries to get the education and training necessary for a job.

There is the related myth that poor people will not work. In other countries, it is assumed that people do want to work, unless they are physically or psychologically impaired. In the United States, despite all evidence to the contrary, there seems to be an underlying assumption that the work ethic does not extend to poor people. But example after example can be given like that of the thousands of "welfare mothers" (recipients of AFDC), who once overwhelmed a meager U.S. program seeking to *require* them to work, with an avalanche of voluntary applications, only to be sadly disappointed when it turned out that there were in reality few jobs available for them.

There is the myth that the elimination of welfare cheating and fraud would save billions. The fact is that large-scale anti-cheating programs will not pay their way, much less buy a bucket of Pentagon pliers or a gross of their toilet seats. Welfare recipients are at least as honest as high-bracket income tax filers, increased auditing of which group would probably prove to be much more cost effective.

There is the myth that if we would just give poor people enough advice, they would quit welfare. Give them advice if it makes you feel better, but money is what they need. For those who can work, of course, a job is their preferred way to get it. There is the myth that, if advice does not avail, making it hard on poor people will help them see the error of their ways and get them up and going. That is like trying to put a punitive tax on snuff; dipping snuff is already punishment enough. So is being poor.

There is a misconception that the concept of charity is the principal basis for welfare and social security: the more fortunate of us should help to take care of the less fortunate, out of the goodness of our hearts. The fact is that these programs are in our own self-interest—and that is the way they should be justified. It is a proveable and proved fact that a society in which people have enough to live on is a more stable society and one in which more people feel allegiant to the system. Right now, we know that most states seem unable to build enough prisons fast enough to hold the torrent of lawbreakers. What we should realize is that this is not unrelated to the recent rise in the number and percentage of Americans who live in poverty. Democracy itself cannot flourish in an environment without amelioration of both extreme wealth and extreme poverty. People without a chance do not make good democrats. Welfare and social security—and the redistribution they entail—perform a fundamentally stabilizing function in the nation's economy, as well. To paraphrase Pogo, "We have met the beneficiary, and he is us!"

Finally, there is the misconception that social security and Medicare should pay their own way—through earmarked and seemingly constantly increasing payroll taxes. This, in effect, pits workers against old people. The resulting conflict grows worse as the percentage of our old people increases. In 1935, there was a strong but unsuccessful effort to convince Franklin Roosevelt to propose that social security be funded out of general revenue (as many other industrial countries do it). Indeed, that was one of the things Alf Landon later advocated in his poorly reported "fraud and hoax" speech.

To grasp the present consequences of continued insistence on full payroll-tax funding of Social Security and Medicare, suppose for a moment that the lawmakers of the thirties had decided instead to fund *National* Security, not social security, through an earmarked payroll tax. Today's officials would have to react periodically to alarms about the eminent "bankruptcy" of defense. They would feel constrained to vote to increase payroll taxes each time they approved a new weapons systems. At budget-cutting time, they would call for a freeze on defense budget COLAs. They would regularly require generals and admirals to contribute an ever larger share of the costs of their own medical care. And defense contractors, rather than welfare and social security recipients, would come to know what it is to be treated like statistics.

II. David Hamilton

The papers in this session are almost as diverse as the many facets of what is referred to when using the term social security in its broadest sense. Blanche Coll in her paper notes that Arthur Altmeyer regretted the more narrow meaning given to the term when it came to refer only to old-age, survivors and disability insurance. And this assertion seems warranted for each of these papers. One deals with public assistance, one with disability insurance, and one with the financing of old-age and survivors insurance. Each is directed to some particular part of the more general problem of income maintenance in an industrial economy.

Certainly it can be said that our Social Security system did not develop out of some consistently held ideology. As a matter of fact, just the opposite. The whole notion of providing income maintenance, of developing an income stream independent of current participation in the work force or of ownership of productive assets, was largely foreign to the prevailing ideology in this nation both at the time of the establishment of our major income maintenance systems and before. And to many today it still seems an alien idea.

It was not ideology that provoked social security. It was technological necessity provoked by the rise of the industrial economy. The diversity of papers at this conference as well as at this session warrant this statement. The industrial economy is the most secure one that human beings have managed to produce. This is testified to by statistics on longevity, infant mortality, and general health and well-being. But if many of the insecurities of earlier forms of economy have been eliminated by the industrial way of life, there are nevertheless new insecurities that, to some extent, are testimony to its very success. The greater proportion of people for whom we must provide income in old age is a case in point.

Overall the greatest economic hazard in the industrial economy is a loss of pecuniary income for whatever cause. To be without the wherewithal to meet the demands of economic and social reciprocity denies to the one so deprived the possibility and, indeed, the right, to participate in any meaningful way in the social life process. This denial may be by virtue of old age and being denied the right to participate in the work force for either physical or institutional reasons; by virtue of not having a parental relationship which gives entitlement to share in an income stream; by virtue of a work related injury denying one the right or ability to participate in the paid work force; by virtue of a nonwork related disability which also denies full participation in the paid work force; by virtue of the failure of the economy to provide income earning employment for all of those able to, willing to, available for, and seeking work; by virtue of an injury sustained in military service in one of today's industrialized military forces (the remedy for this insecurity, veterans benefits, is usually distinguished from other welfare-state measures by going almost universally unchallenged).

The multiplicity of income maintenance programs, which have largely been independent in their origin, and each of which has been established to meet some well established need, taken collectively make up what is referred to as the welfare state. But because each of these was devised independently, as a problem was recognized as significant and not as the consequence of some overall view of a welfare state, the merits of each must be constantly defended. Worst of all each, by its critics, is looked upon as a cost which we can ill afford and only when in a more charitable mood will they admit it to be a social necessity.

That the income maintenance programs constituting what is referred to as social security are looked upon as costs rather than a general social benefit is attributable partly to the separate origin of each program. The papers we have heard today are all well done and thoroughly researched. Each one focuses on some one aspect of the larger problem of social security. No criticism of any of the authors is intended or implied. Each has done his or her assignment well and in a workmanlike manner. I do not know how such a conference could be held without proceeding in this manner.

And in one way it is fortunate that the welfare state was not conceived out of some preconceived ideological concept of a welfare state. Ideologically conceived notions of the good life or of the ideal state or of the ideal social system have long been a pestiferous influence on the human enterprise. Differences over ideologically held ideas in most instances cannot be resolved short of physical violence or repression.

The merits of the notion of the welfare state is that it is non-ideological. It would be difficult to enlist battalions of people to go fight for the welfare state. Slogans in behalf of the welfare state analogous to "Better red than dead" or "Better dead than red" or "Deutschland über alles" are nonexistent. The notion of the welfare state is a recognition that all of the income maintenance programs of which it is composed do form a consistent economic pattern, one that, far from being an economic burden, assures a more stable industrial economy.

For those pioneers who contributed to the welfare state and to social security by devoting their attention to some particular insecurity inherent in the industrial economy, the larger meaning may have seemed quite remote and irrelevant. After all, who could have successfully made the argument that as any one facet, workmen's compensation for example, went, so went the industrial economy? Any one part was such a small part of the whole that such claims would have obviously been considered grandiose. But, and this is a large but, taken as a whole just some such argument may well be made.

Professor Berkowitz in his paper refers to the dismissal of the Murray-Wagner Act in the post–World War II era as "America's ill-considered reaction" to the Beveridge report. I do not deny that such a dismissal is made, but I believe that dismissal of the use of Keynes as an intellectual foundation for the welfare state is indeed ill-advised. Beveridge was Keynes applied.

In the back of *The General Theory of Employment Interest and Money*, J. M. Keynes directed his attention to the economic strategy that his technical analysis, which preceded these comments, suggested. He noted that two flaws existed in an industrial economy organized on a capitalist basis. One of these was its extreme uneven distribution of income and the other was its historic instability. And he suggested that measures to reduce the uneven distribution of income would go a long way toward reducing the instability. It was this part of Keynes that Beveridge picked up on in his famous report as well as in his *Full Employment in A Free Society*.

The essential truth of these notions was fleetingly recognized during the 1950s in the notion of the "built-in stabilizers". It was assumed that the welfare state, including that part devoted to the welfare of farmers, worked in such a fashion as to destabilize automatically the federal budget when the economy faltered. Too much weight was given to the automatic initiation of these measures in making for economic stability, but the thought was going in the right direction. Attention was removed from the cost of each to the economic benefits that derived from the program as a whole.

These notions, however, did not survive the fifties. They were derailed by the military expenditure of the 1960s and by the new conservatism that focused attention on the pecuniary cost element of social security. And given the budget effect of military expenditure it was easy enough to once again focus attention on the cost aspect of social security, welfare state, or what have you. The military effort gave to the eternal critics a welcome opportunity to revive the attack.

Ironically, welfare measures are often viewed by the critics as wholly consummatory and nonproductive while these same critics endorse almost unlimited military expenditure, an expenditure which is one hundred per cent consummatory. It has been described as "produced means for further destruction".

But this fiftieth anniversary of the social security system is no time for apologies. It is time for addressing realities. The matter of cost when focused on the pecuniary side is an argument over how to do the bookkeeping. The real cost of social security is how much of the real goods and services produced in this industrial economy we will allocate to those who have no current pecuniary claims on that output, either from direct participation in the work force or from ownership of property allegedly engaged in producing those goods and services. The word *will* is the critical word. Theoretically only, we could allocate one hundred per cent, which, of course, would end the flow as there would be no goods and services for those who produced the current abundance. But putting it in this absurd fashion draws attention to the fact that we can "afford" social security. At what level depends upon our willingness to support that level. And that of course depends upon social attitudes.

Social attitudes are in turn affected by the general understanding of how any social program works and an understanding of its place and necessity. If it could once and for all be understood how, in a Keynesian sense, social security is both necessary and socially beneficial we could overcome the picky fights over the bookkeeping. As Stuart Chase once put it, anything which is technologically feasible is socially fundable.[1]

This same notion was expressed almost four decades ago by C. E. Ayres who wrote:

Other objections are indeed made, with the greatest vigor and even bitterness. They are capitalistic objections. People who deny the possibility of general unemployment object to social security or any other program for preventing what they deny exists. So do people who attribute unemployment to "government interference." People who maintain that the administration which began in 1933 was responsible for the depression which began in 1929 also object to social security.

If objections such as these prevail, they will make any adequate program of social security "politically" impossible. That does not mean that it is economically impossible.[2]

A long time ago, Gilbert Seldes in his *Your Money and Your Life* called attention to the social necessity of income maintenance in a very dramatic way by stating, "The one luxury the rich cannot afford is the poverty of the poor."[3]

Notes

1. Stuart Chase, *Money to Grow On* (New York: Harper and Row, 1964), Ch. 18

2. C. E. Ayres, *The Divine Right of Capital* (Boston: Houghton Mifflin, 1946), pp. 103–104.

3. Gilbert Seldes, *Your Money and Your Life* (New York: Whittlesey House, 1938), p. 208.

Epilogue

In 1935 long after most industrialized nations had instituted some form of national social insurance, the United States established its social security system. Although numerous reformers had advocated various kinds of social insurance for many years, social security's arrival in the United States was largely due to time and events.[1] The Great Depression of the 1930s shattered the illusion that the United States was somehow different than the rest of the world; it called into question the prevailing ideology of voluntarism, individualism, self-help, and private philanthropy; and it undermined the abiding faith in the market-oriented, free enterprise system. Under the leadership of, and within the parameters set by, President Franklin D. Roosevelt, the architects of social security fashioned a system that was uniquely American. To some extent, as Arthur Altmeyer has pointed out, the American system differed because it was rooted in labor legislation rather than in poor-relief laws.[2] Moreover, while the American architects were imbued with social consciousness and a sense of community, they were also realists and pragmatists. These men and women had one eye on the Southern-dominated congressional committees and the other eye on the Supreme Court; they were also sensitive to American ideology, myths, and character. Many of them cared deeply about preserving the federal system and maintaining the spirit of free enterprise, initiative, and savings. They had a vision of a universal, comprehensive system that would provide a measure of security from cradle to grave and substitute insurance for public assistance. But they were prepared to wait to fill in the gaps. They would establish a foundation that could be built upon the future. The result was a limited, contributory system that was moderately redistributive and that provided only partial protection.

The social security system aroused opposition from both ends of the political spectrum. The left denounced the low benefits, the reliance on individual contributions rather than on general revenues, and the failure to redistribute income. Viewing it as the opening wedge of socialism, the Right fulminated against the expansion of public assistance, the compulsory features, the involvement of the national government, and the demise of voluntarism. The debate continued on and off, for twenty years until social security was safely enshrined in the American system by the Eisenhower administration. By then, whether out of a desire to promote social stability, economic growth, national efficiency, political self-interest, or social justice, a consensus was reached in the body politic in favor of social security. The old controversies were also muted by the postwar prosperity, the acceptance of Keynesian economics, and the broad based desire for security. Meanwhile, benefits were increased, more Americans were covered, and the system was made more comprehensive by adding survivor benefits, disability, and, eventually, Medicare. As a result of the expanded social security system and the programs of the Great Society, the United States began to resemble the welfare states of the European industrialized nations.

America's acceptance of the welfare state began to waver in the mid-1970s. Inflation, the economic slowdown, escalating payroll and income taxes, resentment with skyrocketing welfare rolls, and demographic changes combined to undermine the consensus that had developed during the previous decades. In addition, the revived ideological Right, strengthened by the Reagan victories, raised the old philosophical objections: freedom of choice, voluntarism, and the dangers of the big state. While most of the attack centered on Great Society programs and AFDC, the basic social security programs—old-age insurance and disability—did not escape criticism. Indeed, the short-term financial crisis facing OAI in 1982–83 only magnified the debate and raised serious questions about the long-term viability of the system. The political logjam in Congress and the executive branch produced paralysis until President Ronald Reagan established the National Commission on Social Security Reform. Working in secret and virtually dictating a reform package, the commission dealt with the short-term and long-term crises within the old consensus framework.[3] That stilled the controversy, but by no means silenced it.

The fiftieth anniversary of social security provided an opportunity to reexamine social security's past and confront the issues raised in the recent controversy. The University of New Mexico Conference on Social Security brought together five veteran policy makers and a number of scholars for two days of intense and lively discussion that tended to focus on Old-Age Insurance, but that also touched on other aspects of the complex system of American social insurance. The conversations and formal papers reproduced in this volume revealed some major disagreements that reflected different points of view, degrees of personal involvement and scholarly detachment, the approaches of the various disciplines represented, and the perspectives of several generations. Nevertheless, all of the conference participants shared the basic assumptions that have characterized the general consensus on social security during the past half century: namely, that a broad, government sponsored and administered system of social insurance was necessary in the 1930s and is still justified, that the goal of such a system should be to provide a basic floor of protection against the insecurities of life in modern industrial society, and that the emphasis should be on prevention of poverty rather than on public assistance. In short, they believed that the social security system, though not perfect, has worked rather well over the past fifty years and has served the public good. No one called for the scrapping of social security or a major overhaul of the system, as some critics, representing in particular the ideological Right, have advocated.[4]

As the discussions and essays in this volume indicate, this does not mean that the participants rejected future changes in the social security system. They recognized that social security has evolved over the past fifty years in response to economic, social, demographic, and political developments in the United States. As Wilbur Cohen observed, none of the architects of social security could have predicted all of the changes that have occurred, such as the swelling of the welfare rolls. Further adjustments and adaptations will be necessary in order to maintain the viability of the system and to retain public support. Several participants argued that the agenda in the future will have to shift the emphasis from old-age benefits to the health side of social insurance. On the one hand, the retirement system will have to take account of the growing prosperity of a majority of the elderly and the supplemental protection offered by IRAs and secured private pension systems. On the other hand, the United States must prepare itself for the coming financial crisis in Medicare, the miracles of modern medicine and escalating health costs, an aging population that is living longer, and public sensitivity to the plight of individuals and families stemming from long-term illness and disability. Recently, even President Reagan publicly expressed concern for the problems of catastrophic illness.

Social security has become an integral part of American life; and, though there will be modifications in detail and emphasis, it will likely remain fundamentally the same over the next half century. Those who formulate and administer the changes must be aware of the heritage of the past as well as contemporary and future trends. Their success will depend, in part, on the careful consideration given to the state of the economy, social stability, political realities, ideology, and human values. And while they must appreciate the larger forces that operate in a complex and dynamic society, they must not forget that the fate of millions of individual Americans will be determined by their decisions and actions. Finally, policymakers and the academic community must educate the public about the issues involved and our common stake in social security. It is hoped that this volume, by its assessment of the past and present of social security, will contribute to the development of a sound and serviceable system in the future.

Notes

1. The best review of the efforts of the early efforts of social insurance is found in Roy Lubove, *The Struggle for Social Security 1900–1935* (Cambridge, MA, 1968).

2. Arthur J. Altmeyer, *The Formative Years of Social Security* (Madison, 1968), vii.

3. For an excellent treatment of the National Commission on Social Security Reform, see Paul Light, *Artful Work: The Politics of Social Security Reform* (New York, 1985).

4. For a representative sample of this outlook, see Peter J. Ferrara, *Social Security: Prospects for Real Reform* (Washington, D.C., 1985).

A Chronology of Significant Events in Social Security, 1935–1985*

1935

Social Security Act passed providing for federal old-age insurance, federal-state public assistance and unemployment compensation, and extension of public health services, maternal and child health services, services for crippled children, child welfare services, and vocational rehabilitation services; three member Social Security Board created to administer the Act (August 14, PL 271, Seventy-fourth Congress). Railroad Retirement Act passed (August 29).

1936

Federal unemployment tax of 1 percent of payroll of employers with eight or more employers goes into effect. First public assistance payments made with federal participation under the Social Security Act in some states.

*Compiled by Richard F. Tomasson. I wish to acknowledge two earlier chronologies of significant events in the history of Social Security from which I have freely borrowed: "Significant Events of Social Security, 1935–65," pages 277–87 in Arthur J. Altmeyer, *The Formative Years of Social Security*," Madison: University of Wisconsin Press, 1966; and "Chronology," pages 429–34 in Martha Derthick, *Policymaking for Social Security*, Washington, DC: Brookings Institution, 1979.

1937

Workers begin to acquire OAI credit. Employers and employees begin paying tax of 1 percent on first $3,000 of earnings. Constitutionality of OAI and unemployment insurance provisions of Social Security Act upheld by US Supreme Court (301 US 495, 548, 619). Approved unemployment insurance laws passed by all the states.

1938

All jurisdictions in U.S. making old-age assistance payments under Social Security Act.

1939

Federal Security Agency created with Social Security Board within it. Social Security Act amended to provide benefits to dependents and survivors (OAI becoming OASI), to advance payment of benefits to 1940 from 1942, to revise benefit formula to average monthly earnings basis, to hold tax rates for both employers and employees to 1 percent each through 1942, to tax only first $3,000 of earnings for unemployment insurance, and to increase federal share of public assistance payments (PL 379, Seventy-sixth Congress).

1942

OASI tax rates frozen at 1 percent through 1943. (Increase again postponed in 1943, 1944, 1945, 1946, and 1947, for years through 1949.)

1943

Wartime coverage under OASI provided for seamen employed by or through War Shipping Administration.

1944

Social Security Act amended to authorize appropriation to OASI trust fund from general revenues of any additional amounts required to finance benefits.

1946

Social Security Board abolished and functions transfered to the Federal Security Administrator who created the Social Security Administration with a Commissioner of Social Security to run it. Social Security Act amended to provide OASI benefits to survivors of certain World War II veterans, coverage of private maritime employment under state unemployment insurance, temporary unemployment benefits to seamen with wartime federal employment, greater federal sharing in public assistance payments for a specified period, and larger grants for maternal and child health and child welfare.

1947

Tax rate for employers and employees to be held at 1 percent through 1949, but increased to 1.5 percent each for 1951 and 1952 and to 2 percent in 1952 and thereafter.

1948

Social Security Act amended, over President Truman's veto, to exclude certain newspaper and magazine vendors from OASI coverage. Congress also passed a joint resolution limiting the executive's discretion in issuing new regulations defining who is an "employee" under the Act.

1949

Bureau of Employment Security which administered unemployment insurance transferred from Social Security Administration to Labor Department.

1950

Social Security Act amended to extend OASI coverage to about ten million more persons (including most nonfarm, self-employed persons), to liberalize eligibility conditions, to improve retirement test, to provide earnings credits of $160 a month for military service, to increase OASI benefits by 77 percent, to raise the earnings base to $3600 from $3000, to eliminate 1944 provision authorizing appropriations to the OASI trust fund from general revenues, to establish a federal-state public assistance program of aid to the permanently and totally disabled (APTD), to broaden for federal matching purposes aid to dependent children to include person with whom child is living, and to extend federal matching provisions to aged and blind persons in certain public medical institutions (PL 492, Eightieth Congress).

1951

OASI tax of 2¼ percent of earnings effective for self-employed (1½ times the employee rate). Railroad Retirement Act amended to coordinate railroad retirement with OASI.

1952

OASI benefits increased by 12.5 percent, gratuitous earnings credits for military service extended, retirement test liberalized, and public assistance grant formula liberalized to provide additional funds to the states.

1953

Federal Security Agency abolished; Social Security Administration transferred to Department of Health, Education, and Welfare. Commissioner of Social Security to be appointed by the President with the advice and consent of the Senate. Gratuitous military service credits extended.

1954

Social Security Act amended to extend OASI coverage to farmers, self-employed members of some professions, farm and domestic employees, and, on a voluntary basis, members of state and local government retirement systems (on a group basis) and ministers and members of religious orders; earnings base increased to $4200; OASI benefits increased by 13 percent; tax rates increased for distant future (1970s); retirement test again liberalized; a dropout of four or five years of lowest earnings in computation of benefits allowed; and a "disability freeze" was introduced to protect benefit rights of totally disabled workers (PL 761, Eighty-third Congress).

1955

Gratuitous credits for military service again extended.

1956

Social Security Act amended to provide monthly benefits to disabled workers aged 50–64 (OASI becomes OASDI); to pay child's benefits to disabled children (aged 18 or over) of retired or deceased workers if disability began before age 18; to lower to age 62 the retirement age for widows and female parents, and, on an actuarially reduced basis, for wives and women workers; to extend coverage to self-employed persons (excepting physicians), additional farm owners and operators, and certain state and local government employees; to set up a disability insurance trust fund financed by an additional tax of .25 percent on both employers and employees and a .375 percent on the self-employed; and to reimburse the trust funds for the gratuitous military earnings credits granted veterans (PL 880, Eighty-fourth Congress). The Social Security Act was also amended by extending regular OASDI taxation to members of the military.

1958

OASDI benefits increased by 7 percent, earnings base increased to $4800 from $4200, new tax schedule adopted increasing OASDI tax for 1959 to 2.5 percent, amount exempt from retirement test increased, benefits added for dependents of DI beneficiaries, and the eligibility standard for DI liberalized (PL 85–840).

1960

OASDI tax becomes 3.0, Title I (old-age assistance) amended to provide medical benefits to certain aged persons, age 50 requirement for DI eliminated, and retirement test again liberalized.

1961

Men permitted to retire at age 62 with reduced benefits; minimum benefit increased; benefits payable to aged widow, widower, or surviving dependent parent liberalized; retirement test again liberalized. AFDC eligibility expanded to include intact families with unemployed parents at a state's discretion.

1963

Public assistance functions removed from the Social Security Administration and placed under a newly created Welfare Administration by order of the Secretary of Health, Education, and Welfare.

1964

Eligibility for DI benefits of persons meeting eligibility requirements at time of disability made fully retroactive by permanent legislation.

1965

Social Security Act and the Railroad Retirement Act amended to provide hospital insurance for persons 65 and over (OASDI becomes OASDHI) and persons 65 and over entitled to purchase insurance against the cost of physicians services, half the cost to be paid by the federal government out of general revenues (PL 89–97, Medicare). Also, OASDI benefits increased by 7 percent, tax rate increased to 4.2 percent and earnings base to $6600 for 1966, definition of disability liberalized and retirement test again liberalized, and mandatory OASDHI coverage extended to physicians. Benefits introduced for dependents and survivors aged 18–21 who were full-time students and wife's and widow's benefits to divorced wives when marriage had lasted at least 20 years. Medicaid, a federal-state program for the medically indigent, passed.

1966

Prouty amendment passed providing a flat monthly benefit to certain categories of not fully insured persons at age 72.

1968

OASDI benefits increased by 13 percent and earnings base increased to $7800.

1969

OASDI benefits increased by 15 percent and the OASDHI tax rate increased to 4.8 under a schedule passed in 1967.

1971

OASDI benefits increased by 10 percent, earnings base for 1972 increased to $9000, and the OASDHI tax rate became 10.2 under a schedule enacted in 1969.

1972

OASDI benefits increased 20 percent, automatic adjustments of benefits and the earnings base to take effect in 1975, new formula for calculating benefits introduced, the tax rate increased to 5.85 percent and the earnings base to $10,800 for 1973, waiting period for DI benefits reduced from six to five months, benefits for widows and widowers increased, amount of earnings exempt from the retirement test increased. Special minimum benefit introduced applicable to individuals with long periods of covered employment at a low earnings level. Medicare extended to those receiving DI benefits for at least two years and to insured workers and auxiliaries with chronic kidney disease. Supplemental Security Income passed federalizing assistance to the aged, blind and disabled, to be administered by the Social Security Administration.

1973

OASDI benefits to be increased by 7 percent for March-May 1974 and by an additional 4 percent commencing in June 1974. Earnings base for 1974 increased to $13,200. Automatic adjustments rescheduled to begin in June 1975.

1974-78

Through automatic adjustment based on changes in average earnings, the earnings base was increased to $14,100 in 1975, $15,300 in 1976, $16,500 in 1977, and $17,700 in 1978.

1975

U.S. Supreme Court decision gave fathers with a deceased, disabled, or retired wife the same benefits as a mother in a comparable situation.

1977

The Social Security Act was amended in 1977 to meet an unexpected deficit. The scheduled tax rate for 1978 was left unchanged at 6.05 percent but the rate for 1979 was increased to 6.13 percent and the rates for subsequent years increased. The earnings base, in excess of projected automatic increases, was scheduled to be: $22,900 for 1979, $25,900 for 1980, and $29,700 for 1981. The formula adopted in 1972 was revised because of the increasing replacement ratios arising from the inflation of the 1970s. The regular minimum benefit was frozen at its December 1977 level. U.S. Supreme Court decision did away with the dependency requirement for aged husbands and widowers on the grounds that none existed for aged wives and widows.

1980

Lower maximum family benefit (MFB) for disability benefits than the regular MFB.

1981

Student benefits for youth aged 18–21 to be phased out, minimum benefits phased out for those claiming benefits from 1982, mother's and father's benefits terminated when youngest child reaches 16 (had been 18), and a "Megacap" provision on DI benefits introduced; stricter controls on Medicare costs with higher deductible and coinsurance amounts (PL 97–35). Numerous deliberalizations of AFDC.

1983

Scheduled tax increases moved back; automatic cost-of-living adjustments moved ahead to calendar year basis; taxation of half OASDI benefits of upper income recipients; expansion of mandatory coverage to upper level government employees, new federal hires, and employees of nonprofit organizations; self-employed to pay OASDHI tax equal to combined employer-employee rate; termination of state and local governmental units prohibited; normal retirement age for unreduced benefits to be increased in steps to age 67 beginning in 2000; Medicare to pay a fixed amount for inpatient hospital care according to one of 467 diagnosis-related groups (DRGs) (PL 98–21).

Selected Bibliography of Books on Social Security, 1935–1985

Aaron, Henry J. *Economic Effects of Social Security*. Washington, DC: Brookings Institution, 1982.

Aaron, Henry J., and Gary Burtless, eds. *Retirement and Economic Behavior*. Washington, DC: Brookings Institution, 1984.

Achenbaum, W. Andrew. *Old Age in a New Land*. Baltimore: Johns Hopkins University Press, 1977.

Altmeyer, Arthur J. *The Formative Years of Social Security*. Madison: University of Wisconsin Press, 1966.

American Enterprise Institute. *Social Security: Universal or Selective?* Rational Debate Seminar, Wilbur J. Cohen and Milton Friedman. Washington, DC: AEI, 1972.

Armstrong, Barbara N. *Insuring the Essentials: Minimum Wage, Plus Social Insurance*. New York: Macmillan, 1932.

Atkinson, Raymond C. *The Federal Role in Unemployment Compensation Administration*. Washington, DC: Committee on Social Security, 1914.

Ball, Robert M. *Social Security: Today and Tomorrow*. New York: Columbia University Press, 1978.

Berkowitz, Edward D., ed. *Disability Policies and Government Programs* New York: Praeger, 1979.

Berkowitz, Edward D. and Kim McQuaid. *Creating the Welfare State:*

The Political Economy of Twentieth Century Reform. New York: Praeger, 1980.

Booth, Philip. *Social Security in America*. Ann Arbor: Institute of Labor and Industrial Relations, University of Michigan—Wayne State University, 1973.

Bortz, Abe. *Social Security Sources in Federal Records, 1934–1950*. Washington, DC: Government Printing Office, 1969.

Boskin, Michael J., ed. *The Crisis in Social Security: Problems and Prospects*. San Francisco: Institute for Contemporary Studies, 1977.

Bowen, William G., and others, eds. *The Princeton Symposium on the American System of Social Insurance: Its Philosophy, Impact, and Future Development*. New York: McGraw-Hill, 1968.

Brinkley, Alan. *Voices of Protest: Huey Long, Father Coughlin, and the Great Depression*. New York: Alfred A. Knopf, 1983.

Brittain, John A. *The Payroll Tax for Social Security*. Washington, DC: Brookings Institution, 1972.

Brown, J. Douglas. *An American Philosophy of Social Security*. Princeton, NJ: Princeton University Press, 1972.

———. *Essays on Social Security*. Princeton, NJ: Industrial Relations Section, Princeton University, 1977.

Burkhauser, Richard V., and Karen C. Holden. *A Challenge to Social Security: The Changing Roles of Women and Men in American Society*. New York: Academic Press, 1982.

Burns, Eveline M. *Toward Social Security*. New York: McGraw-Hill, 1936.

———. *The American Social Security System*. Boston: Houghton Mifflin, 1949.

———. *Social Security and Public Policy*. New York: McGraw-Hill, 1956.

Califano, Joseph A., Jr. *Governing America*. New York: Simon and Schuster, 1981.

Campbell, Colin D. ed. *Financing Social Security*. Washington, DC: American Enterprise Institute, 1978.

Campbell, Rita Ricardo. *Social Security: Promise and Reality*. Stanford, CA: Hoover Institution Press, 1977.

Carlson, Vlademar. *Economic Security in the United States*. New York: McGraw-Hill, 1962.

Cates, Jerry R. *Insuring Inequality: Administrative Leadership in Social Security, 1935–54*. Ann Arbor: University of Michigan Press, 1983.

Chen, Yung-Ping. *Social Security in a Changing Society*, 2nd ed. Bryn Mawr, PA: McCahan Foundation, 1983.

Cohen, Wilbur J. *Retirement Policies under Social Security*. Berkeley: University of California Press, 1957.

Coughlin, Richard M. *Ideology, Public Opinion, and Welfare Policy*.

Berkeley: Institute of International Studies, University of California, 1980.

Derthick, Martha. *Policymaking for Social Security.* Washington, DC: Brookings Institution, 1979.

Dixon, Robert G. *Social Security Disability and Mass Justice: A Problem in Welfare Judication.* New York: Praeger, 1973.

Douglas, Paul H. *Social Security in the United States: An Analysis and Appraisal of the Federal Social Security Act,* 2nd ed. New York: McGraw-Hill, 1939.

————. *In the Fullness of Time: The Memoirs of Paul H. Douglas.* New York: Harcourt Brace Jovanovich, 1972.

Epstein, Abraham. *Insecurity: A Challenge to America.* New York: Random House, 1938.

Falk, Isadore S. *Security against Sickness: A Study of Health Insurance.* Garden City, NY: Doubleday, Doran, 1936.

Ferrara, Peter J. *Social Security: The Inherent Contradiction.* Washington, DC: Cato Institute, 1980.

————. ed. *Social Security: Prospects for Real Reform.* Washington, DC: Cato Institute, 1985.

Flora, Peter, and Arnold J. Heidenheimer., eds. *The Development of Welfare States in Europe and America.* New Brunswick, NJ: Transaction Books, 1981.

Gagliardo, Domenico. *American Social Insurance.* New York: Harper & Row, 1949.

Gordon, Margaret S. *The Economics of Welfare Policies.* New York: Columbia University Press, 1963.

Graebner, William. *A History of Retirement.* New Haven, CT: Yale University Press, 1980.

Grant, Margaret. *Old-Age Security: Social and Financial Trends.* Washington, DC: Committee on Social Security, 1939.

Haber, William, and Wilbur J. Cohen., eds. *Social Security Programs, Problems and Policies: Selected Readings.* Homewood, IL: Richard D. Irwin, 1960.

Harris, Seymour E. *Economics of Social Security.* New York: McGraw-Hill, 1941.

Hirschfield, Daniel S. *The Lost Reform: The Campaign for Compulsory Health Insurance in the United States from 1932 to 1943.* Cambridge, MA: Harvard University Press, 1970.

Holtzman, Abraham. *The Townsend Movement, A Political Study.* New York: New York Bookmen's Association, 1963.

Howards, Irving, Henry P. Brehm, and Saad Z. Nagi. *Disability: From Social Problem to Federal Program.* New York: Praeger, 1980.

Joe, Tom, and Cheryl Rogers. *By the Few for the Few: The Reagan Welfare Legacy.* Lexington, MA: Lexington Books, 1985.

Kaim-Caudle, P. R. *Comparative Public Policy and Social Security: A Ten-Country Study.* New York: Dunellen, 1973.

Kreps, Juanita M., ed. *Employment, Income, and Retirement Problems of the Aged.* Durham, NC: Duke University Press, 1963.

Larson, Arthur. *Know Your Social Security.* rev. ed. New York: Harper, 1959.

Leff, Mark H. *The Limits of Symbolic Reform.* New York: Cambridge University Press, 1984.

Leiby, James. *A History of Social Welfare and Social Work in the United States.* New York: Columbia University Press, 1978.

Leman, Christopher. *The Collapse of Welfare Reform: Political Institutions, Policy, and the Poor in Canada and the United States.* Cambridge, MA: MIT Press, 1980.

Light, Paul. *Artful Work: The Politics of Social Security Reform.* New York: Random House, 1984.

Lopata, Helena Z., and Henry P. Brehm. *Widows and Dependent Wives: From Social Problem to Federal Program.* New York: Praeger, 1985.

Lubove, Roy. *The Struggle for Social Security, 1900–1935.* Cambridge: Harvard University Press, 1968.

Marmor, Theodore R. *The Politics of Medicare.* Chicago: Aldine, 1970.

Mashaw, Jerry L. *Bureaucratic Justice: Managing Social Security Disability Claims.* New Haven, CT: Yale University Press, 1983.

McGill, Dan M. ed. *Social Security and Private Pension Plans: Competitive or Complementary.* Homewood, IL: Richard D. Irwin, 1977.

McKinley, Charles, and Robert W. Frase. *Launching Social Security: A Capture-and-Record Account, 1935–1937.* Madison: University of Wisconsin Press, 1970.

Meriam, Lewis. *Relief and Social Security.* Washington, DC: Brookings Institution, 1946.

Mitchell, William I. *Social Security in America.* Washington, DC: Robert B. Luce, 1964.

Moynihan, Daniel P. *The Politics of a Guaranteed Income; The Nixon Administration and the Family Assistance Plan.* New York: Random House, 1973.

Munnell, Alicia H. *Effect of Social Security on Personal Saving.* Cambridge, MA: Ballinger, 1974.

———. *The Future of Social Security.* Washington, DC: Brookings Institution, 1977.

Myers, Robert J. *Social Security,* 3rd ed. Homewood, IL: Richard D. Irwin, 1985. (This volume contains a lengthy bibliography of reports, pamphlets, papers, and articles dealing with Social Security.)

Myles, John. *Old Age in the Welfare State: The Political Economy of Public Pensions.* Boston: Little, Brown, 1984.

National Conference of Social Work. *The Report of the Committee on Economic Security of 1935 and Other Basic Documents.* Washington, DC: NCSW, 1985.

Nelson, Daniel. *Unemployment Insurance.* Madison: University of Wisconsin Press, 1969.

Neugarten, Bernice L., ed. *Age or Need?: Public Policies for Older People.* Beverly Hills, CA: Sage Publications, 1982.

Pechman, Joseph A., Henry J. Aaron, and Michael K. Taussig. *Social Security: Perspectives for Reform.* Washington: Brookings Institution, 1968.

Perkins, Frances. *The Roosevelt I Knew.* New York: Viking, 1946.

President's Committee on Economic Security. *Social Security in America.* Washington, DC: Social Security Board, 1937.

Rejda, George E. *Social Insurance and Economic Security,* 2nd ed. Englewood Cliffs, NJ: Prentice-Hall, 1984.

Rimlinger, Gaston V. *Welfare Policy and Industrialization in Europe, America, and Russia.* New York: John Wiley, 1971.

Robertson, A. Haeworth. *The Coming Revolution in Social Security.* McLean, VA: Security Press, 1981.

Rosa, Jean-Jacques., ed. *The World Crisis in Social Security.* San Francisco: Institute for Contemporary Studies, 1982.

Rubinow, I.M. *The Quest for Security.* New York: Henry Holt, 1934.

Schlabach, Theron F. *Edwin E. Witte: Cautious Reformer.* Madison: State Historical Society of Wisconsin, 1969.

Schlesinger, Arthur M., Jr. *The Coming of the New Deal.* Boston: Houghton Mifflin, 1959.

Schottland, Charles I. *The Social Security Program in the United States,* 2nd ed. New York: Appleton-Century-Crofts, 1970.

Schulz, James H. *The Economics of Aging,* 3rd ed. Belmont, CA: Wadsworth, 1984.

Stevens, Robert, and Rosemary Stevens. *Welfare Medicine in America: A Case Study of Medicaid.* New York: Free Press, 1974.

Shore, William. *Social Security: The Fraud in Your Future.* New York: Macmillan, 1975.

Starr, Paul. *The Social Transformation of American Medicine.* New York: Basic Books, 1984.

Stein, Bruno. *Social Security and Pensions in Transition.* New York: Free Press, 1980.

Steiner, Peter O., and Robert Dorfman. *The Economic Status of the Aged.* Berkeley: University of California Press, 1957.

Stewart, Maxwell S. *Social Security*, rev. ed. New York: W. W. Norton, 1939.

Tomasson, Richard F., ed. *The Welfare State, 1883–1983*. Volume 6 of *Comparative Social Research*. Greenwich, CT: JAI Press, 1983.

US Department of Health and Human Services, Social Security Administration. *Social Security Programs Throughout the World—1983*. Washington, DC: SSA Publication No. 13-11805, 1984.

US Department of Health, Education, and Welfare, Social Security Administration, Office of Research and Statistics. *Public Attitudes toward Social Security, 1935–1965*. By Michael E. Schiltz, Research Report No. 33. Washington, DC: Government Printing Office, 1970.

Weaver, Carolyn. *The Crisis in Social Security: Economic and Political Origins*. Durham, NC: Duke Press Policy Studies, 1982.

Witte, Edwin E. *The Development of the Social Security Act*. Madison: University of Wisconsin Press, 1962.

———. *Social Security Perspectives*. Madison: University of Wisconsin Press, 1962.

Woytinsky, W. S. *Labor in the United States: Basic Statistics for Social Security*. Washington, DC: Committee on Economic Security, 1938.

———. *Earnings and Social Security in the United States*. Washington, DC: Committee on Economic Security, 1943.

Notes on
Participants

W. Andrew Achenbaum, born in 1947 in Philadelphia, Pennsylvania, is professor of history at Carnegie Mellon University and a senior scholar at the University of Michigan's Institute of Gerontology. He is the author of *Old Age in a New Land* (1978), *Shades of Gray* (1983), and *Social Security: Visions and Revisions* (1986).

Edward D. Berkowitz, born in 1950 in Passaic, New Jersey, is associate professor of history and director of the Program in History and Public Policy at George Washington University. He has written on social welfare policy and history, including a forthcoming study of public policy toward disability for the Twentieth Century Fund.

Eveline M. Burns, (1900–1985) born in London, England, was a pioneering social analyst and planner, who in 1934 joined the staff of the Committee on Economic Security. She was a prolific author on Social Security and social welfare, including *Social Security and Public Policy*, a basic text for social security analysts. She was Professor Emeritus of Social Welfare at Columbia University.

Wilbur J. Cohen, (1913–1987) born in Milwaukee, Wisconsin, was the first employee of Social Security. He was Secretary of Health, Education, and Welfare under President Johnson and played a central role in the passage of Medicare and Medicaid. He was Professor of Public Affairs at the Lyndon B. Johnson School of Public Affairs at the University of Texas and co-chair of Save Our Security, a national coalition of groups concerned with Social Security and health care.

Blanche D. Coll, born in 1916 in Baltimore, Maryland, published her first article in social welfare history, "The Baltimore Society for the Prevention of Pauperism," in the *American Historical Review* in 1955. After joining the Department of Health, Education, and Welfare she analysed the pre–New Deal state-local system in *Perspectives in Public Welfare* (1969). She is presently completing a history of post-Depression social welfare, with an emphasis on the public assistance titles under the Social Security Act.

Richard M. Coughlin, born in 1948 in Buffalo, New York, is associate professor and chairman of sociology at the University of New Mexico. He has written on comparative social policy, including *Ideology, Public Opinion, and Welfare Policy* (1980). Currently, he is studying the effects of demographic and economic change in the second century of the welfare state.

Thomas H. Eliot, born in 1907 in Boston, Massachusetts, as counsel to the President's Committee on Economic Security in 1934–35, participated in drafting the Social Security Act. After its passage he became General Counsel of the Social Security Board. Later he was a representative in Congress from Massachusetts, practiced law, taught political science, and was Chancellor of Washington University.

Gary P. Freeman, born in 1945 in Atlanta, Georgia, is associate professor of government at the University of Texas at Austin. He makes comparative analyses of the public policies of the Western democracies, particularly comparing US policies with those of the European nations. He is the author of *Immigrant Labour and Racial Conflict in Industrial Societies* (1979).

David Hamilton, born in 1918 in Pittsburgh, Pennsylvania, has been a professor of economics at the University of New Mexico for thirty-seven years. He is the author of *A Primer on the Economics of Poverty* (1968) and *The Consumer in Our Economy* (1962). His *Evolutionary Economics* was published in a Japanese edition in 1985.

Fred R. Harris, born in 1930 in Walters, Oklahoma, is professor of political science at the University of New Mexico. He practiced law in the 1950s in Lawton, Oklahoma, was a US Senator from 1964 to 1973, and a contender for the Democratic nomination for President in 1972. He is the author of a number of books on a variety of subjects.

Mark H. Leff, born in 1949 in Cincinnati, Ohio, joined the Department of History at the University of Illinois at Urbana-Champaign in 1986 where he teaches American history and public policy. He is the author of articles on public assistance and Social Security financing. He is also the author of *The Limits of Symbolic Reform* (1984).

Charles E. McClelland, born in 1940 in San Antonio, Texas, is professor of history at the University of New Mexico. He is a specialist on Central

European social and cultural history and the author of *The German Historians and England* (1971), *State, Society and University in Germany* (1980), and the forthcoming *The Rise of Modern Professions in Germany, 1840–1940*.

Robert J. Myers, born in 1912 in Lancaster, Pennsylvania, began his federal service in 1934 as junior actuary with the Committee on Economic Security. He was Chief Actuary of the Social Security Administration during 1947–70 and later was Deputy Commissioner of Social Security. He was Chief of Staff of the National Commission on Social Security Reform appointed by President Reagan in 1981. In 1985 he published the third edition of his *Social Security*.

Gerald D. Nash, born in 1928 in Berlin, Germany, is Presidential Professor of History at the University of New Mexico. He is a specialist in twentieth century U.S. history. He is the author or editor of more than a dozen books in U.S. history, most recently *The American West Transformed; The Impact of World War II* (1985). He is co-editor of this volume.

Noel H. Pugach, born in 1939 in Brooklyn, New York, specializes in U.S. diplomatic history at the University of New Mexico. He has published articles in his specialty in numerous journals. He is the author of *Paul S. Reinsch: Open Door Diplomat in Action* (1979). He chaired the Planning Committee for the UNM Conference on Social Security and is co-editor of this volume.

Gaston V. Rimlinger, born in 1926 in Strasbourg, France, holds the Reginald Henry Hargrove chair in economics at Rice University. His research and publication have been mainly in economic and labor history and in the comparative history of the welfare state. He is the author of *Welfare Policy and Industrialization in Europe, America, and Russia* (1971). His current research is the history of the American hospital system.

Charles I. Schottland, born in 1906 in Chicago, Illinois, was both dean of the Florence Heller Graduate School for Advanced Studies in Social Welfare and president of Brandeis University from which he retired in 1979. Earlier, from 1954 to 1959, he was U.S. Commissioner for Social Security. Currently he is President of both the American Society on Aging and of the National Senior Citizens Law Center and Chairman of the Arizona Governor's Council on Aging.

Richard F. Tomasson, born in 1928 in Brooklyn, New York, is professor of sociology at the University of New Mexico. He is the author of books and articles on the Scandinavian societies and is editor of *Comparative Social Research*. In recent years he has been studying comparative social security. He is co-editor of this volume.

Index

Subject Index

333

Name Index

Index